CAUSEWIRED

CAUSEWIRED

Plugging In,

Getting Involved,

Changing the World

Tom Watson

WILEY

John Wiley & Sons, Inc.

Published by John Wiley & Sons, Inc., Hoboken, New Jersey.
Published simultaneously in Canada.

For general information on our other products and services, or technical support, please contact our Customer Care Department within the United States at 800-762-2974, outside the United States at 317-572-3993, or fax 317-572-4002.

Wiley also publishes its books in a variety of electronic formats. Some content that appears in print may not be available in electronic books.

For more information about Wiley products, visit our web site at www.wiley.com.

Library of Congress Cataloging-in-Publication Data:

ISBN 978-0-470-37504-4

Printed in the United States of America

10 9 8 7 6 5 4 3

To Mom and Dad,
for the work, the wisdom, and the words

Contents

About the Author   *ix*

Foreword   *xi*

Acknowledgments   *xv*

Introduction   *xix*

Chapter 1:   Lost in the Flood: Wired Causes Rise   1

Chapter 2:   Friending for Good: The Facebook
                 Philanthropists   23

Chapter 3:   Signing up to Fight Evil: The Network Acts   41

Chapter 4:   Portfolios for Change: Peer-to-Peer
                 Philanthropy   59

Chapter 5:   Defined by Causes: The Public Lives
                 of Millennials   79

Chapter 6:   From the Bottom Up: "The Order Is
                 Rapidly Fading"   95

Chapter 7:   Spare the Paperwork: The Quick Rise
                 of Flash Causes   119

Contents

Chapter 8: Heralds of Change: Giving Goes Open Source   137

Chapter 9: Aspiration and Activism: Armies
of Online Leaders   159

Chapter 10: Distributing the CauseWired Future   179

Websites   *199*

Further Reading   *207*

Notes   *211*

Index   *227*

About the Author

Tom Watson is a journalist, media critic, entrepreneur, and consultant who has worked at the confluence of media technology and social change for more than a decade. During his long career as journalist and blogger, Tom has written for the *New York Times, Huffington Post, Industry Standard, Inside, Worth*, and *Contribute*, among many other publications. He writes about politics and media on his own popular blog, *My Dirty Life & Times*, and is the founder and editor of *Newcritics.com*, a group blog on popular culture. Tom is chief strategy officer of Changing Our World Inc., an international philanthropic services company that provides a wide range of consulting services to nonprofits, corporations, foundations, and individuals in philanthropy. Tom is the publisher of *onPhilanthropy.com*, Changing Our World's extensive online resource for philanthropy professionals. Before joining Changing Our World, Tom was co-founder and co-editor of *@NY*, the pioneering Internet news and information service that chronicled the rise of New York's Silicon Alley new media in the mid-1990s. Early in his career, Tom was executive editor of the *Riverdale Press*, a Pulitzer Prize–winning newspaper in the Bronx, where he covered politics and won more than a dozen state and national awards for excellence in journalism. Tom is a member of the board of directors of the Drum Major

Institute for Public Policy, a progressive think-tank based in New York. He holds a degree in English literature from Columbia University, where he served as adjunct professor of new media at Columbia's Graduate School of Journalism. He lives in Mount Vernon, New York, with his wife, artist Beryl Watson, and their three children, Veronica, Kelsey, and Devon.

Foreword

By Jean Case

Way back in the 1970s, when causes were still causes but *wired* referred to a college student pulling an all-nighter, a TV commercial for an add-water-and-stir cup-of-noodles product had as its tag line the famous question: "Is it soup yet?"

Today, in the worlds of philanthropy, social activism, business, and even politics and policy making, this question is especially ripe for asking. We are at a juncture where blended forms of civic engagement and business activity—supported and spurred by new social web technologies—are being used by both individuals and organizations to create and expand a rising culture of giving and a coming together of ingredients that can create powerful opportunities for positive change.

CauseWired is so timely in its arrival and spot-on in its focus. A new generation of givers—the *Net-native millennials*—is emerging, and a fresh generation of nonprofit, foundation, and business leaders is already taking the helm. But do we understand what these changes will mean? Do we know as donors, foundations, nonprofit and business leaders, policymakers, and volunteers how we should participate in this change? What more do we need to know in order to capture this opportunity to motivate and engage more people and increase giving of every kind, everywhere?

These questions have occupied a great deal of recent effort at the Case Foundation (as graciously noted in this book), and will consume more of our efforts and resources in the future. In 2007, we launched several projects to better understand how people were engaging using Web 2.0 and social web tools. First, we watched with great interest as more than 5,000 people applied to earn four $25,000 grants from us, and then observed in near amazement as more than 15,000 online voters decided who would get those grants. Later, we launched twin "giving challenges" with our partners *Parade* magazine and Causes on Facebook, asking people to use online tools, including widgets and social networks, to spread the word of their cause and encourage online donations through Network for Good and Global Giving. More than 80,000 people gave more than $1,750,000 in the six weeks the challenges ran.

These efforts, and our observation of the many others noted in this book, help confirm our hunch, which underlies *CauseWired*'s well-explored premise: Giving has in fact changed. It is still changing, right before our eyes and in ways that will forever alter the relationships between people and the causes that motivate them.

Tom Watson has been there all along, exploring the nuances of what these new approaches might mean to the philanthropic sector, commenting on efforts to harness their power, and helping the sector make sense of it all.

From every direction, new opportunities to get involved are being presented and developed by a new breed of civic leaders and entrepreneurs. And though the debate over how best to blend business models and nonprofit missions continues, the integration of entrepreneurial thinking and online tools into philanthropic ventures and the equally important integration of giving and nonprofit sensibility into corporate cultures is well underway.

CauseWired does a wonderful job chronicling exactly that—the imaginative and bold ways people have chosen to make their voices and their causes heard using new tools, new technologies, and new social relationships.

What is more, it provides an instructional narrative for anyone who wants to play a role in building this new culture of giving. Finally, it makes clear that it is time to get moving because *it's soup* and *it's now*.

■ ■ ■

Jean Case is the CEO of the Case Foundation (www.casefoundation.org).

The Case Foundation was created by Steve and Jean Case in 1997. The Foundation invests in individuals, nonprofits, and social enterprises that aim to connect people, increase giving, and catalyze civic action.

Acknowledgments

Several key events led directly to the beginning of this project, and it is by way of thanking those involved that I acknowledge an author's debt to the people who encouraged its completion. Two of those events were conversations: Susan Carey Dempsey, my partner in building and running onPhilanthropy.com these past eight years, used her singularly strong brand of persuasion to get me to "make the call" that got this book under way. Almost a year earlier, our boss at Changing Our World, Mike Hoffman, urged me during a visit to the racetrack, his favorite place, to pursue a bigger writing project. My entire experience at Changing Our World has nourished the ideas that went into this book, and provided the perspective on fundraising and philanthropy needed to see the larger picture. Our company, created as a small consultancy by Mike and my brother Chris Watson nearly a decade ago, has grown into one of the world's leading firms working in philanthropy and nonprofit management—and it has always pursued ideas and innovation. I cannot name everyone from the company here, but I would like to thank longtime colleagues Joann Zafonte, Tony Smith, Steve Manzi, Mary Beth Martin, and Kieran McTague for their encouragement. Our interactive services group, led by Jenn Thompson, Garth Moore, and Bob Carter, was enthusiastic and generous with ideas. And I must acknowledge a debt to Dr. Susan Raymond for helping me to understand the changes afoot in international philanthropy.

The outline for the book came from a speech I was honored to give at the annual Conrad N. Hilton Humanitarian Symposium in New York in September 2007, an invitation that came from the generous Judy Miller and Jean-Marc Moorghen and the Hilton Foundation. Another event that month also sharpened some of the ideas for the book: Hacking Philanthropy was a private roundtable discussion organized by my friends at Union Square Ventures, Fred Wilson and Brad Burnham. The perspectives shared that day at Columbia are sprinkled like insightful little flowers throughout this book. I would also like to recognize the organizers and staff of the Clinton Global Initiative, the Milken Institute Global Conference, and the Skoll World Forum. I have felt most welcome at all of these important conferences and benefited mightily from the ideas shared in those venues. The staff at *Contribute* magazine, led by editor Marcia Stepanek, gave me the title *CauseWired* by cleverly placing it over an article I penned for them a year ago—and it stuck.

Several bloggers, writers, and analysts were generous with their knowledge, time, and encouragement. First among equals is my longtime collaborator Jason Chervokas, a fine writer and an old friend who knows me to the core, and did not hesitate to push me rather firmly when I needed it. In similar fashion, Andrea Batista Schlesinger gave several friendly shoves and looked over some of the text. The insightful philanthropist Maureen Baehr helped me organize my thoughts at the outset. Howard Greenstein provided instantaneous and generous expertise in social media whenever he was asked, which was often. Lyndsay Reville and Will Schneider were very kind in organizing an ad-hoc focus group on the cause-related values of young professionals and Marie Molese and her team have provided crucial logistical support. Author Allison Fine gave me valued advice on both the book business and the sector, in which she is a leading voice. Tech bloggers and online cause evangelists Beth Kanter and Marnie Webb were inspirational in their day-to-day enthusiasm. Further ideas and plain old encouragement came online and off from (in no order at all) Lance Mannion, Eric Goldberg, James Wolcott, Peter Daou, M.A. Peel, Bruce

Bernstein, Elana Levin, Craig Dyer, Lindsay Beyerstein, Tom Watson (the British version), Jon Swift, Robert Tolmach, Joe Green, Ben Rattray, Peter Deitz, Mark Hanis, Phil Cubeta, Tom Kissane, Charles Best, Jason Paez, Peter Watson, Andrew Rasiej, Lucy Bernholz, Scott Edward Anderson, Doug Tween, Mario Morino, Micah Sifry, Jean Case, Tom FitzSimmons, Joe Solomon, Matt Flannery, Dawn Barber, Greg Spradlin, Allan Benamer, Sean Stannard-Stockton, Jed Emerson, Larry Aronson, Premal Shah, Nate Ritter, Jason Calacanis, Vinay Bhagat, Robert Greenwald, Andras Szanto, Nicholas Kristof, Brendan Tween, Blue Girl, and many others.

From the first early-winter conversation at a coffee shop in Hoboken to the completion of this book, Susan McDermott, my editor at John Wiley & Sons, has been the model of encouragement and professionalism—proving that patience is indeed a literary virtue. Her colleague, Dexter Gasque, is a talented production editor who undoubtedly improved this book.

Speaking of patience, my family is the center of this book. They helped me survive five furious months of writing every single weekend in my upstairs lair, and they put up with my moods and occasional outward frustration. My daughter, Veronica, in addition to providing real in-house insight into the role of causes in the lives of millennials, helped with some typing. My boys, Kelsey and Devon, provided great good cheer and the occasional sandwich and coffee delivery. And my dear partner in life, my wife Beryl, was the firm and loving rock I leaned the project on; without her, I could never have attempted this book. They each have my love and affection always.

Introduction

The business pages are filled with stories of startup companies and massive valuations. Google grows ever more rapidly into a global powerhouse. The reach of social networks such as Facebook stretches every day. Americans are living more of their lives in public, creating vast lists of online "friends" and professional colleagues, and sharing their experiences, their taste in music, their political choices, and even their personal lives.

No trend is hotter than the rush to create social networks, the vast, intertwined next generation of the Web that promises real-time connection and communication. Americans of all ages are taking part, but no group is more enthusiastic—and more empowered—than the so-called *millennials*, that demographic slice of our society that has never known life without the Internet. These young men and women now entering the workforce for the first time have lived much of their lives online, and they bring with them in their introduction to the national economy and our society great expectations for lightning-fast communications, openness and transparency, and the ability to change the landscape quickly.

At the same time, the world is a smaller place. Genocide in remote villages in the east African region of Darfur is covered by Google maps that show the devastation and religious cleansing, while hundreds of bloggers write about the terrible story—not merely passing along links from mainstream media organizations, but urging action and placing a premium on their own opinion. On Facebook, the fastest-growing online social network in the world, hundreds of thousands of people—students, young professionals, political action committees, and even gray-haired CEOs and captains of industry—signal their support for stopping the slaughter and helping the victims by placing badges on their individual profiles. Video sharing brings the story home, and thousands of digital photographs are traded and posted on blogs and social networks. Keywords and tags allow anyone interested in the topic to explore a massive cultural document—the living expansion of the topic in public consciousness—through blog networks and search engines. Darfur becomes more than a yellowing news-clipping down in the backroom of the public library, more than a research report, and more than a news story from far away. It becomes a cause. More accurately, Darfur becomes *CauseWired*.

This term, first employed in this book, is important for anyone interested in the public consciousness to understand. For consumer marketers, causes are a vital path to successful brands. Never before have consumers cared more about the ethical righteousness of companies. For employers, it is also a vital concept: Studies show that talented young people want to work only for companies and organizations they believe contribute to the public good. For nonprofit organizations and the philanthropists who support them, a grasp of the coming influence of social networks in causes will be, frankly, key to survival in a world where your grandfather's style of check-writing charity no longer applies. For government and anyone involved in politics, the hopes and dreams of the "Facebook generation" and their older, early-adopter counterparts are crucial aspects of winning electoral support in elections ranging from national presidential contests to the vote for local council seats.

Well-informed and interested consumers will seek a better understanding of the very trend they are creating. This is expected; after all, anyone who is CauseWired understands that fact quite clearly. This group discusses the very trends in which it is involved with a transparent self-awareness that is really unprecedented in public discourse. CauseWired consumers are superinformed consumers who expect to create and support causes, change politics, and have personal involvement in the brands they support economically.

■ ■ ■

While many books have covered the impact of digital media—from blogs to video to the rise of user-generated content—this one attempts to track the impact on causes, from the charitable to the political, and provide a roadmap for anyone serious about understanding the real impact on society of the social web. It will also introduce readers to a fascinating cast of characters, a band of social entrepreneurs who believe in the power of technology and communications to change society and solve many of our global problems. You will meet young founders of online enterprises such as Kiva.org, Causes on Facebook, DonorsChoose, and Change.org. You will also be introduced to bloggers, media analysts, political operatives, and social activists willing to experiment with new forms of communications to raise both money and awareness and to support a wide range of causes. It is my belief that this core group of pioneers will change the way humanity views philanthropy and activism, as well as how we go about trying to improve life on this planet. Yes, this group is a bunch of do-gooders out to change the world; but their idealism is tempered, I think, by a willingness to employ the basic scientific tool of trial and error. In other words, they seek either to succeed or to fail in a spectacularly illuminating fashion. Spending time with them through all the modern channels of communications over the past several months has been both a great personal pleasure and something of a salve to an older soul laden with creeping doubts as to the efficacy of hope.

This book also suggests strongly that what some refer to as *online social activism* and others call *peer-to-peer philanthropy* is quickly becoming a sector, bound together by a growing critical mass in usership and an expanding acceptance in the worlds of philanthropy, politics, activism, and marketing. Indeed, the brief period of creation of the past few years (perhaps dating to the beta launch of DonorsChoose in 2000) is giving way to the next evolutionary phase of growth, and the permanent mooring of several important financial models on our greater economy.

Yet, it is that early phase of creation that attracted me to this project. If anything, it reminded me almost viscerally of that period in the mid-1990s when I was at the center of a new and exciting sector just coming into bloom. In those days, when Jason Chervokas and I founded an online newsletter called @NY to chronicle the rise of the commercial Internet in the world's media capital, the aroma of creativity and experimentation wafted deliciously through the media labs of lower Manhattan. For a young journalist such as myself, the blend of technology and artistic expression was intoxicating and every day held a new surprise, some unexpected success or some semi-tragic failure. The common goal of making something from the vast new digital network was itself fuel for the crowd of entrepreneurs—a group as diverse and iconoclastic as any I have known. "Silicon Alley," as it was facetiously named by the more capital-endowed Valley denizens three thousand miles to the west, fairly teemed with underemployed artists, writers, photographers, producers, and editors trying to make their way in the new medium—or just trying to remake themselves.

The nascent online social activist sector (allow me to call it *CauseWired* to please my publishers) is more serious and less given to frivolity than the old Internet startups of my living memory. But the energy and the drive and the willingness to take chances—to launch rather than to plan—is pungently reminiscent to this story-loving journalist's nose. There is just something there.

Part of that something is hype, of course. The world of connected online media, also known as *Web 2.0*, may score awfully high on the hype meter of skeptical business writers, but the sheer number of users is still staggering. Technorati, the leading search engine for blogs and social media, currently tracks more than 112 million socially wired sites at the time of this writing, and a quarter-billion pieces of tagged media. Facebook reported more than 67 million members by the end of the first quarter of 2008, and MySpace, its older cousin, now owned by media baron Rupert Murdoch, tops 100 million users. YouTube, the video-sharing service now owned by Google, serves more than 100 million videos a day and boasts at least 2.9 million user channels. Some analysts began to suggest early in 2008 that the social media sector was nearly mature, that growth was flattening out, and that the pace of use of even Web giant Google had slackened.

Yet, even as the newness of social media began to wear off, and the wired world accepted the always-on, always-connected nature of modern digital life, one area saw a burst of energy and entrepreneurial spirit: the nexus between media technology and causes. Online organizing changed the course of the 2008 presidential campaign with tens of millions in contributors supporting candidates, in particular the socially powered online campaign of Illinois Senator Barack Obama. Kiva.org, the nonprofit startup using a social network to direct loans from everyday people to small-scale entrepreneurs in the developing world, grew from zero to more than 270,000 leaders in less than three years, making loans of $26,149,810 as of March 2008—$25 at a time. DonorsChoose, hot-housed in a Bronx public school just after the millennium, came of age with direct gifts of more than $25 million to school teachers. GlobalGiving, a Washington, D.C.–based nonprofit founded in 2002, has funneled more than $6 million to 900 projects around the world. Causes on Facebook leveraged social networking's most popular hub to sign on 12 million users and raise $2.5 million for 40,000 different charitable and political causes worldwide. A new army of startups took the field, with names such as Change.org, BringLight, ChangingthePresent, FirstGiving, Fundable, GiveMeaning, GlobalGiving, allvoices.com, MicroGiving, Razoo, Zazengo, Helpalot, PledgeBank, DemocracyinAction, SixDegrees, Care2, ThePoint, and PincGiving.

■ ■ ■

Clearly, the numbers in the CauseWired movement are approaching critical mass. This is an excellent time to produce a brief account of the impact of social networks on charity, politics, and consumer movements—one that explains the trend, offers real-world stories of success, and introduces the reader to some of the people, famous and almost unknown, powering this movement.

This book is very much a product of the movement and change it describes. Much of the work for this book has been supported by a blog I launched at www.causewired.com—a virtual headquarters for research, interaction with sources, reporting, and collecting links. It is the place where this book came together, at least partially in public. I used the social-bookmarking tool del.icio.us.com to track key sources, and Google docs for notes and writing. Some of the interviews for the book were conducted on Facebook itself. I made broad inquiries to key players on Twitter, and I used the contact-management tools at LinkedIn.com to track down key players. In no way could *CauseWired* have come into existence otherwise; it is the story of what people do online to try to change the world for the better. To accurately report that, I had to be in the middle of it. Just as international correspondents seek the frontlines and political reporters the backrooms, I spent countless days on the network I hoped to profile. However, unlike the war reporter, I picked up a rifle or two. I became a Kiva donor. I participated in DonorsChoose contests, signed up for Change.org, recruited supporters for various Facebook Causes, and made a few contributions. I joined Razoo and talked about everyday good works, I traded badges and widgets, I actively participated in the early stages of the 2008 elections (I was for Clinton), and I blogged a lot. Like George Plimpton's first-person participatory reporting in the world of professional sports, I was the Paper Lion among the millennials. But, unlike the brilliant Plimpton, I had put on the pads before. I was more the aging veteran suiting up with the spry young draft choices, than the total novice taking the field for the first time.

■ ■ ■

This book attempts to provide insight into the sum of many millions of personal experiences. But it is collected by one person, and in the spirit of the network of networks and the open-source nature of our media-obsessed lives, it must begin with a short download. My experience is singular as well, and I bring my own prejudices, my own judgment, and my own biases and self-interest to the writing—in the parlance of the network, my own profile. And a book, even linked to a blog or an ongoing discussion, is media in its oldest form: a construction of one mind, designed to be consumed by many. It is (according to Markos Moulitsas, the outspoken and controversial founder of the progressive-activist superblog, DailyKos) "the anti-blog."

My recent obsession with wired causes is really the culmination of a long personal journal rather than an overnight discovery. My online life began way back in the 1980s, with the advent of dialup bulletin boards. Entirely text-driven and slow as molasses, these boards required users to dial in modem to modem to participate in virtual communities that gathered around certain topics, like gaming, sports, or technology. Indeed, I particularly remember the first online fundraiser I ever participated in—the voluntary donation of $10 (by overland mail, of course) to support the hardware needs of a decidedly not-for-profit (in the informal sense) board operator. After those days, it was ISPs like Prodigy and Pipeline, and their accompanying access to Usenet groups in the early 1990s. Many early Internet users still believe Usenet, which predated the commercial Web, was a golden era for online discourse, idea-sharing, and community. A self-policing free-for-all divided into endless topic groups (including a wide variety of environmental, social, religious, and political causes), Usenet linked hundreds of thousands of people behind computer screens across a wide network and connected them by shared interests.

In retrospect, it is easy to see that growing up in the 1960s and 1970s, I was a child obsessed with media; but no one was analyzing my consumption, least of all me. "He watches an awful lot of television," was the phrase most often employed. And it was true. Yet, I was also a huge fan of radio. The voices were magnificent—Marv Albert calling the Knicks, Bob Murphy and Lindsay Nelson bringing the Mets from the exotic climes of Los Angeles right back to my bedroom. Even the stentorian tones of CBS radio announcers updating the war in Vietnam gave me a shiver—the news of the world coming to me over this tiny handset powered by a single type A battery. The radio was on every morning and every night, and the television (more regulated by my parents) in the hours in between. And when neither was going, records were stacked six at a time in the "solid-state" single-unit stereo set up in our bedroom. The sociological study of the *always-on* media phenomenon became popular in the 1990s, but by the late 1960s, I was always plugged in.

Then there was *print*, as they call it now. My mother remembers my stubborn resistance to reading as a kindergartener, but once I gave in, I never stopped. Then, too, we were a newspaper family. My father caught the bus every day for the ride into downtown Yonkers, where he worked in the composition department of the old *Herald Statesman*; he literally put the paper together, and I was fascinated with the smell of wax and the vast, industrial computers that I saw when he took us in for visits to the office. These early behemoths huffed and chugged noisily just to produce a dainty piece of thin, paper tape with a series of coded holes in it; that paper, fed into another machine, produced the columns of type that were pasted onto layout sheets by hand. It was a hands-on production, a flurry of X-acto knives, pica poles, and rolls of border tape. It was my first introduction into the messy production of media, the creation of something wonderful that arrived on our doorstep every afternoon.

No wonder that I gravitated toward newspapers, less as a formal career than as the only logical choice I could make. As a college kid working the nightshift in the sports department of a suburban daily, covering high school and college games and filing on-deadline copy (sometimes by calling it into the sports desk) was both brilliant training and entirely intoxicating. I moved to news after college at one of the nation's great community newspapers, the *Riverdale Press*, and put down roots over a decade of reporting and editing. My time at the *Press*, a family-run Pulitzer-winning weekly covering the neighborhoods of the northwest Bronx, also taught me a great deal about community organizing and instilled in me an abiding respect for activists and community organizers, those people who take it on themselves to stand for a cause. That collision of media and causes was formative for a young whippersnapper of a journalist. On any given day, somebody with a cause would simply walk through the door and demand to speak with one of the reporters or editors. And we would be required to sit down and listen, to dig deeper and decide whether that cause was newsworthy, to report and try to find balance in the opposition, and then to take our lumps after publication, when we very quickly learned that no news story about an issue people have a strong passion for can possibly satisfy everyone. It was a grinding, humbling experience. The causes then were ecology and overdevelopment, crime and street repairs, education and health care—the same causes millions of Americans still organize around today. But the tools of cause organizing were petitions and letters and editorials, protests and street marches, phone banks and advertising. True organization took deep commitment from an active leadership, many in-person meetings, and long hours of planning and knocking on doors.

By the early 1990s, my growing interest in online networks had blossomed. New York was a place where a chronically underemployed subset of creative types—writers, artists, photographers, designer, actors—was coming face to face with the Internet. These talented young people were throwing themselves into creating projects, experiments, virtual art installations, ezines, newsletters, and communities. Chervokas and I smelled a story and we jumped in, meeting in lofts with entrepreneurs who did not really understand that they had started a business, artists who wanted to change the nature of media, and a growing group of financiers who believed that the Internet was the next massive American investment opportunity—that it would, in the parlance of the day, "change everything." Chervokas and I launched @NY in the summer of 1995, less than a year after the debut of Netscape Navigator, the first commercially viable Web browser, and Yahoo!, the first Internet portal. We were journalists, enthusiastic about the story we had latched onto, not businessmen. Almost despite our best efforts to sink it, @NY grew with the times. The experience was entirely formative. It created a permanent network of friends and colleagues, and it revealed a hidden entrepreneurial side to my worldview. Besides, stoking the growth of small webshops and webzines in New York (a continent away from the epicenter of the digital explosion in California) was a cause in itself. Working the network, exchanging links, finding advertisers, breaking stories, analyzing the numbers, digging into IPOs, and dreaming about the future—all the while freelancing for publications like the *New York Times* and the *Industry Standard* to support our money-starved venture—created a vortex of connected activity that informs everything else I do online.

A few years later, another story captured my attention: using the Internet as a force for social change, as a way of linking donors with causes, as a method for organizing to fight disease or rebuild communities. Changing Our World, Inc. was a tiny startup crammed into a steamy four-room suite above Grand Central Terminal in 1999, but from the start its creators knew they wanted to build a company that leaned forward, rather than looking back. Chairman Michael Hoffman and his partner Chris

Watson (my younger brother) leveraged their fundraising and nonprofit management careers to create a new kind of consulting firm, and Susan Carey Dempsey and I teamed to build onPhilanthropy.com, an online center for analysis of trends and best practices that are rapidly changing the nonprofit sector. For five years, we have produced the annual Summit onPhilanthropy, a gathering of nonprofit and foundation leaders in New York that brings together some of the top people in the field under the Changing Our World banner. The company and its incredibly diverse workforce of committed consultants and experts has provided the best possible vantage point to observe the changing face of philanthropy, both in the United States and abroad. Moreover, through its clients and campaigns, the company is an active leader in that rapidly changing world, and it has been my privilege to get my hands dirty in the service of those clients. At Changing Our World, I have learned how nonprofits work, how they raise money, and what challenges they face. I have seen online causes grow rapidly after September 11, 2001, and I am well aware that the landscape is shifting (or as Bob Dylan might say, "The order is rapidly fading"). Then, too, my own home is part of the story, part of what convinced me to work on this project. My three children have never known a world without an online network and their experience and enthusiasm informs this book. My eldest, Veronica, is 16 and heavily involved in online causes; you will hear from her occasionally. My sons, Kelsey, 13, and Devon, 10, certainly believe that they can find anything they want online, and that the way to *organize* anything is through the network.

■ ■ ■

That is my identity trail, a summary easily discerned from four years of posts on my blog or my long Google tail of bylines and stories and links. *Personal identity*, that digital trail, is at the center of the CauseWired movement, and it is the part of this story I find most compelling. I do not believe there is a good, impersonal, purely journalistic or academic way to cover this movement; you have to plunge in directly to understand it. So you may come across more personal stories in these pages. You may hear more about my own causes and my own experiences as I try to illustrate the bigger trends. I think that is appropriate. This is a time when super-wired, always-on, live-life-in-public young Americans wear their causes like style choices. Everything is open, searchable, available, and out in front.

Causes matter to today's consumer. Causes matter to companies, they matter to stock prices, and they matter to sales and brands. The early signs of this media-based *cause revolution* are everywhere, and this book identi-fies some of the best examples of the cause culture in action—bringing real-world stories to readers. New online interactions are connecting people as never before in human history, and those connections transcend the more obvious social activities such as sharing music, flirting, trading photos, and posting crazy homemade videos. Hidden behind those more shallow, everyday actions are deep changes in the way consumers band together to seek changes in society. This powerful (and positive) trend will have a huge impact on several large-scale areas of American life: consumer marketing, nonprofit organizations and personal philanthropy, and political and social causes.

■ ■ ■

The central goal of this book is to convince you that rapid advances in media and technology, in the ways people communicate, are changing how people support causes and how we respond to that underlying human impulse to help others, improve our communities, and change the world. If I can convince you through examples, stories, research, and my own experi-ence that this change is afoot, and that it is important to the future of char-ity, politics, social investment, and consumer marketing, I will have done my job and earned the price you have paid my publisher for this book.

There is a secondary goal: I would also like to get you thinking about how this will all take shape, what the landscape might look like in a decade, and the manner in which today's young people will be tomorrow's leaders, online and off. Here, there is more of a moving target; predicting the future is a fool's game, but it is so much fun that we will take a crack anyway. In doing so, the key is asking the right questions. If the framework for arriving at some forward-looking conclusions is correct, then the conclusions themselves can be recalculated and adjusted as conditions shift. There is an old maxim about starting a garden: Get the bones of it right—the beds, the exposure to the sun, the paths, the general layout—and then you can shift the plants year to year, season to season, as you learn about what works and what does not work. I rather like that metaphor for the realm of digital media. As I write this paragraph on a breezy June afternoon in 2008, I have no idea what some wily entrepreneurs are cooking up in some corner of the world, or what some cadre of digital inventors is coding. It may be a new variation on social networking, a new way to spin the Web, some new flower of innovation. But if we set up some rock-solid questions now—if we get our paths in order—we will be ready for those promising seedlings next spring, or the spring after that.

No matter how cleverly written, a book is not an interactive medium. Unlike the thousands of blog posts I have written over the past five years, I cannot go back and change a few words, add a link, or drop in a pithy quote. Although editions might change (if I am lucky), this is essentially a finished work—a moderately verbose snapshot of the digital landscape of causes put down during a certain time period. Yet, there is something gratifying about a medium with the permanence of a book. If I am successful, this book will do more than sit on the bookshelf; it will stimulate conversation and perhaps inspire a few people to launch themselves down the path of wired social change.

In many ways, writing this book has been like shooting at a moving target. When I began, Facebook was the darling of financial analysts and sociologists the world over, fat in both market cap and reputation as a game-changer. When I completed it, Facebook was still a giant in the social networking space, but it had lost some of its reputation as "the next Google" as the company struggled with privacy concerns and advertising, and its ultimate revenue model took time to develop. By the time you read this book, Facebook may have been sold for billions. But that does not matter to the premise of *CauseWired*; this is not so much about companies (do not look to me for investment advice; I still have some stock certificates of late-1990s dot-com companies that have the value of Confederate currency). The book is about large numbers of users, what they do online, and how they are changing the relationship between communications and causes. To me, Facebook is incredibly valuable as the largest online lab for these forces of change. I do not care if it ultimately has a successful IPO or sells at a bargain-basement price to Rupert Murdoch; I care about how people use it to answer that most human of questions: "What can I do to change the world?" The Internet itself is a social network; the companies that use it to create markets are interesting, but the great networked collaboration—the *conversation*—is much more compelling.

■ ■ ■

In 1980, the guitar-smashing, anthem-writing rock star Pete Townshend of the Who wrote a song for his solo album, *Empty Glass*. The song was called "Rough Boys," and it came from a searing moment in the studio when Townshend, by then seen as an aging relic of an earlier age by some critics, reacted with a fury to the rise of punk rock in Britain and the United States. It was a time of smaller labels, smaller venues, and tremendous invention and change on the rock scene, when the music was boiled down to its essence by a network of young, angry musicians who abhorred both the big, flabby, arena-filling stars of the 1960s and 1970s and the mind-thumping, empty pulse of disco. In truth, it was a very short moment in the history of pop music, soon eclipsed by the rise of indie and grunge rock and the massive growth of hip-hop. The punks did not age well, and whereas Townshend is still writing new songs and experimenting with both technology and music, the punk era vanished more than two decades ago, seen only in glimpses these days in fond tributes by younger acts.

But "Rough Boys" captured something else, perhaps the instinctive reaction of an old rebel to the next generation. At the time, it was taken by some as a dismissal of punk rock acts like the Clash, Sex Pistols, Dead Boys, and Heartbreakers (and as a signal of Townshend's own sexual ambivalence). However, I think it has worn well as a totem of change, transcending those early critical judgments and surviving as an (only slightly grudging) appreciation of new energy and experimentation. "Rough boys," Townshend shouted, "Gonna get inside you . . . Gonna get inside your bitter mind . . . I wanna see what I can find."

Completing this book, I am 46 years old, and although an early adopter of media technology with a long career of online publishing and experimentation, I cannot be considered a member of the CauseWired generation, that core group of young millennials using Internet media and networks to support causes and bring about changes. I am either a last-second Boomer or an early Gen-Xer, a shoulder generational type with an obsession for media. There are many thousands of us, and we helped to pioneer the creation of a commercial Internet. We are still plugged in and still obsessed, but we are giving way to a new crop of inventors, organizers, and amateur social scientists. Still, that long online history and that continued obsession makes us older adopters the perfect partners to help the CauseWired generation and to provide some perspective on the rise of online social causes. Watching the growth of online causes and how quickly a generation that has never known a nonwired moment of consciousness has connected the use of technology with the pursuit of social change, I had my Pete Townshend moment. A good portion of this book is my attempt to get inside that movement, to see what I can find.

Mount Vernon, New York

September 2008

1

Lost in the Flood: Wired Causes Rise

The images of New Orleans and its neighbors on the Gulf of Mexico were stunning, and they hit America like a sickening punch. Hurricane Katrina formed over the Bahamas, crossed westward over Florida, picked up strength over the warm water of the gulf, and, on August 29, 2005, it roared ashore in Southeast Louisiana. Winds of 125 miles per hour battered the coastal communities, ripping down trees, shredding small buildings, tossing ships from their moorings, and laying waste to broad stretches of the coastline. The winds were devastating.

Then came the water.

Churned by intense low pressure and powerful winds, the storm surge swept over the coast, ripping through the Mississippi cities of Waveland, Bay St. Louis, Pass Christian, Long Beach, Gulfport, Biloxi, Ocean Springs, and Pascagoula.

But Louisiana was even worse. The water overwhelmed the aging and under-engineered flood-control system of New Orleans. The levees failed, and more than 80% of the city flooded. In many respects, one of America's cultural gems, a multicultural city known for its music and its food and its style, ceased to exist.

We all saw the terrible human cost. More than 1,800 people died in Hurricane Katrina, making it the most deadly Atlantic Storm in nearly eight decades. Government failed; indeed, the federal government seemed almost disinterested in the fate of an iconic American city for days, as thousands of people—mainly those too poor, or sick, or elderly to escape the storm surge—were trapped in their homes or in waste-clogged, sickening, makeshift community centers such as the Superdome. Bodies floated down flooded highways or lay bloated on ruined stretches of neighborhood streets. The U.S. Coast Guard began a widespread rescue operation, and gradually aid began trickling into the region. Refugees streamed from the region to shelters to the west in Texas or in the states to the north. Whole neighborhoods were emptied. Hospitals closed. Businesses failed. The population dwindled to half of its pre-storm levels. New Orleans was brought to its knees while a nation watched on television.

■ ■ ■

Online, the reaction was frenzied. Political bloggers excoriated the federal government and the response of the Bush Administration, concentrating much of their anger at the President, who seemed slow to react, and the action of his political appointee, Federal Emergency Management Agency director Michael D. Brown. Among liberal-leaning blogs, there was pure fury. The DailyKos, a progressive, large-scale weblog with many authors run by Markos Moulitsas, the U.S. Army veteran and political activist who founded the site in 2002, provided a typical online tableau of grief and anger in the days and weeks after Katrina. It published diary after diary by writers who were watching cable television news and blaming their national government, and George W. Bush, for a slow response and lost lives. Here is a typical heartfelt and emotional blast of anger from diarist Hunter, published three days after the storm hit, while refugees still awaited food and clean water and bodies still littered the streets:

> We have witnessed two disasters this week. The first was an act of nature. The second was not. The second disaster, still ongoing, is unforgivable.
>
> That's the only word that comes to mind, a word I keep repeating to myself. These deaths, these men, these women, these infants dying now in these hours didn't have to happen. They did not have to die waiting for convoys to gather outside their city or for reservists to stand alongside their shattered police forces. They did not have to wait in darkness and fear for help to arrive, only to struggle for days without that help ever coming.
>
> This is not politics. This is not partisanship.
>
> This is unforgivable.

Thousands of bloggers published thousands of posts about Hurricane Katrina and New Orleans. The shocking video was sliced and diced and redistributed on YouTube, a new video service founded less than five months earlier—and many amateur videographers added their own intense stories to the mix. On Flickr.com, a new photo-sharing site launched just 18 months earlier, photographers posted images of the damage, visual stories in digital still pictures of a dying city. And websites around the country posted links and banner ads to raise money via the American Red Cross and other major national charities.

By December, according the BloggersBlog site, the total number of English-language Katrina blog posts had passed the 500,000-post mark on Technorati. There are over 468,000 posts on BlogPulse and over 900,000 posts on IceRocket.com.

Indeed, the networked online community of Americans lit up with a mixture of shock, concern, disappointment, and anger. There was a palpable feeling, and I remember this quite vividly, that we were all so connected, so empowered by the online medium, so wired for good. Outside of the political ramifications and the issue of blame for governmental failure, the reaction to Katrina was almost as unanimous as the reaction to the attacks of September 11, four years earlier. And yet, in those four years, a new, better-connected Internet had begun to emerge—one that emphasized not an old-style publishing model of merely posting articles and photos and videos, but rather the possibilities of great social partnership among anyone with a connection.

This was Web 2.0, a still-emerging platform of companies, technologies, and communities—and in 2005, a new way of thinking about the Internet as a series of social networks. In the old model, content providers created things for other users to read or watch; it was very like old media moved online, complete with advertising and subscription rates. Group interaction was limited to email lists and bulletin boards, and there was no simple and integrated method for sharing that content—and those ideas.

This new *social web* placed a value on human interaction and an underlying technical configuration that allowed websites and applications to share information—and users to define their own experiences. Wikipedia—the massive, user-generated Internet encyclopedia and itself a Web 2.0 icon—has one of the most concise definitions of this chapter in new media development, which was hitting its stride just about the time Katrina came roiling ashore in August 2005:

Web 2.0 refers to a perceived second generation of web-based communities and hosted services—such as social-networking sites, wikis, and folksonomies—which aim to facilitate creativity, collaboration, and sharing between users.

Geekspeak aside, people were talking—writing blogs, sharing links, and using tags and keywords to build huge stories and connect themselves and their ideas to the world. Katrina provided the cause, the first large-scale combination of need for assistance and the desire to help, the Web-ready conflagration of compelling stories, angry politics, and the philanthropic case for support.

On my own blog, I railed against government incompetence like everybody else and used the description of one particularly moving photograph—a picture taken by Bruce Chambers of the Orange County Register and widely distributed, reproduced, and tagged by users—to describe my frustration:

> There have been many brilliant, shocking images coming out of the Katrina disaster and its aftermath, and there can be no doubt that the photographers who documented the struggle in New Orleans will see their work praised and rewarded for years to come. But it's more than two weeks since the storm; I didn't expect to be shocked, moved, saddened, angered, and touched deeply by a new photograph. Yet there it was, and even in a middle seat on the shuttle down to DC on business today, pressed in by work and competing elbows, it took my breath away.
>
> The picture shows a rescue team emerging from a white, two-family house in New Orleans. A big husky guy in U.S. Army fatigues with the name Ramos on his chest holds the truly emaciated body of a naked, elderly black man. The victim's head lolls back at a strange angle; consciousness does not dwell there. His ribs and breast-bone are prominent, and his body is smooth; age appears only in the well-worn hands and the ancient feet. He wears an oxygen mask and is hooked up to an IV drip. The team has taken the time to drape a towel across his genitals. Clearly, the man's life hangs in the balance, but this group of rescuers saw the need for some slight dignity.

Then there is the face of Ramos. It is a powerful face, late 30s I'd guess, going to jowls. A man who likes his cold ones and his football (pure conjecture, but it's my blog). Ramos is hell-bent to save the dying man, that much is clear. All camo fatigues and determination, he is the face of a real Federal response to disaster. His energy is the abundant source of movement in the photo, the complete contrast to the limp, thin victim.

There are others: A woman with a navy shirt that apparently reads New Orleans Medic holds the patient's legs as the group descends some concrete steps. She wears a blue handkerchief on her head, and her brown braids are the only sign of youth and beauty in the picture. Her colleague, a man in dark shades, holds the victim's shoulders aloft. They are local EMTs, supporting the shoulders and the legs of a man being rescued by the Federal response team. A hand with a camouflage cuff, the rest unseen, holds the IV bag.

This is New Orleans two weeks after the flood. Two weeks.

The post started a conversation. Other blogs picked up my description, and the Tattered Coat blog called the photo "the Katrina pieta," a fitting title.

At my blog, frequent commenter Tony Alva (his blogging nom de plume) shot me his thoughts: "We ought to be most thankful that there are people that are motivated to carry out their duty and do it with care no matter what has led them to the point they're at. And perhaps, that we don't forget these people. Maybe we should inspire to be more like them." Tony, I knew from our longstanding but entirely virtual relationship, was about my age, married with kids, and politically more conservative than I am. He did not like the political finger-pointing that dominated much of the blog posts after Katrina and did not hesitate to say so.

Another commenter said it reminded him "of the image of the raising of the U.S. flag on Mt. Surabachi on Iwo Jima." Another called it "Shocking and stirring. All the horror and goodness in one image." The discourse was tough but generally polite, as it usually is on my blog, where I write about media, politics, sports, and miscellany on a semi-regular basis. It is a personal site, and the discussion reflected the opinions of the small group of regulars whose company I am pleased to enjoy, plus the usual newcomers who find me when a post is highlighted elsewhere. In the vast and horrifying Katrina chapter, it was one small conversation, but it felt important to me, and I felt connected to others, to a wider circle—and in some ways, to a bigger cause.

All around the blogosphere, there were thousands of conversations like this one—some angry, some bitter, some incredibly sad, and many of them moving and vital and personal. To me, the virtual conversation around Katrina was a milestone in the context of social media and public discourse. It transcended the more partisan tone of the first "blogger election" the year before because it brought people together for a cause greater than an electoral triumph. Reading through those posts from the late summer and early fall of 2005 is instructive—they show the power of shared content, linked stories, tagged media, and interconnected conversations. Media expert Mark Glaser wrote an instant coda to the watershed Internet moment in mid-September 2005:

> As the water finally starts to recede in New Orleans, the watershed for online journalism has been laid bare. Hurricane Katrina brought forth a mature, multi-layered online response that built on the sense of community after 9/11, the amateur video of the Southeast Asian tsunami disaster and July 7 London bombings, and the on-the-scene blogging of the Iraq War.

The blogging of Hurricane Katrina also clearly showed the limits of online support for disaster relief. Millions of dollars were directed to the American Red Cross, which many Americans later came to believe did not perform particularly well in the storm's aftermath. The lack of electricity in the devastated areas kept many amateur journalists from covering the storm or its immediate aftermath. Meanwhile, some of the mainstream media—derided as an article of faith by bloggers—performed heroically, particularly the local press. Nola.com, the large-scale website of the *Times-Picayune* newspaper, became the online ground zero for reports from the city and was cited for its blogging when the paper won two Pulitzer Prizes (one for public service) for its coverage of Katrina. And most of us followed the horrific story on cable television, as that old-time dinosaur of 24-hour news CNN particularly distinguished itself.

Yet, I think Nola.com's role in the Katrina story transcends the old "we report, you read" formula for big news coverage—and it was central to how Katrina played out online, among the blogging community and a world of donors who wanted to help but felt powerless. After Katrina hit, reporters in the field updated the *Times-Picayune*'s blog on a continuous basis. Traffic exploded from about 800,000 page views on a normal day to more than 30 million a day in the aftermath of the disaster. As evacuees scattered north and west of the region, they eventually were able to get their local news from the ongoing blogging at Nola.com. Accepting the Pulitzer, editor Jim Amoss paid tribute to the blog's contributors, "who were integral to everything we published, and made us an around-the-clock vital link to readers scattered across the nation."

Reading just the headlines to Nola.com's blog posts of September 1, 2005, can bring a shiver to the back and a tightness in the throat—there are a mix of posts, some filed by reporters and some by residents:

People Needing Rescue—Thursday A.M.
Diana Puerto Analla in Gretna is missing
Missing sister Thelma Brown
Ellen Thomas looking for family
3–4 adults need help on Jefferson Ave.
Looking for Lakeisha Milligan
Fats Domino okay?

Searching for 6-year-old grandson
Residents trapped at UNO
Tulane Univ Med Center physicians need rescue
Searching for 9 Missing Family Members
Rescue needed at St. Mary of the Angels School
Murders in the Streets

There are dozens more. However, rather than being pinned to trees and lampposts and makeshift bulletin boards—as such pleas were, after September 11, 2001, in New York City—these posts became part of the flow of information out of New Orleans. They were read all over the world, and made their way into news reports and simple blogs posted by the tens of thousands of other bloggers. Nola.com's onsite, open-source, straight-to-the-public model—blending the stunning professionalism of its staff with raw reports from residents—combined with other reports and other photographers and video sources to build a national story that did not go away.

Indeed, the online reports flashed through the blogs so quickly that bloggers were often several steps ahead of the government in understanding the deepening crisis. There were times when the slow and seemingly broken disaster relief mechanisms of federal and state governments and the large relief agencies stood in stark contrast to the lightning-fast distribution of images and stories from the scene. This drove a high level of outrage among the wired classes, from national television anchors to lone bloggers. If they could see, almost instantly, what was happening—and share that information with millions of people online—why was it that the government could not react more quickly? Three weeks after the storm, the blogger who runs the People Get Ready blog wrote about returning to the city:

The city is a ghost town, or more accurately, a police-state ghost town where the inhabitants are eerily missing, replaced by a militia monitoring the movements of its own members.

It looks like an atomic bomb went off in New Orleans. Cars are strewn around in random ways straddling curbs, on the neutral grounds, some upside down. Skiffs, canoes, pirogues, and even small cruisers were beached. Everything once covered in floodwaters is now covered in an ash-brown dried mud. Anything that was once green is now dead and desiccated, coated in that same ash-brown dried mud.

In areas where significant flooding occurred (even Uptown), cars and houses are striped with grime along their sides—green and brown and ash in color, like dirty rings in a bathtub, or the great strata of millennia at the Grand Canyon, each set of rings telling a story of catastrophic loss. But the rings are everywhere. Across the expanse of entire neighborhoods, the trail of rings can be followed, from one house to the next, from one car to the next, across a fence or a tree or a row of bushes.

I drove into my neighborhood down Jefferson from Claiborne Avenue. A week ago, this area remained flooded with black water and was impassable. Now, everything was bone dry. A barricade on Jefferson Avenue forced me to duck into a side street. Then I continued down Joseph Street. Garbage lined both sides of the street where, obviously, lots of other people like myself had found a way into the city, their destroyed furnishings piled into high mounds on the street. There was litter scattered on the ground everywhere along with downed wires and dead tree limbs.

At each house, as I moved down the street, I looked to see where the water line was. I knocked on almost every one of these doors in the last election cycle as the captain of my precinct for the Kerry campaign. I tried to remember the faces that came to open particular doors, the doors to houses that were cuter than others, or the doors to houses whose yards had been given a little extra attention.

The water line was like a death sentence. For those whose houses were built on slabs or which were only raised marginally on short piers, every furnishing would be found destroyed, and many family heirlooms or irreplaceable objects of sentimental value. And this is just Uptown, which was spared the worst flooding.

I drove just past my house to park in a small clearing of debris in the street. My body's danger mechanisms kicked in as I stepped out onto the street. I felt a thin film of sweat develop, and my heart started to beat faster. The air was humid and filled with that smell of rotting swamp even though the ground was completely dry now.

■ ■ ■

In late summer 2005, the concept of online social networks was still a new one. Yet as the informal network of Katrina bloggers showed its reach, the potential of social networks in the cause of helping others showed its power. Photographs appeared on Flickr.com, a photo-sharing service that is now part of Yahoo, and many thousands linked to them, reposted them, and commented on them. Craigslist, the online classifieds provider, carried missing-persons posts and helped refugees find shelter in new cities. More than two dozen sites for people desperately trying to reconnect with friends and family members were launched.

Money was quickly raised. The Austin-based software company Convio, which helps nonprofits communicate with their online communities and raise money, set a single-day record for fundraising on August 31, 2005. Convio customers involved in providing disaster relief services to hurricane victims collectively raised nearly $14 million online—including the American Red Cross, American Humane Association, American Society for the Prevention of Cruelty to Animals, Feed the Children, Navy–Marine Corps Relief Society, Texas SPCA, and UJA Federation of New York.

By mid-September, of the half-billion dollars raised for Katrina relief, $265.1 million came through online donations, reported the Red Cross.

Simply following the "Katrina" tag on Flickr, YouTube, or Technorati brings instant access to an incredible cultural document, a huge trove of reporting and reaction, stories of human triumph and fragility. It is a vast document, one that has never existed before—a document created by millions of Americans, many of them young and totally at home with social media, with leaving a part of themselves in public view. You can call that massive cultural document a *tale*, a *story*, a *web*, or a series of conversations. You can call it a *social network* or a *metafile* or just a very large search result. You can even call it an annotated, hyperlinked epic online *prose poem*.

I would call it a *cause*. To be more specific, it is a souped-up, superwired, socially networked cause—a cultural development that will change how corporations approach consumers, how charities ask people for money, how candidates seek votes, and how ordinary Americans view their place in the world. Many of the people becoming involved in online causes are doing so simply because doing things online is what they know—they have never known an unwired world, a world where you could not change your Facebook photo or your skin or your instant messaging handle at any time.

The bloggers and journalists and "friends" who talked about Katrina online, and took action, and raised money brought an emerging consumer technology trend into sharp focus. They had become *CauseWired*.

What do we mean by *CauseWired*? How far does it reach? Who does it involve, and what does it encompass?

First, let us look at the *cause* part. To me, causes are situations that motivate people to try to change some part of the status quo; causes are, by definition, progressive. They are what drive people to seek change. But I also favor the widest possible definition for the purposes of this study. That change can be fairly conventional—what we have always thought that charities and nonprofit institutions were about: healing the sick, feeding the hungry, protecting the environment, fighting injustice, educating the young. These areas, at least in the United States, are dominated by established 501(c)3 tax-exempt organizations and religious organizations. Many of these groups have pivoted sharply in recent years and adopted cutting-edge technology in their fundraising and donor-cultivation activities. They realize that as the donor pool gets younger and more open in its connection to causes, they must evolve quickly or be left behind.

Certainly, large nonprofits are part of the story, but they are not the whole story. Unless you have been hiding away from the tumult and national argument, you are undoubtedly aware of the effect that online organizing has had in recent politics. Millions of Americans have signed on as virtual supporters and they have contributed tens of millions of dollars to their candidates; all the while, a new class of activist-journalists drives debate and challenges the mainstream media's view of the national polity from behind the dashboards of their blogs. Then there are the *flash causes*—quick and fast-moving drives to organize people online to take action, in response to a disaster or news story, for example. Finally, there are the social entrepreneurs, a rising class of visionaries that are building online activism into plans for a new generation of change-agent organizations.

What is *wired* about this movement?

Surely, nonprofits and politicians have been raising money online for more than a decade now. (And *wired* just does not cut it in a media landscape so dominated by wireless technology.) Yet, there is something about the current environment that makes wired causes so compelling right now, as opposed to a few years ago. First, *wired* does not just mean the cords attaching your computer to the wall, or the high-speed cable inside that wall and leading out to the street. It means the people on the vast network of networks. Never before have we all been so wired—that is to say, so closely related. Email was the "killer app" of the first decade of the commercial Internet—and it remains a vital connector.

But we've moved well beyond it, to a far more connected Internet. On any given day, I stay in touch with hundreds of people—real friends and Facebook friends—and they keep track of me, through Facebook, via Twitter (a short-messaging service that limits posts to 140 characters), or by subscribing to blog feeds or Flickr feeds or YouTube accounts. That wired (or *wireless*, of course, but it makes for an inferior metaphor) infrastructure of personal interaction and its growth over the last three years creates fertile ground for fast-moving social activism online. It allows for a kind of charitable involvement that is both personal and open to the world, what microfinance pioneer Susan Davis terms "the philanthropy of you."

There is another force in the wiring as well. We are living in a time of widespread experimentation involving causes—call it *social entrepreneurship*, *venture philanthropy*, *social enterprise*, or whatever term strikes your fancy. At its core, this movement favors a tolerance for risk in seeking social change. It is no accident that two of the best models for changing how society engages in philanthropy are web-based, social network-friendly, and highly viral—the microfinance site Kiva.org and the targeted philanthropy enterprise DonorsChoose. The ability to tap vast databases and provide a personal donor or lender experience is at the forefront of online social activism. Together they form what Ben Rattray, founder of the innovative giving portal Change.org, calls "the mega-public," a vast and interconnected army of people who, at least in part, want to change the world.

Technology makes it possible, of course—new protocols and software "hooks" that allow websites to talk to each other, that break down the barriers and silos that held back true online collaboration in the early days. The authors of *Wikinomics: How Mass Collaboration Changes Everything*, Don Tapscott and Anthony Williams, describe that model for widespread collaboration:

Call them the "weapons of mass collaboration." New low-cost collaborative infrastructures—from free Internet telephony to open source software to global outsourcing platforms—to allow thousands upon thousands of individuals and small producers to cocreate products, access markets, and delight customers in ways that only large corporations could manage in the past. This is giving rise to new collaborative capabilities and business models that will empower the prepared firm and destroy those that fail to adjust.

Tapscott and Williams, who focus primarily on consumer markets, foresee something of a golden age ("a critical turning point in economic and social history"), and it may well be possible to extend their view of online collaboration to causes. Wikipedia, the massive, free online encyclopedia that is written and edited entirely by its own user community, is emblematic of this possibility. In seven years, that community has built Wikipedia into a strong consumer brand—the fifth highest brand ranking by the readers of brandchannel.com—with over 10 million articles in 253 languages, comprising a combined total of over 1.74 billion words by March 2008. Yet, Wikipedia is itself a wired cause, run by the Wikimedia Foundation, Inc., a nonprofit organization headquartered in San Francisco. To its most ardent volunteers, Wikipedia is a vital cause, a rallying point for online social activism: "Imagine a world in which every single human being can freely share in the sum of all knowledge. That's our commitment," reads the foundation's credo. Wikipedia's 75,000 active users write and edit and check facts—and they support the cause of knowledge using a set of digital tools unavailable a decade ago. They are part of a hidden economy, or "prosumers" as futurist Alvin Toffler calls them— amateur or semiprofessional volunteers and activists, passionate in their work and contributing real value to the greater society. In terms of social activism, they're part of Ben Rattray's increasingly powerful mega-public.

Not to put too fine a point on it, much of that mega-public is young. The headlines and the ubiquitous B-roll footage do not tell a particularly compelling story about the priorities of young people these days.

To the popular press, young Americans are "generation clueless"—millions of selfish, naïve, and coddled starlet types staggering through their lives intentionally blind to the suffering of others, to world poverty, to the great issues of our day. To some degree, this reputation is hard earned.

However, the generalization of a materially obsessed generation masks a vital and important movement—a subtle shift in priorities and aspirations that will have a huge impact on the future of philanthropy. At no point since the student movements of the 1960s have young people worn their causes so openly—but this time around, the Facebook Generation is not fighting the establishment. They own it. For today's superwired, always-on, live-life-in-public young Americans, the causes you support define who you are. Societal aspirations have so permeated the "net-native" population that causes have become like musical tastes, style choices, and "blog bling."

Take Facebook. In less than six months during 2007, its Causes application (a bit of code you can easily add to your online profile) attracted more than two million members, who combined to support tens of thousands of nonprofits and political causes. Causes was created by Project Agape, a for-profit startup backed by venture capitalists in California. The company was co-founded by Sean Parker, a managing partner at The Founders Fund and a co-founder of Napster, Plaxo, and Facebook, and Joe Green, who comes from a background of grassroots organizing, having worked on the ground in political campaigns on the city, state, and presidential level. Causes allows organizations to raise money and gather supporters within Facebook. Said the founders, rather boldly:

> This is a natural evolution of social networking. Leveraging real-world social networks is an important part of activism, fundraising, and political campaigning. This is especially true of grassroots activism, local-chapter style nonprofit organizations, and the walks/runs used by many charities to raise money. Given all this, it's a bit surprising that online social networks haven't been more aggressively leveraged until now.

The money raised did not nearly match the level of involvement at first. Cancer research at Brigham & Women's Hospital, for instance, had attracted more than three million members by April 2008, but they had contributed just over $60,000, or two cents per member. The Save Darfur coalition had more than 840,000 members and $16,000 in donations, or the same two cents per member. One of those members was my teenage daughter, and many of her friends have joined the cause as well. They may not be raising huge sums, but they've made the cause of aiding victims of African genocide part of their public lives, and they're not shy about telling others or signing them up. Her old man may work in the philanthropic sector and have a decent understanding of the trends, but I suspect that my daughter and her friends will create a philanthropic future that's very different, indeed.

Sites such as Kiva, MySpace, LinkedIn, DonorsChoose, Change.org, and Facebook hold the promise of connecting social entrepreneurship with mass markets of consumers—of linking the motivation behind philanthropy with the aspiration to bring about change. The result may change how developed societies come to view charity and causes— particularly as young people begin to "wear" their causes as public manifestations of their personalities, like clothing and music.

Recent announcements of philanthropy initiatives on sites as diverse as buttoned-up professional network LinkedIn and the freewheeling MySpace, where members will be invited to help battle malaria, show that social-network members ranging from geeked-out middle school kids to resume-swapping career-climbers are all adding the charitable impulse to their digital profile building. Beyond the social networks, there's also a growing recognition that philanthropy and social causes can be a rewarding career path. At onPhilanthropy.com, where I'm the publisher, a group of young professionals has formed Future Leaders in Philanthropy (FLiP, as we call it), a "mashed-up" community that includes a blog, a Facebook group, and in-person networking events. More than 2,000 people have signed up, subscribed, or attended a happy hour to discuss their careers in the sector.

Jean Case is CEO of the Case Foundation, which she created with her husband, Steve, founder of America Online and one of the nation's pioneers in the media technology business. The Case Foundation is heavily involved in priming the pump for online causes, getting more people involved and keying activism. She talks regularly about the optimism she feels about the younger generation of activists, noting that almost half the world's population is under 25. Many are getting deeply and personally involved in causes in a way that has never happened before. "We are seeing such a huge opportunity to engage individuals at all levels," she said, at the Wealth & Giving Forum in 2007, an annual gathering of family foundations. "And this space has not yet been fully tapped. Social networking opens up exciting opportunities to bring people together and to define themselves by what they care about. . . . I think we'll look back at philanthropy as this quaint time when rich people wrote checks and we'll be living in a time when philanthropy is part of everyday life."

Causes matter to today's consumer. Causes matter to companies, they matter to stock prices, and they matter to sales and brands. A 2007 survey conducted by cause-marketing company Cone Communications found that 83% of Americans say companies have a responsibility to help support causes, and 87% would switch from one brand to another if the other brand is associated with a good cause. But I believe that the *net-native generation* is also applying this principle to individuals, including themselves. The concept of a personal brand is everywhere. It turns out Andy Warhol had it wrong, probably because he was commenting on an era dominated by TV networks and tabloids—an era that has passed. We will not all have our 15 minutes of fame; we will have lifetimes of slight notoriety within our personal networks, some small, some large. And one factor in how we rank is our public support for the causes that are close to us. It is easy to see how today's young workers want to bring their causes with them to the office. This is a growing professional field. Even in other fields, doing well and doing good are becoming ever-more intertwined.

American philanthropy nears $300 billion a year, holding steady at around 2% of GDP. Of that, the confluence of the net natives and online donations is a tiny ripple in a vast ocean—estimated at between $6 and $8 billion at the most.

I believe that will change. The combination of what the next generation expects and what it has access to will change the nature of philanthropy and giving and causes. It is often observed by fundraisers that the Baby Boomers heading toward retirement and asked to make contributions to causes expect two things: personal involvement and results. You can see that both in the explosion of 501(c)3-registered organizations and in foundations. The trend-watchers tell us that writing a check isn't good enough for many of today's major donors. This is driving innovation in information sharing and communications. Sites promoting acts of generosity and kindness, such as Kiva, DonorsChoose, ChangingthePresent, Global Giving, Razoo, Social Actions, DoSomething, Karmadu, Change.org, FirstGiving, and WorldChanging.com, and the philanthropic efforts of social networks like Facebook, LinkedIn, Friendster, MySpace, and many others are making the public adoption of causes part of the social-networking experience.

The central thesis of this book is very simple: New technology and the human urge to communicate will create the basis for a golden age of activism and involvement, increasing the reach of philanthropy and improving the openness of politics, democratic government, and our major social institutions. Whether that golden age materializes and becomes a force for great change will be largely dependent on how well that technology is used, how open the network remains, what voices rise to lead its movements, and whether the increasing onslaught of digital communications turns out to be a tool for good or an abstraction of entertainment and frivolity. In short, the public commons is changing; it is being rewired and supercharged with the powerful fuel of information and instant conversation. What happens on that new digital commons over the next quarter century will be the legacy of those who gather there.

I wrote, back in 1995 (for the online newsletter @NY, which Jason Chervokas and I created that summer), that the Internet is not a mass medium—it is a medium of the masses. There is no Super Bowl Sunday online, and no CBS Evening News with Walter Cronkite as in the America I grew up in, where up and down the street each living room glowed with families watching the same news on the same television program at the same time. From the moment in the middle 1990s when the Internet became a vast consumer medium, that programmed nirvana of one event, one massive audience, one huge shared experience evaporated like the morning mist over the water in late summer. With few exceptions, the era of singular experience ended as America Online carpet-bombed dialup disks across the landscape and Netscape downloads spun the server meters to infinity.

Day by day, minute by minute, on whatever device in whatever setting we find ourselves colliding with media these days, our experiences are all different. No two people enjoy the same path to information, to entertainment, to communication.

The social web rallied after Katrina, spontaneously at first as people connected around the news story, and then more formally. Three years later, Katrina and its aftermath remains a wired social cause. Looking back along the many blog posts, public photographs, uploaded videos, user comments, and feed tracks, you can see a vast cause coming to life online— a cause that transcended geography and race and age.

The devastation left by Hurricane Katrina, physical and social, is still prominent in the CauseWired world. Three years after the storm, there are dozens of online efforts to raise money for the storm's victims and to help New Orleans regain its footing. It is a sign of Americans' generosity and desire to help; but it is also a signal of just how easily a wired cause can permeate the consumer consciousness and become part of how we interact.

Type "support hurricane Katrina" into Google, and you get more than 600,000 results—links to organizations aiming to help those left homeless and a community still damaged by the storm. Many are sponsored results, either paid advertisements or links donated to nonprofits by Google, which maintains a large program to donate traffic to causes. They include links to Network for Good, the online donation center for nonprofits; OxfamAmerica, the spinoff of Europe's largest antipoverty organization; the Urban Institute, which is studying the rebuilding of New Orleans; the Phoenix of New Orleans, a nonprofit organization devoted to rebuilding and recovery of the centrally located Lower Mid-City neighborhood; the brilliant Squandered Heritage site by community organizer Karen Gadbois, who is determined to preserve historic homes under repair from demolition by overly aggressive public agencies; and Friends of New Orleans, a nonprofit that says it is "looking for a million friends to declare their support for New Orleans and surrounding parishes."

On Facebook, the Hurricane Katrina Relief Foundation cause had more than 1,110 members. It was created by a high school student in New Jersey (not the Foundation itself, just the Facebook cause) whose class went on a mission trip to the stricken city. On the cause's main page is a YouTube video that shows a series of slides taken on the trip in St. Bernard Parish and parts of the Lower Ninth Ward. And on YouTube, the student's amateur video got this response from a New Orleans resident: "Thanks for the video. I will soon be moving back to N.O. It seems as though most of the United States has long forgotten New Orleans. We don't really want pity or money from you, just don't forget about us. May none of you ever have to experience anything such as Katrina in your lives."

■ ■ ■

Years after Katrina came ashore, the social web still connects people who were hurt with people who want to help. The immediate response to the disaster was a terrible failure, a national object lesson in neglect, poor policy, and cultural disconnections. But the CauseWired community still connects, still raises money, still keeps its eye on New Orleans, and still considers the rebuilding of the city and the lives of its residents an important, national (even international) cause.

One small corner of this large, interconnected cause was a site called Hellicane, a blog dedicated to poetry about Hurricane Katrina. It still collects poems about the storm, or about the people of the Gulf, but as I linked back across the Katrina-inspired social network, which touched millions and raised millions, I came across one bit of verse that seemed to me to stand for the billions of connect bytes and the people who came together online and off. It is part of a poem by Jill Eisnaugle, called "Time of Greatest Need":

> Even when the worst is finished
> And the toll has last been known
> Kindness shall not be diminished
> And you'll never walk alone

2

Friending for Good: The Facebook Philanthropists

When Eric Ding was in high school, doctors found a baseball-sized tumor in his chest and told him he had only a few years to live. But Ding survived and dedicated his life to medical research. Ding was born in China, and is a naturalized American citizen. At 25, he is one of the nation's next generation of great medical researchers. As a doctoral candidate at Harvard University, where he earned dual doctorates in epidemiology and nutrition, Ding led a two-year investigation into the safety of the pain reliever Vioxx and its sister drugs, a case that drew national attention, and he is deeply involved in cancer research at Harvard, part of the movement to bring treatments and eventual cures to patients more quickly than in the past. His accomplishment in this vital field at a young age is enough for him to be considered one of the rising stars in leading-edge health care.

Eric Ding is also a living example of successful social activism in the Internet age, a leading member of the CauseWired movement. "Ever since my own battle with a large tumor as a teenager and the death of a grandparent and close mentor from cancer, I've wanted to start a campaign to increase the pace of cancer research. As a scientist, I know the wheels of cancer research don't always spin quickly or efficiently, particularly funding," he says.

In 2007, Ding was looking for a way to quickly gather public support and funding for breast cancer research at Brigham & Women's Hospital, one of the flagship hospitals of Harvard Medical School. Some of the work at Brigham & Women's was done in conjunction with the Nurses' Health Study, the largest and longest-running study of women's health in the world, a program with more than 120,000 subjects studied continuously since 1976. Some of the most important research related to estrogen, trans-fats, heart disease, and many forms of cancer originated from the Nurses' Health Study and its sister study with another 120,000 women. Ding was no stranger to online communities, and he looked for a solution to quickly gaining mass support for his cause—a platform to develop a new source of funding and activism.

The platform was *Causes* on Facebook.

■ ■ ■

Causes was launched by veteran Internet entrepreneur Sean Parker and political organizer Joe Green in March 2007. It was one of the first outside applications to reside on Facebook, the fast-growing online social network that began as a way for Harvard students to meet each other, socialize, and build virtual lists of friends. Causes allowed nonprofit organizations and political campaigns to tap into Facebook's rapidly expanding community of millions of users, and its launch coincided neatly with Facebook founder Mark Zuckerberg's decision to open membership in the community beyond college students. Facebook membership was exploding; young professionals were building large personal networks, and everyone was looking for the next thing after sharing photos and building friends lists. Causes on Facebook was something new. It had no website of its own, no online presence except for the section on Facebook.com that offered users the opportunity to add the Causes application to their profiles. One click did that. Then Facebook members could add their names as supporters of various causes, contribute money, and bug their friends to sign up. In terms of usership, Causes was an overnight hit. It was easy to say yes to friends asking for virtual support, donations were not required (only suggested), and the investment boiled down to a few seconds and a click or two. In three months, more than a million Facebook members signed up. Many of them quickly hooked into Eric Ding's cause.

"It got started as my idea to reach out to the public, who I know are very energetic and passionate, for funding and advocacy," says Ding. "I knew Facebook was a popular medium, but the idea to reach people didn't come to light until I came across the Causes app. I was also fortunate in being one of the first causes established on Facebook Causes, as well as benefiting from the enormous public sentiments of support for breast cancer research—which was the original name of the campaign during the first two or three months."

Breast Cancer Research quickly jumped to the top of the Causes charts and stayed there. Soon renamed "The Campaign for Cancer Research," and using the pink ribbon as a symbol, Ding's cause took off as users passed the campaign to their friends. A year after it launched, Ding's cause had signed up 3.1 million Facebook members. Everyone, it seemed, knew somebody in his or her family who had battled cancer. The cause was ubiquitous. The goal was very simple:

> Cancer is preventable and treatable—someday nobody should die from cancer. We believe in preventing cancer and promoting cancer survivorship. All donations *directly* benefit cutting-edge cancer research at Harvard Medical School.

Comments on the cause's "wall" (the simple public bulletin board that goes with every profile on Facebook) showed the wide appeal of Ding's campaign: "A friend has just passed on. It is beatable, but sometimes, no matter how much you fight, you sometimes can't win; that is why the support is needed. What you are doing is great. Have faith and keep it up."

With a few lines of code, a small digital picture of a pink ribbon, and his own list of friends, Eric Ding had created a channel that caused three million people to make cancer research a small part of their Internet lives. However, there was a caveat to his success: The Campaign for Cancer Research raised only $62,000 in its first year, or roughly two cents per Facebook supporter. This was clearly not enough to make direct-marketing fundraisers sit up and take notice. Indeed, the pattern was the same across the top causes just below Eric's—1.8 million members and $22,000 for Stop Global Warming (1.2 cents), 1.3 million members and $22,000 for Animal Rights (1.6 cents), a million members and $10,000 donated for the Society Against Child Abuse (about a penny), and 850,000 members and $17,000 donated for Save Darfur (2 cents).

Eric focused on the size of the supporting group, not how much came through Facebook in dollars and cents:

> The best invention of all in Causes is the ability to mass email all the members in the cause, as well as separately send announcement notifications to everyone as well via their notification box on

Facebook. I would say that such mass-messaging feature for us absolutely makes the application truly invaluable—for a cancer campaign—it's hard to even put a sticker price on 3.1 million emails to members who are all interested in cancer.

Ding has a point: Where else could he have amassed a database of online users interested in cancer research so quickly, and at almost no cost? But Eric's story does not end with three million "friends" and $60,000 for a research program. Leveraging the response to Causes, Ding is in the process of creating the O Campaign Foundation (the O symbolizes "full circle") and plans to launch an Internet-based cancer study to spur evidence-based cancer education using what Eric calls "real science-based knowledge, not shady snake-oil remedies." The Foundation will also establish a set of prizes for breakthrough achievements in cancer research, "sort of like the X Prize, but for step-wise critical achievements rather than a grander Nobel-level prize," says Eric.

For Eric Ding, the experience has been worth it and it has advanced his original goal: to spur cancer research. "I'm more of a scientist rather than a social networking sociologist," Eric says. He continues:

However, being relatively young and rather in tune with the social networking trends, I indeed feel it holds tremendous opportunities for the future. People sincerely want to help and join to help fight cancer—yet the average lay individual has very little clue what it actually takes to find various treatments for various cancers—all of which are very different and biologically heterogeneous and complex. As a scientist peering out, I have been very surprised how many myths people hold about cancer and how many snake-oil miracle cures people believe in that apparently spread like wildfire on the Internet and virally via social networks. It's quite disturbing to a scientist like me. But I hope our work will be able to help dispel [them] someday. . . . All in all,

I feel very fortunate in being in a critical place where I can help bridge the gap between academia, science, and the lay populace to do greater things for cancer research.

There is lesson in Eric Ding's experience with Causes on Facebook in one short year. While the program might not raise buckets of money for individual causes, it creates attention. It builds a channel for branding a new cause, for creating a movement. It is only a year old. When you consider the two big metrics of Ding's cancer campaign, one pales beside the other: $62,000 will not go very far in the labs at Harvard, but 3.1 million people may indeed help change the game someday. What Eric Ding was doing with Causes on Facebook was not about building a fundraising campaign.

It was about building an audience.

■ ■ ■

Joe Green and Sean Parker are an unlikely pair of revolutionaries. In fact, they are unlikely partners entirely. Parker is the hard-charging entrepreneur with a string of well-known startups behind him and a reputation in Silicon Valley as a young man in a hurry. Green is the progressive grassroots community organizer who ran for the local school board, worked on the Kerry campaign, and took his inspiration from Cesar Chavez. Together, their for-profit startup company aims to create nothing less than the worldwide platform for organizing social causes online.

Launched in May 2007 on Facebook, their Causes application attracted more than 11 million users on the popular social networking site within a year. Causes is part of Project Agape, a for-profit company backed with venture capital and named for the Greek word that has come to mean brotherly love or acts of charity. In one short year, Causes on Facebook showed just how quickly social networking could spread causes ranging from research into breast cancer to ending the genocide in Darfur to raising a few bucks for a local soup kitchen. Its growth was exceedingly viral; the social network spread each cause (in reality, a bit of text, a logo, and a donation mechanism) through easy adoption and light peer pressure.

Causes was almost instantly accepted by the mass Facebook audience at the moment that Facebook decided to open its platform to outside developers. In the mix of goofy contests, souped-up virtual graffiti walls, hot-or-not quizzes, celebrity news streams, music applications, and con-verted board games, Causes stood out quickly as an easy choice to make for a Facebook user. The proposition was simple: Add the Causes applica-tion, pick something worthy, and tell all your friends about it. Then those friends told friends, and so on. No other development in the CauseWired world showed large-scale viral growth so quickly. Causes on Facebook proved that a broad social network could support online social activism—at least at the cursory and admittedly shallow level of publicly adding a cause to your social profile.

By the time Sean Parker, 28, co-founded Causes on Facebook, he had several major Internet startups behind him and was among the lead-ing entrepreneurs in online viral marketing and social networking. He was also a well-known personality among the Valley digerati. Tech blogger Om Malik tagged him "Sean 'wild boy' Parker," and wrote about "Silicon Valley's bad boy," and Valley chronicler Michael Arrington said he was "larger than life." Some of that reputation came from Parker's singular success at a young age in a series of prominent Internet ventures. Parker was just 19 when he helped Shawn Fanning create Napster, the file-sharing Web service that helped to revolutionize the distribution of music. Launched in 1999, Napster took off like a rocket as millions of music files were ripped from CDs and traded freely using peer-to-peer file-transfer technology. Napster use peaked at more than 26 million users worldwide in 2001, but by 2002, foundering under the weight of successful lawsuits by the record indus-try, it was bankrupt and had to shut down. In 2001, Parker founded Plaxo, an online address book service, with Minh Nguyen, Todd Masonis, and

Cameron Ring. The service grew to more than 15 million users. In 2004, he became the founding president of Facebook and a year later left to become a managing partner of the Founders Fund, a venture capital fund in San Francisco.

Joe Green brought none of the glamour and high-speed lifestyle of Silicon Valley's fortunes, market caps, and stock prices to his partnership with Sean Parker. "If you'd told me five years ago that I'd be running a business of any type, I'd have said you're insane," he says. Green's interest lay in progressive politics, and away from big-time capitalism; he liked to joke that the cities in which he had spent all of his adult life from college onward—Berkeley, Cambridge, and Santa Monica—are each also known as "the People's Republic of. . . ." However, he did bring experience in community organizing, and a deep respect for real-world social organizing.

What Parker and Green did have in common was a strong desire for social change through networks. They shared a core belief that the Internet could connect people in the service of that goal like nothing else in history. They also shared a common Facebook friend.

■ ■ ■

Mark Zuckerberg launched Facebook from his Harvard dorm room in February 2004 and built it into a leading social networking platform, prompting *Forbes* magazine to call him "the world's youngest self-made billionaire." He was also Joe Green's roommate at Harvard.

Green recalls working on the Kerry campaign in New Hampshire during the summer of 2003 and thinking about social networks and organizing activists. "That's when I first saw Friendster and I thought, here is this map of how everyone knows each other." Friendster is a social networking service founded in 2002 that eventually grew to 50 million users, but peaked in the United States well before sites like MySpace and Facebook became household names. The service had much of what drives online social networks: profiles, photos, and lists of friends and contacts.

Green was intrigued at its application on political and social activism campaigns: "That fall I was thinking about it a lot. I asked my roommate about creating a social network for politics, but he was more interested in a social network for college students."

Green went off to work for the Kerry–Edwards campaign in the general election, canvassing neighborhoods in rural Arizona for the unsuccessful Democratic ticket, but he continued to think about combining old-school organizing and new-media social tools. He set out to build something on his own. After the election, he founded essembly.com, a nonpartisan political social networking website that would let people connect with one another based on political opinions. The site was deliberately small in scale and by invitation of other members, and it was designed to encourage intelligent discourse while discouraging flame wars and personal attacks. Its design around small groups of dedicated voices—using political statements called *resolves* to start discussions—hearkened back to Green's personal experience as an organizer, which began in high school in Santa Monica, California. Green described the formative experience on the progressive political blog MyDD:

> I first got active as a senior in high school. Santa Monica had a living-wage campaign—one of the first that covered not just city employees, but everyone in our tourist zone. The campaign barely lost but we got a lot of students at our high school involved, many of whom had parents who cleaned hotel rooms in beach hotels for like seven bucks an hour.

At Harvard, he studied under Marshall Ganz, a professor of public policy and a well-known organizer who spent 16 years working with Cesar Chavez and the United Farm Workers. The lesson was an important one:

> Here was Cesar Chavez trying to take pretty much the most powerless people in the country, the people who are closer to serfs than we've had for a long time, with almost no legal rights, and organizing them.

But first you had to convince them that it was even possible for them to have any impact on all-powerful forces. And once you did, there were no shortcuts. You start with a small number of people, just speaking one-on-one in a meeting, and you share your personal story, then you convince them to have a meeting, and it's through these existing social connections of family and friends and church that you grow these movements. Basically, you're organizing yourself out of a job.

In thinking about modern media technology and old-school activists, Green was struck by the potential of online social networking in organizing support for causes. "One of the hardest parts of organizing is sitting down with the address book and figuring out who everybody knows; the transparency of connections struck me—if we had one of these networks where you knew how everyone was connected, it would be very powerful."

Not long after the 2004 election, Green met Sean Parker through his old roommate, Mark Zuckerberg, and in the summer of 2006, the two found themselves brainstorming something new at the Coffee Bean in West Hollywood. "We were looking at a very broad solutions base. We felt that social networking is important, that it represented a fundamental transformation of community online." Parker's work on Plaxo, in particular, showed them a path. "Sean taught me that deliberate viral engineering, how you turn your users into propagators through careful optimization, was very important. He had this in the back of his head already, how to move it." At first, they looked at building a social network for causes from scratch, but decided to pursue distribution for their idea first. Quite naturally, they did it through their mutual friend's little startup, which had morphed into one of the fastest-growing online communities ever, moving quickly beyond the college community it was designed to serve.

■ ■ ■

Earlier communities on the Web promoted more of a widespread free-for-all, an anonymous or pseudonymous experience. Identities were free-flowing, and much of the early online growth stemmed specifically from a user's ability to guard his or her real name. As the famous *New Yorker* cartoon of a wisecracking canine pointed out back in 1993, "On the Internet nobody knows you're a dog." Anonymity was big in the first years of the commercial Internet, continuing the pattern established by the bulletin boards of the 1980s and Usenet, the vast, interest-based community of users.

As the social web began to grow quickly after the turn of the century, parts of the new social web—which placed an emphasis on the personal experience online not just of consumers but of creators—began to emphasize *authenticity*. Bloggers used pseudonyms, but they were meticulously open in moderating discussion. Amateur photographers took pride in their portfolios on Flickr, and linked to other photographers. Sites like del.icio.us created a system of open bookmarks held together by personal identity. Gradually, it became possible to stitch together a personal identity online that was quite authentic, whether it used a pseudonym or not. And that identity was not limited to a single site or service; now you created your "best you" (as my teenage daughter describes personal online profiles), through your blog, your comments on other blogs, your Facebook or MySpace profiles, your LinkedIn or Plaxo contact information, your music playlists at lastFM or Pandora, your del.icio.us bookmarks and Digg votes, your FriendFeed posts, and your videos on YouTube. It was a kind of freedom to both create and be recognized for creation that had not existed before on such a vast scale.

"Three things changed, ultimately, to move us from the intimate, voyeuristic Internet to the public, exhibitionist Internet," says media critic Jason Chervokas:

First, always-on Internet connectivity and mobile Internet connectivity stitched the Net deep into the seams of everyday life. Second, high-bandwidth Internet access completely opened up the medium not only to video and audio, but also to hybrid forms like mash-ups and file-sharing and media-rich user profiles. No longer was the Net a replica of written correspondence, but a multimedia, multichannel, new way of communicating—neither one-to-one nor one-to-many, but any-to-any both in terms of people and in terms of types of communication. Finally, there was a generational change. As old media guys, we dragged our experiences and presumptions onto the Net, even as we tried not to. The second- and third-generation entrepreneurs started building more Net-native kinds of experience.

Technology, bandwidth, digital tools, and a common will toward self-expression created increasing freedom online. As Charles Leadbeater described it in his book, *We-think*:

> Freedom is a slippery idea, but I believe that the web will be good for freedom of expression in four respects. These are: the freedom to think what we like, to form and express ideas independently; the freedom to shape our identities, to be who we want to be; the freedom as consumers to choose and buy what we want; and the freedom to express ourselves through creating things that matter to us.

That new social web provided social proof of who you were; you gradually created one solid but multilayered identity across the entire Web, rather than many identities on many different sites or services. Yes, you probably portrayed an idealized view of yourself, but the more you contributed, tagged, commented, and linked, the truer the picture of your "real" identity became—the more trustworthy your profile appeared. That profile was continually validated, not by your own statements but by the online actions of your friends. They added you to friends lists, linked to your pictures, commented on your posts, argued with you, invited you to attend events online and in the real world—and that created a record of your "life" in the digital realm.

That record is a *social graph*, as Facebook's Zuckerberg called it when he opened the site's architecture to outside developers in 2007. He meant that each person's network transcended one site or service, even one as large as Facebook. Media consultant Stowe Boyd argues that "every person has a social graph, and parts of their social graph may be represented within various online social networking applications, but the social graph in its entirety cannot be encompassed in any tool; it is too rich, broad, and open for that."

Moving social activism online should take advantage of that social graph, Green and Parker believed. As they worked on their service, the idea of opening it to that connected world spanning many sites and services and feeds was very appealing, because it solved one of the key obstacles to organizing activists—the limited nature of going door-to-door with a petition in your hand. Author and philanthropic consultant Allison Fine believes that the biggest obstacle to organizational success is "the lack of power—both perceived and actual—felt by activists. This state of being is overcome in the Connected Age by the opportunity for organizations both to be self-determining, to set out their own pathway, and to involve large numbers of people in their efforts in new and meaningful ways."

■ ■ ■

Instead of a website, Causes became a service—a database run with open-source software that allowed it to be portable. Causes simply allowed any user to create a cause, tell her friends about it, create a list of supporters, and raise money. The first platform was an easy choice, according to Joe Green: "On Facebook, the social proof is there. We have friends in common, I look at photos of you with people I know, I find out what you look like, I'm convinced it's you—and it's enough to convince my friends that it's you, so it grows."

That real identity is crucial to philanthropy, social activism, and political organizing. Contributions require receipts. Nonprofits like to keep records of their donors so they can ask for more money at another time. Activism lives on real contact information that can be used again. Political contributions are important public records. Occasionally, anonymous campaigns— boycotts for instance, where the action is the *absence* of a person's presence or money—can succeed. But in the larger landscape of social change, where nonprofits raise money and politicians run for office, identity matters. Facebook has generally been a stickler for true identities. Further, its size and its expansion outside of college networks to include regional networks, corporate networks, and other organizations changed its demographic dramatically, from a service for people under the age of 22 to a network of connected consumers of any age. By the middle of 2007, Facebook had more than 42 million active users and more than half of them were outside of college campuses. As Green says, "distribution is everything at the beginning; once you have distribution you have social data."

Once you have social data, you have the opportunity to use it for social causes. In the test bed of Facebook, the ability to bring social pressure to bear (of the very lightest kind, of course) is part of the equation. When you sign up for a cause (Darfur, or global warming, or Eric Ding's campaign for cancer research), that choice shows up in the *mini-feed* that is a part of every member's profile. In the traditional charity world, big-ticket events raise money from social consciousness: the desire for peer recognition among the black ties and ball gowns, the need to be known for helping your alma mater or the local hospital. Causes on Facebook mimics that very public namedropping, but at the tiny cost of a click or two. It creates an instant form of organizing for charity that has never existed before. In other words, it lowers the bar for involvement, dramatically dropping the acquisition cost for acquiring potential supporters. Charities seeking to raise money through direct mail are known to pay a premium for each dollar raised from a brand-new donor; the cost may be $1.30 or $1.50 to acquire each new dollar. While the money raised on Causes is small so far, the acquisition cost per public supporter is almost zero.

Once a group comes together around a cause, they are already wired for mass communications. Cause owners can message the entire group with ease and at almost no cost. In the end, that may be the true value of innovations like Causes to social activism. As New York University sociologist Clay Shirky wrote in his fascinating study of groupthink, *Here Comes Everybody: The Power of Organizing Without Organizations*, "activities whose costs are higher than the potential value for both firms and markets simply don't happen. . . . New social tools are altering this equation by lowering the costs of coordinating group action. The easiest place to see this change is in activities that are too difficult to be pursued with traditional management but that have become possible with new forms of coordination."

The other key factor with Causes is the social validation that is welded to each nonprofit, candidate, or campaign created on Facebook. Causes do not spread just because they are good; they spread because people spread them. This seems simple and rather obvious, but it is the secret sauce behind the rise of all the online social networks. In short, people like being asked nicely by other people they know to do things for them; that request validates the relationship. This precept is as old as recorded civilization. The third-century B.C. Roman Republic poet Quintus Ennius wrote: *Amicu certus in re incerta cernitur*; it means, "A sure friend shows himself in an unsure time." This has come down to us as "A friend in need is a friend in deed," the English proverb dated by the *Oxford Dictionary of Quotations* to the eleventh century. The very word *friend* comes from the Old English and is closely related to the word *free*.

As *friending* enters the lexicon with a helpful shove from MySpace and Facebook, the essence of something freely given empowers the idea of social causes—as does the idea of public recognition for that gift. To Joe Green and Sean Parker, the appearance of a Cause in someone's Facebook mini-feed drives public social validation.

"There are really two things we're trying to accomplish here," says Green. "Causes is equal-opportunity activism. We want to empower individuals. If they have something they want to change, they have the tools to try. The second thing is we'd like to introduce market dynamics and increase the efficiencies of the nonprofit world."

While the funds raised in the first year were small (especially compared to the massive online haul of Democratic candidate Barack Obama, for example), the reach itself among a group of highly motivated, mostly young, socially networked, would-be activists was pretty impressive. "If you say that in nine months [Causes] raised two million dollars from sixty to seventy thousand individuals, you may say that's nothing in the big picture. But now eleven million people are using the model," says Green. "Now you start to pay attention."

New media analyst J.D. Lasica wrote in his forward-looking 2005 book, *Darknet: Hollywood's War Against the Digital Generation*, that "it's inevitable that participatory culture will prevail in the long run." Causes on Facebook is certainly part of that culture, supercharged by the idea of *public recognition on the social graph.*

"It certainly doesn't hurt to be recognized for what you do," says Green. He continues:

In the charity world at the high end, there is surely a healthy dose of social validation behind the biggest gifts. At the lower end, on a cancer walk, say, getting people to give to charity is the aim, but the incentive to recruit is the cause itself. Simply the idea of growing a cause to immense size is very powerful, and to have that based on social connections is even stronger—the idea that they're coming back because of the people they're volunteering with.

■ ■ ■

By the middle of 2008, Causes was poised to move beyond Facebook. The company raised $5 million in venture capital to fund its expansion and created Causes on MySpace, Facebook's more chaotic and entertainment-oriented social networking cousin (and now a unit of Rupert Murdoch's News Corp). It also announced that it had raised $2.5 million for its non-profit partners, while involving 12 million social network members in supporting its causes.

What is fascinating about Causes is the overt use of the very factors that drove the growth of MySpace and Facebook and other social networks. On the surface, these sites can seem like frivolous places for sending fake toys, silly quizzes, and virtual cocktails to friends (some of whom you barely know in the real world), and not very useful for the more profound issues we deal with as a society. But like many Web communities, original intent is co-opted by experimentation and shifting community norms, and the online social networks are now being used for things they were never explicitly designed for. More so than other social networking sites, for example, Facebook has become a hotbed for political causes, which are advanced through user-created groups and third-party applications that help raise visibility for these initiatives, from local campaigns to international issues.

When Facebook came to life as a way for Harvard students to stay in touch and plan their social schedules, I am sure no one foresaw the brilliant use of the networking principle by young graduate student Eric Ding to build a new medical research foundation with three million online supporters in a few months' time. The cause itself drove that growth: Facebook was merely a very fertile host.

Says Joe Green: "The cause is potentially one of the most viral things in the history of the Internet because the entire purpose of a cause is to grow."

3

Signing up to
Fight Evil:
The Network Acts

To western ears, the tragedy in Darfur holds complex origins but simple and horrible outcomes: death by famine, by war, and by mass murder; rape used as a weapon; ethnic cleansing. It is a repetition of the long history of "man's inhumanity to man."

Decades of drought, deadly dustbowl conditions, and simmering tribal and political tensions created an environment for civil war in the Darfur region of western Sudan in February 2003. In the years since, as many as 400,000 have died, according to United Nations estimates, and millions more have been displaced. As the conflict grew and accounts of horrific human rights abuses began to make their way into the media from the

41

African nation, many worried that once again the world would stand by while genocide was perpetrated on the helpless.

The usual human rights organizations pressured western governments and worked to support poorly provisioned African peacekeepers. But the growing Darfur genocide took place against a new communications landscape in the developed world, one that was beginning to use online tools and digital media assets to move governments, raise money, and empower activists—young, superwired people like Mark Hanis.

A junior at Swarthmore College, a liberal arts college outside of Philadelphia, Mark and fellow student Abena Mainoo organized Genocide Awareness Month in April 2004, "to promote awareness of genocide and show the campus community it doesn't just affect faraway places but our everyday lives as well." That year marked the tenth anniversary of the Rwandan genocide, and PBS presented a special program, *Frontline: Ghosts of Rwanda*, which recalled in stark detail how 800,000 people were murdered in 100 days as the rest of the world seemed to stand by helplessly. The comparison to what was unfolding in Darfur was obvious. Hanis is Jewish, and all of his grandparents were Holocaust survivors, so he believed passionately in the cause of stopping genocide in the modern world—of international intervention—and he found a welcome audience in his fellow college students.

Hanis is also a natural organizer, and his Swarthmore commemoration spread into something more permanent, as students focused on the growing ethnic cleansing in Darfur, Sudan, and on raising money to support the African Union peacekeepers. Hanis founded the Genocide Intervention Fund, which raised $250,000, recruited more than 100 colleges to join the effort, and involved thousands of students. He recruited celebrities like Mia Farrow and Don Cheadle, worked with former President Bill Clinton, and was featured in an op-ed column by crusading *New York Times* writer Nicholas Kristof, who was impressed with the online organizing against genocide: ". . . out of the miasma of horror that is Darfur, something uplifting is taking place. Ordinary Americans are finding creative ways to respond to the slaughter, so that they personally inject meaning into those traditionally hollow words: Never Again."

The scope of involvement is impressive, and one that is hard to envision without the tools of online social activism. Social networks Friendster, MySpace, and Facebook are at the center of a strategy that from the start had a longer-term goal than a typical letter-writing effort or fundraising campaign. "We're building a permanent political constituency against genocide," Hanis told Kristof in 2005, and today he has done just that. The original fund has grown into the Genocide Intervention Network (GI-Net), an international organization that is at the forefront of efforts to stop the killing in Darfur and beyond. Using targeted advocacy campaigns online, with software that matches legislators' constituents with donations amounts, GI-Net members helped pass the Darfur Peace and Accountability Act in 2006, and advocated for an increase of $50 million in funding for the African Union peacekeepers. Its STAND program is a nationwide, student-led organization that mobilizes high school and college-age young adults through more than 800 campus chapters. Formed out of the rapidly growing student movement to protect Darfur, STAND works to unify this anti-genocide movement under one message by providing students with informational, educational, and organizing resources, empowering them through an extensive network of impassioned student activists and advocating for a change in the world's mentality toward genocide. In 2006, as part of its "Time to Protect" campaign, STAND students raised more than $100,000 for civilian protection in Darfur. In 2007, STAND activists dramatized the link between China's economic and diplomatic support of Sudan and the Darfur genocide by forming a human chain spanning 12 blocks in New York City, and calling on the state of New York to "break the chain" and divest from Sudan. GI-Net also manages a campaign to encourage financial divestiture in Sudan and thereby pressure the government there, runs an anti-genocide hotline, and publishes a legislative scorecard tracking Congressional votes.

■ ■ ■

The Genocide Intervention Network is part of a larger group of organizations fighting genocide in Darfur and elsewhere. The Save Darfur Coalition has become a ubiquitous online cause, and has more than 180 member organizations, including GI-Net, and boasts the involvement of more than 130 million people.

That includes me. Sometime in 2007, I added the Save Darfur Causes badge to my Facebook profile. So did 27 of my contacts (or "friends," though I barely know some of them), along with more than 80,000 other Facebook members. Our involvement on Facebook seems very slight to me; indeed, we have contributed only a little over $16,000 via the online contributions system. Yet the money seems secondary to awareness. The number of online users reached by the various tools employed by the Save Darfur Coalition, including the Genocide Intervention Network, is impressive, but it took a brief conversation with my teenage daughter to really understand that reach.

"Dad," she said one evening as we both sat pounding on our laptops, "do you think we should boycott the Olympics?"

Now, this question was posed before the movement to protest Chinese involvement in Sudan by threatening to stay out of the Beijing games had received much media attention. Indeed, news-obsessed as I can be, I was still fairly clueless.

"Why should we?" I asked. And then I learned about the coalition's effort to use the Olympics to bring pressure on the Chinese to halt trade with the Sudanese government unless it ended its complicity in the region's tragic conflict. The Save Darfur badge, it turns out, was the most popular cause among my daughter's Facebook friends. "They join Causes but they don't donate any money," she told me. "But they'll send you chain things." In other words, my daughter's schoolmates and her network of online friends were sharing messages and email about genocide in Africa. And that is how she learned about Chinese involvement in the Sudan, and the movement to use the Olympics to pressure the world's largest country and fastest-growing economy. That is how I came to read a letter of protest from the coalition to President Hu Jintao of the People's Republic of China—a letter signed by Nobel Laureates, Olympic athletes, current and former government officials, business leaders, human rights activists, and public advocates that included this appeal to the Chinese government:

As the primary economic, military, and political partner of the Government of Sudan, and as a permanent member of the United Nations Security Council, China has both the opportunity and the responsibility to contribute to a just peace in Darfur. Ongoing failure to rise to this responsibility amounts, in our view, to support for a Government that continues to carry out atrocities against its own people. As host of the 2008 Olympic games, China has a special role to play in ensuring that its actions this year are commensurate with the Olympic ideals of peace and international cooperation.

The atrocities in Darfur continue to intensify. Of the seven million inhabitants of Darfur, hundreds of thousands have already died due to the conflict and 2.5 million have been displaced. Rape and sexual violence have been and continue to be used as weapons of war against untold numbers of girls and women. The Government of Sudan has also been involved in the forced relocation of people from refugee and Internally Displaced Peoples camps. Without homes to return to those displaced are left vulnerable to further attack.

We recognize some efforts by China in 2007 to increase diplomatic pressure on Sudan—notably through its support of the passage of UN

Security Council Resolution 1769, calling for the deployment of a UN-AU hybrid peacekeeping force to Darfur. At the same time, however, we note with dismay that the Chinese government worked to weaken the resolution before it passed. China also doubled its trade with Sudan in 2007, providing resources that make it easier for that government to continue to carry out its atrocities. China's military relationship with Sudan also continues.

The letter was part of a widespread campaign to put pressure on the Chinese, which it organized online with a message that millions of social network users could easily understand and pass along: "China's efforts to polish its international image can't hide the fact that it has not done enough to stop genocide in Darfur. The games China is playing in Beijing cannot hide the games that China is playing in Darfur." And all those badges, text messages, and emails brought about some real-world action in addition to the money raised: In April, when the Olympic torch made its only stop in the United States in San Francisco, anti-genocide activists launched the "Darfur Day of Action: Carry the Olympic Torch to Darfur." Their argument against participation in the Beijing Olympics struck a chord and the protests became a national news story.

Yet, it really wasn't personal.

■ ■ ■

Darfur has jumped to the top of the wired-causes roster in the past two years because of committed leaders like Mark Hanis; but it has also benefited from the canny use of a variety of technological tools and organizing techniques, many of which are aimed at getting people to take some kind of action. Posting a badge or adding a cause to Facebook or MySpace is just the beginning, the easiest action to take—in many ways the wide top to the funnel of real activism. "The biggest lesson about organizing online is complementing it with offline organizing," says Hanis. "The Internet at the Web 2.0 revolution requires offline social capital to reach its true potential. We need to have people have meaningful experiences and that largely comes through offline. So, after all the clicking, emailing, viewing, and posting, people need to get up from their chairs and step outside."

One of the ways to "step outside" doesn't actually require marching in a demonstration or attending a hearing—it just requires a telephone. The integration of telephone canvassing with online organizing has changed the way organizations and campaigns get volunteers to "call their Congressman." In the spring of 2008, when GI-Net wanted to pressure the U.S. government to make good on the funds it owed to pay for the Darfur peacekeeping mission, it used a hybrid system that literally teed up telephone activists and controlled the message as well. Every volunteer who signed up via Facebook, MySpace, or the organization's website got a simple set up instructions:

1. Call 1-800-GEN-OCIDE.
2. Dial your five-digit Zip code when prompted.
3. Choose to connect to either your representative (1), your senator (2), or the White House (3).
4. Listen to the talking points provided before the call connects.
5. Speak for a couple of minutes to a secretary in the official's office. Don't forget to say your name and where you're from!

More than 11,000 people made the call. Making it easy for volunteers to get their talking points down correctly was central to making an impact with federal officials; rolling the system out to 800 high school and college chapters gave it real power. Save Darfur coalition member GI-Net offered many ways for people to get involved. Web 2.0 tools included applications for Facebook, MySpace, the blogging platform LiveJournal, video-sharing portal YouTube, photo-sharing service Flickr, short-message-system

Twitter.com, and giving portal Change.org. The organization also used a series of single-purpose sites separate from the main website. For instance, www.AskTheCandidates.org asked supporters to "act now" and "sign the petition to all candidates and stay up to date on where they stand on Darfur" during the 2008 presidential race. A "Rapid Responders" program called on activists to download a plug-in to the popular Firefox Web browser that delivers real-time news alerts on Africa, and then prompted them to vote the stories in higher placement on user-driven meta-sites like Digg.com.

Somewhat counterintuitively, the key to pushing Darfur to the top of public consciousness online was using sophisticated technology to present a simple message: "Thousands are dying and you can help them. The tools are very easy to use. It will take you a few minutes. We only need a few dollars. Tell your friends." In that framework, hundreds of thousands will get involved; more than 800,000 added the Facebook Causes badge to their profiles. However, a vibrant and potentially powerful subset of those light users will dig deeper; of those 800,000 Facebook supporters, more than 4,000 wrote personal emails to local representatives in a matter of hours after the group sent an appeal to its group list on Causes.

A fine example of simplicity and direction in online cause promotion was The Nature Conservancy's "Plant a Billion Trees" campaign, which aimed to "restore and plant one billion trees by 2015 in Brazil's Atlantic Forest, one of the greatest repositories of biodiversity on Earth." The cause itself is compelling, especially to today's green consumers and environmentally conscious young people. The Atlantic Forest spanned across eastern Brazil, northern Argentina, and eastern Paraguay, and was once twice the size of Texas. More than 93% of the forest has been lost to development. The remaining land is home to 1,180 vertebrate species (mammals, amphibians, reptiles, fish, and birds) representing 5% of the vertebrates on Earth. More than 800 of those species are unique to the region, and more than 60% of all of Brazil's threatened animals call this forest home. It is a complex story of overdevelopment, international politics, and ecological science. The Nature Conservancy's program is large scale. It featured a multimedia content initiative that includes Planet Green, the first-ever 24-hour television network dedicated solely to green lifestyle programming, all supporting efforts to restore and plant one billion native trees on 2.5 million acres and connect more than 12 million acres of new forest corridors in the Atlantic Forest—in seven years.

But the request for action that reached my social network was small and simple: Build a widget. When I say *build*, I really mean "click on a cute but threatened species, log into Facebook, and tell your friends about it." It is deceptively simple, and aimed at encouraging people to learn more and possibly take the next step of getting involved. The organization aims to "get people off the mouse and onto the keyboard," says digital marketing director Jonathon Colman. "This means that we see a lot of value in commenting, linking, tagging, and the like; sometimes more so than just an empty visit to our site. I feel that someone who's engaged enough to write a sentence or two or to participate in a conversation or to upload a photo with a caption is a person who's inspired and compelled enough by our mission and success to take the next step."

The Darfur cause represents an example of a networked approach to social change; it is not a single organization, but a coalition. Much of its membership is virtual. Its costs are distributed; indeed, much of the labor cost is assumed by online volunteers, the activist equivalent of Toffler's prosumers. The growth of the coalition in several key metrics—members, money raised, influence—was rapid, and in direct response to the immediacy of the crisis in Africa. As Leslie Crutchfield and Heather McLeod Grant wrote in their landmark study of new models for charitable organizing, *Forces for Good: The Six Practices of High-Impact Nonprofits*:

. . . a network strategy is a more highly leveraged approach to achieving social change. The traditional way to scale an organization's impact is to build and fund new locations one by one. Expansion takes longer, requires more capital, and attains power slowly. But by scaling a network, nonprofits distribute the costs, scale more quickly, and have more immediate power through collective action. Networks wield additional public influence over large situations; they offer a larger distribution platform for services or ideas.

That distribution platform can change how a news story is presented, and power the creation of an international cause. In February 2008, Cyclone Ivan slashed across the African island of Madagascar with winds of more than 125 miles per hour, bringing heavy rains and massive destruction across the island. Government officials reported that the cyclone left around 190,000 people homeless and caused heavy damage to crops, roads, and public buildings. More than 80 people died. The storm hit Madagascar during an unusually heavy rainy season, so the ground was already saturated and flood damage had been sustained from previous storms. The Republic of Madagascar, formerly the Malagasy Republic, comprises the world's fourth largest island, a poor nation in the Indian Ocean that nonetheless enjoys vital importance as a center of somewhat fragile biodiversity.

In the west, media coverage of the cyclone, a storm roughly the size and strength of Hurricane Katrina, was minimal: a few wire-service stories and postings on sites like AllAfrica.com. In the United States, there was little coverage and no video on the cable news stations. I learned about Cyclone Ivan by reading Beth Kanter's blog. Beth is a self-described "Web technology evangelist" and one of the world's leading experts on the effects of social media on nonprofit organizations. She's a prolific blogger with a vast network of online correspondents, and I am always surprised by what turns up in her feed; her curious mind and extraordinary linking powers bring in some fascinating stories. It was Beth who told me about the work of blogger Joan Razafimharo and, by extension, the social venture known as Foko Madagascar.

Foko Madagascar was formed quickly after the gathering of the exclusive TED conference's regional expansion into Africa in 2007. The conference's theme was "Africa, the Next Chapter." Several social entrepreneurs and bloggers pooled their activism to start the Foko project, to help support Madagascar's development. That work took several forms: a biodiversity initiative (Madagascar has some of the highest biodiversity in the world and is home to as many as 12,000 plant species but struggles with the use of fire as an agricultural tool by poor farmers on the island); a women's craft-skills program aimed at helping poor women to make additional income from embroidery, sewing, and weaving; and a blogging project. In partnership with the Rising Voices initiative, the Foko Blog Club is teaching young people in Madagascar blogging skills. Rising Voices is a project of Global Voices, the "nonprofit global citizens' media project" founded at Harvard Law School's Berkman Center for Internet and Society, a research think-tank focused on the Internet's impact on society. It aims to "spread the tools and techniques of citizen media to communities that are underrepresented on the conversational web."

Lova Rakotomalala, Foko's project manager for health, described the goals of the blogging project on Foko's blog:

> We all know too well how actively participating in the global conversation through digital media can have a major impact in our way of thinking and approach toward development and global awareness. Joining the global conversation is critical on many levels. Firstly, it fosters the exchange of ideas with projects with similar goals such as the former and current rising voices grantees. Many creative ideas have been tested in different settings all over the world; learning from the rest of the world's experiences can only help our project be more efficient in achieving our goals. Secondly, it allows Malagasy people to illustrate and directly share with the rest of the world their perspectives on issues that they'd know best. Thirdly,

joining the global conversation will expand the network of people with similar interests nationally and internationally, connecting them and promoting positive collaborations.

In February 2008, the effort to connect developing regions like Madagascar to the wired world came into sharp focus. Joan Razafimharo covered the cyclone on her own blog and sent out calls for help to her network of digital friends. The Foko blog group kept track of YouTube video coverage and posted many links to blogs worldwide. One particular post from author and blogger Chris Mooney on his blog, The Intersection, stood out:

> When Britney shaves her head, everybody hears about it. When Ana Nicole Smith dies, everybody hears about it. But when Madagascar gets struck by a record six tropical cyclones in one season, killing hundreds and displacing perhaps as many as a hundred thousand, not to mention jeopardizing food supplies for many more, does it garner major and sustained U.S. press coverage?

Yet, the hundreds of people who read Beth Kanter's blog daily or subscribe to her RSS feed or follow her on Twitter heard about the Madagascar disaster. The bloggers at Foko (whose motto is "It takes a village to raise an idea") had fulfilled (at least in a small way) one of the main goals of the new organization: to join the worldwide dialogue by blogging their way into the flow of news. Links directed aid through the United Nations World Food Programme. It was not necessarily revolutionary, but it did show the power of one blogger telling a compelling story to a larger audience—a blogger with a real point of view and not content to sit on the sidelines.

■ ■ ■

Going outside the traditional paths of information distribution can quickly create a cause where none existed before. Using the power of the network to distribute a story, to sign people up to support a cause, and to occasionally bring them into the street is at the heart of the CauseWired revolution. Allison Fine, author of *Momentum: Igniting Social Change in the Connected Age*, wrote: "Social networks are the perfect renewable energy source." As one prominent film director discovered, the network can change the one-way nature of filmmaking into an interactive platform for creating and supporting causes.

In a profile of director and political activist Robert Greenwald, the *New York Times* said that "a visitor to Greenwald's office could be forgiven for thinking that he had stumbled across a dot-com start-up. It is a 24-hour-a-day operation, crammed with computers, monitors, cables, digital recorders, DVD-burners, and high-bandwidth Internet lines." Greenwald's Culver City operation is a far cry from the commercial Hollywood studios where he once worked. Greenwald has been nominated for three Emmy Awards, including *21 Hours at Munich*, about the massacre at the 1972 Olympics, and *The Burning Bed*, the critically acclaimed television movie about domestic abuse starring Farah Fawcett. He directed *Breaking Up* with Salma Hayek and Russell Crowe, as well as *Steal This Movie!*, the well-regarded biopic of 1960s activist Abbie Hoffman. But for all his success, Greenwald may never have as much impact in the movies or on mainstream television as he does on YouTube.

Greenwald founded Brave New Films in 2004, and quickly began producing documentaries attacking America's political right wing. He partnered with large online networks such as MoveOn.org to distribute the films on DVD or via the Internet. To political progressives, Greenwald's *Outfoxed: Rupert Murdoch's War on Journalism* on the media baron and *Iraq for Sale: The War Profiteers*, which looks at the profits behind the war in Iraq, are viewed as classics in film activism. Then he started making small, "instant videos" on social issues and political themes. The videos give the filmmaker the ability to move quickly, to experiment, and to take chances. "Since we decided one year ago to focus on the short video pieces, rather than the traditional full-length documentary," he told in an exchange on Facebook in the early spring of 2008, "we have been working and experimenting with both content and distribution."

Viral distribution was key; the studio posts the pieces on its website—sometimes spinning off mini-sites under a distinct Web address related to the content—and on YouTube. Activists, bloggers, and the merely curious do the rest. Using a bit of code attached to most YouTube videos, liberal bloggers can easily show a Greenwald video on their own sites. Very quickly, Greenwald's operation has evolved from an acclaimed documentary studio—with large budgets and long production schedules—to something with more power and reach. His short films are made quickly and distributed even more quickly.

Moreover, they arrive with comments, with arguments, with a vibrant back-and-forth exchange in real-time that makes the causes Greenwald selects that much more compelling: "The Internet has not changed the audience, but using the Internet to reach an audience has changed everything, radically. We know in a few hours after sending a video out if the audience embraces it, hates it, wants it changed, or wants more of it. They email, they blog, they pass it around—or not."

One of Greenwald's videos is called *When the Saints Go Marching In*, and it is a tribute to the people of New Orleans as well as an indictment of inaction in the aftermath of Hurricane Katrina. Brave New Films posted the four-minute minidocumentary, with its well-marbled Louisiana voices and images of domestic American destruction, on August 28, 2007, and viewership quickly climbed to over 100,000 on YouTube. However, the video was more than Katrina handwringing two years after the disaster. Its purpose was to rally public support for the Gulf Coast Housing Recovery Act of 2007, a proposal by Senator Chris Dodd of Connecticut to speed the process of replacing housing in New Orleans' hardest-hit neighborhoods.

The short video was tied to an online petition signed by more than 23,000 people on the Brave New Films site, and another 100,000 people through MoveOn.org. Just before Thanksgiving 2007 Greenwald delivered the signed petitions to the offices of Louisiana Senator David Vitter, a Republican seen by housing advocates as a legislative roadblock to the proposal. Together, the video and the petition touched hundreds of thousands of people and became part of a larger online conversation about government priorities after Katrina. While the legislation was opposed by the Bush Administration and remained stuck in the Senate, the housing coalition, dedicated to one-for-one replacement of lost homes in New Orleans, grew and gained power. Less than 10 minutes of total video, produced at small cost and distributed and consumed by thousands of online activists (some old hands at government arm-twisting and some entirely new to the process), changed what merely a decade ago would have been an arcane process played out behind closed doors in committee rooms.

"People want to be effective," says Greenwald. "People can go to Brave New Films, they can be local distributors, local producers. We've had people design posters. . . . We've had people find all sorts of ways to use the film for social change. As you guys branch out and as your reach expands, there are ways for people to really get involved." Further, the process has clearly invigorated the 63-year-old film veteran: "I wake up in the morning and I can get involved in a way that is not just sending an email to someone about how angry I am. I can actually do something."

■ ■ ■

Craig Dyer is a second-generation Christian missionary who runs Bright Hope International, a worldwide organization that serves people who earn less than $1 per day, but it is the third generation of the family that got him on Facebook:

My fourteen-year-old daughter introduced me to Facebook. She has over four hundred Facebook friends and I was curious to see how the site worked. I know there has not been a huge level of success with fundraising through networks like Facebook, but I believe the real worth is in exposure and branding. When we first planned our Facebook campaign, I got four of our youngest staff members (twenty-somethings) together and we brainstormed on how best to frame our message to most effectively reach their age group.

Founded in 1968 by Craig Dyer's father, Dr. Kevin Dyer, Bright Hope International is an Illinois-based Christian relief and development ministry committed to helping those living in extreme poverty. According to the organization's mission statement,

> Bright Hope does three things: helps the poor produce a product they can sell; empowers pastors and evangelists to share the love of Christ in poor communities; and provides relief to people in crisis. Bright Hope International works through churches and partners in 42 countries around the world. In situations of immediate crisis, we provide food, clothing, and medicine. Bright Hope helps thousands of the poorest families in the world break out of poverty and come to know the Lord Jesus as Savior.

Missionary work overseas, with its vast network of volunteers, donors, and churchgoing supporters, is a natural testing ground for online social activism. The natural ingredients for success are omnipresent: a built-in group of socially connected people, growing numbers of young members, and a widespread desire to change the world for the better. The same urge to foment change that drives the anti-genocide campaign around Darfur also empowers young missionary supporters in their organizing, and the principle is the same: Gather people online to promote actions offline.

Craig Dyer, building a movement of young Christians to support the poorest of the poor around the world, echoes Mark Hanis, the grandson of Holocaust survivors devoting his life to bringing modern meaning to the phrase "never again":

> At Bright Hope we are planning both networking activities and also live events that will convert the energy created by the network into impact and life change. I have a desire to motivate and engage younger generations to impact the poor.

For an organization like Bright Hope, reaching the next generation of missionary supporters is crucial, so Dyer is basically recruiting that generation where they live. "By using this technology," he said, "we can reach them in a way that is familiar and comfortable. It is crucial to utilize Facebook, and other web-based networks, for maximum exposure at little cost. We could never afford to do this through print or mail. Through this medium we can get our message out to an audience who seems to really want to help the poor and disadvantaged—but they may not know how to do so."

The returns for the organization (which has an annual budget of more than $2 million, according to philanthropy tracker Charity Navigator) are small, but the network is growing, and to Craig Dyer, that is what counts: It is all about seeding the passion for a worthwhile cause. Connecting online is just the start.

"Young people want to have relationships that are meaningful and significant," he says. "Internet social networks are great at enhancing communication between people, but I think young people, desire deeper relationships."

4 | Portfolios for Change: Peer-to-Peer Philanthropy

Across the street from the southeast corner of the Bronx Zoo, just a few yards from the tall electrified fence that contains three acres that zoologists use to recreate the natural habitat of the man-eating Siberian tiger, stands Wings Academy, also known as HS 684, a small public high school that holds classes in a blocky industrial-style building down the block from the elevated 180th Street subway station. The school sits on the northern end of West Farms, a hardscrabble urban neighborhood once as rural as its name suggests, where more than half the population now lives below the poverty line. The school was one of five smaller schools the Board of Education created out of the wreckage of James Monroe High School, a failed large-scale Bronx high school beset with crime and plummeting test scores. Among the thousand schools in the nation's largest public school system, Wings Academy was seen as a good-news story when 24-year-old Yale graduate Charles Best became a history teacher there in 2000. The year before, the *New York Times* had praised the school as "innovative," a place where the aim of emphasizing individual student achievement was being recognized. Test scores were rising. Attendance was up. The school was growing.

However, as Best, a young teacher just starting his career, quickly discovered, supplies and other assets that a suburban high school would take for granted simply could not be found in the city's public school system. Nevertheless, instead of hitting his head against the all-too-hard bureaucratic wall, Charles Best created a system for filling teachers' needs for added materials to better teach their students. In the eight years since its modest creation in the Bronx, DonorsChoose.org has built a model of online social activism that is shaking some of the foundations of old-school philanthropy:

> It grew out of conversation in the teacher's lunchroom—there were books we wanted students to read, art supplies for a project, a trip we wanted to take the students on and we couldn't provide them. There were no resources, and we were spending our own money on copy paper and pencils.

So Best, who is tall, thin, and intensely focused and uses his hands as he describes the venture almost like he is trying to shape it in virtual clay before a listener's eyes, began to noodle with a way to raise money for the items teachers felt were essential for decent education. He quickly came to believe that establishing a close tie with the classroom and with the young people would be important for potential donors. However, managing what would be a fast-growing and ever-changing list of needs on the one hand, with a potentially wide pool of donors on the other, demanded a solution, and a website became the obvious choice:

> I thought there must be a helluva lot of people who want to improve their public schools but figure if they write a hundred-dollar check to the school system, it just goes into an institutional black hole. So why not let them choose the project, see where their money was going, and hear back from the classroom . . . that was the genesis.

■ ■ ■

The first website cost less than $2,000 to develop and launch, and DonorsChoose lived on its rudimentary 1.0 version for several years. It had to: Best had launched DonorsChoose just as the Internet sector went bust, with many of the early big-name Internet companies tanking on Wall Street. There was not a lot of excitement for online startup ventures, nonprofit or otherwise. What had seemed like the endless promise of the commercial Internet in the late 1990s ran up against a lack of real profits by 2000. Then came the September 11 attacks and the economy's subsequent dip. In the Bronx, Charles Best got along with volunteer hours put in by committed fellow teachers and the high school students themselves:

> Every day, for three months, they would come after school and volunteer to stuff, stamp, and hand-address letters to people all over the country—letters telling people about DonorsChoose.org and asking them to check out the website and consider a donation. We got the addresses out of the alumni directories for my high school and college. My students sent 2,000 letters, which generated $30,000 in donations to projects on DonorsChoose.org.

DonorsChoose percolated along on a small scale, connecting individuals with projects in New York public schools. In 2002, a grant from Time Warner allowed DonorsChoose—by then a registered 501(c)3 charity—to hire its first employee. It was relatively well-known within the growing world of social enterprise (some referred to the site as the "eBay of philanthropy"). It had been the subject of articles in *Newsweek* and the *New York Times*, which reported that over two years the site had attracted "some 170 donors, more than half of whom live outside New York State, [who] have financed 215 teacher proposals on DonorsChoose, channeling $120,000 to projects that benefited more than 12,000 students." It was relatively small scale, but impressive for a startup. Indeed, one program officer at a prominent foundation worried aloud that "all the publicity is going to overwhelm them, just like the hype ultimately killed the Internet boom."

But the publicity was just getting started. In June 2003, Oprah Winfrey signed on with DonorsChoose, and did a nationally televised segment on the tiny organization.

"It really was Oprah who catalyzed all sorts of expansion opportunities," says Best, who remembers that his site reacted by crashing from the massive influx of new traffic. Just as constant were media inquiries and offers of partnership using the DonorsChoose model. To Best's credit, while he made the leap for greater funding at a scale he hadn't previously been able to contemplate, he held off on changing the model or expanding beyond providing assistance to public school systems. In other words, Best was able to steer DonorsChoose through the hype and remain on course to try to prove its underlying model. This took some fortitude and eventually forced a couple of key decisions—one strategic, the other personal.

Following an offer from a donor that was too good to pass up, DonorsChoose expanded to serve public schools in North Carolina as well as New York. Beyond the influx of resources, the expansion was appealing because it was limited; it was a chance to test the model beyond the New York City school system Best knew so well as a teacher, to see whether

DonorsChoose had a shot at long-term sustainability. In addition, Best knew his days of serving two masters were over. "I was beginning my fifth year of teaching and waking up every day thinking I was not being as good a teacher as I wanted to be." Best went full-time, and DonorsChoose continued its strategy of contained growth.

Meanwhile, the Internet sector came back with a whole new model: Web 2.0. Big portal sites and properties that tried to recreate newspapers and networks online were out; individual profiles and content sharing were in. Google's ascendancy decentralized the Web experience through search, diffusing the one-to-many old-school model of publishing, and helping to create the peer-to-peer social Internet of today. Weblogs sprouted everywhere, creating a new-content network on every topic under the sun, including philanthropy. Says Internet pioneer and online consultant Howard Greenstein:

> Web 2.0 is a term used to describe several technical and cultural trends that have changed the web. Web 2.0 sites tap the collective intelligence of users—a trend sometimes called the "wisdom of crowds" from the book of the same name by James Surowiecki. The more users contribute, the more Web 2.0 sites get additional content and increase in popularity. . . . Web 2.0 technologies tend to evolve over time. They start as "alpha" or "beta" software and improve, modifying the typical software development cycle of long prototypes and occasional releases.

That pretty much defined DonorsChoose.org. Created amid the wreckage of the first Internet boom, DonorsChoose helped to define new models for online philanthropy when the second wave hit; with its new emphasis on individual users and direct consumer communications, the Web had come back to DonorsChoose, rewarding Best's patience and his vision. The opportunity now seemed clear and wide. Six years after founding DonorsChoose at a small Bronx high school, Charles Best faced both his thirtieth birthday and a momentous decision—one that would change DonorsChoose forever.

Best had also acquired a friendly rival on the top tier of online social enterprise: one that seemed to grow, as Best put it succinctly, "just by virtue of its awesomeness."

■ ■ ■

When Jessica and Matt Flannery first became engaged in 2003, the Stanford alums signed up for a 13-week preengagement class at their church. Jessica was working at Stanford's Business School in the Public Management Program, and Matt was an erstwhile high-tech entrepreneur toiling as a software engineer for Tivo, the digital video recording pioneer then still in startup mode.

In the class, recalled Matt, "They make you talk about big things like kids, money, family, and career goals. We scored pretty well on our tests until midway through the course when we got to the page in our workbook that asked, "What are your career goals?" Matt answered: "I want to live in the Bay Area and be an entrepreneur." Jessica's answer was decidedly different: "I want to go to Africa and do microfinance."

They got married anyway, and Jessica's work at Stanford eventually opened up a new view of entrepreneurship to the impatient Matt Flannery:

> She would come home talking about things like "Social Return on Investment" and "The Double Bottom Line." For me, this was an interesting but academic discussion. One night, she invited me to come hear a guest speaker on the topic of microfinance, Dr. Mohammed Yunus. Dr. Yunus spoke to a classroom of thirty people and shared his story of starting the Grameen Bank. It was my first exposure to the topic and I thought it was a great story from an inspiring person. For Jessica, it was more of a call to action that focused her life goals.

Yunus, of course, was by then a star of international social enterprise—the famous Bangladeshi author of the best-selling autobiography, *Banker to the Poor,* and founder of Grameen Bank, which pioneered the idea of tiny loans to millions of poor entrepreneurs, mostly women. He was a living inspiration for a growing class of social entrepreneurs around the world, a group that included Jessica Flannery. Within six months of her marriage, she was in Africa working for the Village Enterprise Fund, which helps start small businesses in East Africa through small grants and loans. Her job was to measure the impact of the agency's loans and grants and to report on a case-by-case basis on the effectiveness of small amounts of capital. Matt found his way over for a month-long visit, and was struck by Jessica's work with small entrepreneurs and the basic business challenges that did not seem all that different from the familiar world of Bay Area technology startups back in the United States. An idea began to take shape:

When we were out there in Africa, without a ton of money, I read *The Warren Buffett Way.* And I thought, he's a guy who has so much leverage and can make such an impact, you can see the financial leverage he has. I had the same sort of desire. I was this would-be businessman who wanted to have a lot of leverage over some convenience store in Uganda with fifty bucks.

For the Flannerys, the time together in Africa proved formative, as Matt described it in the MIT journal *Innovations* in 2007:

I followed Jessica with my camera through Kenya and Tanzania. Most of our days were spent tracking down entrepreneurs and conducting interviews at their places of work in rural villages outside of major centers like Dodoma, Tanzania, and Kakamega, Kenya. Using a set of culturally specific questions, Jessica worked to ascertain the quality of life of those she interviewed, some of whom had started small businesses and others who had not. I witnessed firsthand the painful decisions familiar to anyone who has lived in poverty—whether to pay school fees, put food on the table, or buy medicine for a child suffering from a curable sickness. These are the trade-offs mothers and fathers are making each day in that part of the world. Confronting them firsthand for a month left a lasting effect on me. The emotional impact of a close confrontation with poverty combined with my more intellectual interest in business problems. I spent a lot of free time interviewing entrepreneurs about their barriers to growth. The challenges seemed quite familiar and understandable to me, even as an outsider.

With strong religious backgrounds, Matt and Jessica were used to the idea of sponsoring poor children in Africa. They started talking in terms of sponsoring businesses. The idea of individual stories was incredibly compelling:

For instance, in a village outside of Dodoma, there was no convenience store. Villagers would walk or bike several miles every day to a nearby village to buy household items. Why not just start a store in that village? The answer, more often than not, was access to start-up capital. The $500 needed to buy an initial inventory and start a store was too great a barrier. So everyone walked.

In another case, a fishmonger sold a half dozen fish on the side of the street every day and brought in barely enough income to feed her seven children. She purchased the fish from a middleman who would come from the lake about two hours away. Because of this, she made only a very small profit each day. Why couldn't she just make the two-hour journey to the lake herself and save three-fold on every fish she sold? She couldn't afford the bus ticket and had, in fact, never left her village.

Why not connect the fishmonger with someone willing to provide her with a loan to expand her business by such modest means as a bus ticket? Why not create an online marketplace—a peer-to-peer lending institution—to tell the fishmonger's story, and leverage the smaller loans of many interested lenders? Why not use market forces and new media technology to create a kind of self-regulating community of lenders who would share those stories, and build their own portfolios of loans?

That initial thinking led to almost a year of spreadsheets, business planning, meetings with potential investors, and Web development. By the early spring of 2005, it was coming together. All that was needed was the name. Recalls Flannery:

> I learned at Tivo that a short, memorable brand can be incredibly important in launching a company. There is always a tension between using an English word that has an obvious meaning and using something less obvious that you can create meaning and affinity around. Jessica and I preferred the latter and were focused on East Africa. We spent a week consulting two sources—the Swahili dictionary and Register.com. We chose *Kiva* because it has an appropriate meaning—"unity" or "agreement"—and because it was available. In fact, it was being held by a squatter at the time, but I was able to buy it from the squatter for a clean $600. That was perhaps the best $600 I ever spent.

In April, the couple sent an email to everyone on their wedding invitation list announcing the beta launch of Kiva.org. Among the seven businesses listed on Kiva seeking loans was the fishmonger from Uganda, Elizabeth Omalla. Kiva users could sign onto the site, read the stories of entrepreneurs seeking funds to expand their businesses, and sign up to be virtual lenders. They could follow the progress of the businesses they funded, and they would be notified when the loans were paid back. In short, they could follow a story of hope and development in a small business in east Africa from their computer screens. Within just a few days, they raised $3,500 in increments of $25 and $50. Kiva worked.

For months, it stayed quite small. Matt Flannery remembers that he knew virtually everyone in the site's database personally, and they had a single partner agency in Africa. That had an upside: The couple could get feedback quickly from people they trusted. They could make changes rapidly. And they could measure the connection between everyday people in the United States and small-scale entrepreneurs living in poor communities half a world away. Then a stranger arrived on the site: Premal Shah, then a product manager at PayPal, the micropayments site that was part of eBay. He had been working on the idea of creating a microcredit enterprise using eBay and its massive community of users when he came across Kiva. "We saw Premal as a missing piece of the puzzle," said Flannery. "Jessica and I were confessional, careful, thorough, strategic, and technical. Premal was passionate, charismatic, brilliant, wildly enthusiastic, and reckless." For his part, Shah saw Kiva as "almost like kindergarten for international philanthropy."

Kiva grew slowly; it expanded to support 50 entrepreneurs in Uganda. The team put out a press release and a few bloggers picked up the story. Matt kept his day job, and Jessica started grad school. Then one morning, the traffic exploded. All the loans were sold out, and $10,000 had been raised in a few hours. Looking at the logs, Matt realized that Kiva had been featured on the front page of the DailyKos, a leading liberal political blog with more than a million readers daily. There were many emails to respond to, and not just from lenders trying to help. Flannery had inquiries from microfinance agencies around the world, from Bulgaria and Rwanda to Nicaragua and Gaza.

Exhausted and exhilarated, Flannery took a walk to gather his thoughts:

As I walked, I was consumed by an overwhelming feeling: pain. For the first time, I connected with how much it actually hurt to not fully pursue a passion that had been ignited a year and a half earlier in East

Africa. I felt weak and extremely light-headed. I couldn't deny myself what every muscle in my body wanted.

The following Monday, Matt Flannery quit his day job.

■ ■ ■

At DonorsChoose.org, there are more than 18,000 classroom projects in need of funding on a warm spring day in April 2008. Visitors can review projects needing funding by several variables: region, the size of the project in monetary terms, grade, subjects, and other categories. There is also a prominent search box, allowing visitors to query the database for anything under the sun. I type in "Mark Twain" and look over the results, 15 in all. One headline grabs my attention: "My Wonderful Eighth Graders Need Novels!!!" So I click and read on:

> I am an 8th grade English and History teacher at a public middle school. My students come from predominantly low-income families. They are bright, eager, and wonderful students, but unfortunately, my school cannot afford all the class sets of novels I would like to have for my students.
>
> I have great ideas and activities in mind to use in teaching my students some of the classic novels of literature. Each of my classes has approximately 32 students. However, without each student having a copy of the book, teaching and learning becomes a difficult task. As a young teacher, class sets of novels are something I could keep throughout my career as a teacher in urban schools, and share with needy students for many years to come!

The teacher is asking for a set of classic novels, including *The Adventures of Huckleberry Finn* by Mark Twain, one of my favorites. I can easily recall the thrill of reading *Huck Finn* for the first time. The cost is $518.

It is a compelling case, and it is from a Bronx middle school. Early in my career as a journalist, I spent a fair amount of time in Bronx public schools, including several in areas where most residents lived at or below the poverty line. Many of the kids are immigrants or the children of immigrants, and providing great American literature resonates strongly. So this donor chooses.

What is interesting to me is that DonorsChoose also includes a 15% fee with each donation—or more accurately, it starts the transaction by counting 15% of the gift as administrative overhead for DonorsChoose. It is a model that will eventually lead to a self-sustaining future for the organization, as regular users will fund the operations as well as the classroom needs.

What is also striking is the sheer volume of activity on DonorsChoose. After seven years of trial and error, sweat, and server crashes, Charles Best and his organization arrived at a crucial moment in the late summer of 2007—DonorsChoose.org went national. Every public school in the United States (or more accurately, every teacher) can now use the website to raise money for materials and other educational assets. It was a bold move, but it was time, and Best's biggest worry came to nothing.

"We thought we'd cannibalize our donor flow," he said. The old version of the site had "had donors in all 50 states, so we figured as soon as they had the opportunity to support local schools, New York and North Carolina would see a decline, but our success rate has gone up." Before going national, about half the projects listed were funded. After the expansion, it increased to a full two-thirds.

Best realizes that even after all the growth DonorsChoose has seen, many of its users are still what might be termed early adopters in new philanthropy: "About half of our donors come to our site because they care about public school students. Another half cares not so much about public school, but about the ability to see where their money is going and to hear back from the students."

One of those early adopters is Fred Wilson, a prominent venture capitalist and blogger in New York. Just after DonorsChoose went national, it launched a "bloggers challenge" to promote online campaigns. Fred promoted the cause on his well-trafficked personal blog, A VC. Wilson asked readers to give to technology-oriented projects, like LCD projectors, computer stations, smart boards, video cameras, and software. More than $18,000 from 93 donors was raised for classrooms around the country. Wilson, who invests in Internet companies and loves to test new models, finds the DonorsChoose model compelling: "The benefit-to-pain ratio is about the highest I've ever seen. The kids and teachers seem to get great outcomes and I can deliver it in about 30 seconds."

That benefit-to-pain ratio (and some timely mass-media exposure) has fueled real growth at DonorsChoose. As the U.S. presidential race raged in the spring of 2008, comedian Stephen Colbert, host of Comedy Central's hilarious *Colbert Report* (a fake conservative news magazine that skewers politicians and the media with pure abandon) decided to raise both consciousness and funds through DonorsChoose. While Senators Hillary Clinton and Barack Obama battled over key swing-state votes in Pennsylvania, Colbert announced "the only straw poll that counts," asking followers of each candidate to show their support by raising money to support projects in Pennsylvania public schools in each candidate's name. Through blogs and the Comedy Central site, the "Celebrate the Democralypse" effort raised more than $100,000, and marked the second time Colbert had chosen to partner with DonorsChoose to push charity while hyping Colbert Nation. During the host's brief stint as a "candidate" in the South Carolina primary, he also raised money for public schools through the site.

A lot of the money raised by DonorsChoose is "new money," or so it seems. Seventy percent of donors who answer the site's survey question say it is the first philanthropic gift they have made to public schools. There is a wrinkle to the DonorsChoose giving pattern, what Best calls the "long-tail donor," a nod to the string of hard-to-find "non-hits" that increasingly power online sales of media on sites like iTunes and Amazon, as popular-ized by *Wired* magazine's Chris Anderson in his book, *The Long Tail*. The idea is that many donors discover their DonorsChoose projects through esoteric searches for specific items that interest them, as with my search for *Huckleberry Finn*. The best estimate is that as many as half the DonorsChoose supporters connect to classroom projects through searches on phrases like "Moby Dick" or "therapeutic horseback riding." When *Fortune* magazine's senior editor, Jeffrey O'Brien, wrote about DonorsChoose in February 2008, he became a long-tail donor, as is clear from his description of how the process works:

> For example, a biology teacher in Oregon submits a funding proposal for $703 to buy 20 chest-waders for high schoolers who operate a salmon hatchery on the Coquille River. A prospective donor concerned about both science education and salmon depletion (like me) can search on "salmon" and fund the whole project or whatever he can afford. DonorsChoose.org then buys the materials and ships them to the teacher. The teacher and students, in turn, provide regular progress reports.

Best sees one potential hurdle to future growth: the investment of time that his model requires:

> We offer a much more rich and rewarding giving experience, but it's also a more time-consuming experience. It requires more proactivity than a direct mail opportunity. One of our users described her experience as her "substitute for volunteering," the connection was so personal. But it can be a thought-requiring, time-taking process.

The growth curve is impressive: More than $25 million has been donated through the site since its inception, but more than $13 million came during the 12 months from mid-2007 to mid-2008. Best is look-ing for better ways to improve communications on his network, to make giving as easy as possible while keeping the rewarding personal experience. He has already met one of the big milestones for DonorsChoose: opening the service to all public schools in the United States. The next big milestone is *self-sufficiency*, the Holy Grail of the social entrepreneurship movement. He believes the site will cover all operating expenses through earned income within three years.

There is the looming question of how else to use the model. Does DonorsChoose expand to other sectors or countries? Does it allow healthcare organizations to create projects? Does it open the funding doors to schools in India? Best and his board know they will face that question somewhere down the road, even as they focus on attaining full-scale sufficiency in U.S. public education.

With many years of data now on its hard drives, DonorsChoose is beginning a more rigorous regression analysis to study donor patterns—from financial demographics to regional differences. That research should be incredibly valuable to the next generation of online social entrepreneurs. Although DonorsChoose is the toast of that innovative community, Charles Best is realistic about its size and reach in a world where the $300 billion American philanthropic market would rank as the world's fifty-seventh largest economy. "We're still a really small community, and in fact we're still casting about for the right terms—is it citizen philanthropy, peer-to-peer philanthropy, an online social marketplace? This is still early."

■ ■ ■

Premal Shah is listening intently, pausing only to take a few notes. Around the table in the big upstairs room at Casa Italiana, the Italian studies center at Columbia University, housed in an imposing 70-year-old Florentine palazzo on Amsterdam Avenue, are some of the top people from the worlds of high-tech investment, social entrepreneurship, philanthropy, and Web 2.0 startups. The occasion is a private conference called "Hacking Philanthropy," staged by the New York venture capital firm Union Square Ventures.

The voices in the room include Craigslist founder Craig Newmark, international philanthropist and investor Ray Chambers, Idealist.org founder Ami Dar, investor Jonathan Soros, blogger Anil Dash, activist-entrepreneur Andrew Rasiej, journalist Micah Sifry, and the event's organizer, venture capitalist Brad Burnham. Charles Best is across the table, and the conversation is all about scale: how to take great experiments like Kiva and DonorsChoose and use them to change American philanthropy.

This is all great for Shah, a clear-eyed veteran of eBay and PayPal and Kiva's operations guru—except for one thing. He has run out of causes for Kiva's swelling network of micro-lenders to support. Quite simply, by the early fall of 2007, Kiva had outgrown itself (temporarily, of course), a near-victim of its own success. The supply of loans offered by people impressed with the Kiva model has outstripped the demand for loans among the microfinance agencies Kiva partners with in developing nations, so Kiva has capped the loans at $25 and is seriously considering issues of scale on which the entrepreneurial brainpower in the room is eminently qualified to offer advice. However, there is nothing grim about Kiva's business challenge at all; it is a good problem to have.

"So the way I view Kiva, this is almost like kindergarten for international philanthropy," says Shah. "Matt designed the lowest friction, most . . . addictive, compelling type of experience that people are looking for and gets them hooked into that system. . . . I think you can create that kind of Howard Dean–style broad-based community support effort in something that typically is overlooked by most Americans."

Kiva's problem is one a lot of social entrepreneurs would love to have. Philanthropy adviser and blogger Sean Stannard-Stockton said that the dilemma is

. . . a great example of how strongly donors respond when social capital markets are created. I believe figuring out how to connect donors and nonprofits via marketplaces will result in temporary supply/demand imbalances. This is a normal reaction to creating liquidity in a market that did not have it before. . . . Kiva's problem is not that there are too few people in the world who need microfinance, but that they've turned on the supply spigot and need to figure out how to turn on the demand spigot.

In the two years since Matt Flannery quit his day job, Kiva.org grew into the world's best-known online micro-lending service, a pioneering organization linking Web users in the United States with small-time businesses in the developing world. Kiva and its founders appeared with Oprah, sat in on the *Today* show, and had a starring role in Bill Clinton's book, *Giving*. The site has empowered almost 270,000 lenders and facilitated $26 million in loans across 40 countries; Kiva has goals of lending $100 million within the next two years and a cool billion over the next decade, all through small-time lenders such as my daughter and myself.

For her fifteenth birthday in 2007, Veronica got the usual cards and trinkets, clothes and video games—and a Kiva gift certificate. I had joined Kiva months earlier, loved the experience, and wanted to pass it along to my increasingly socially conscious teenager. Together, we have developed a thriving little Kiva portfolio of social investments. Our loans helped businesses in Mexico, Ghana, and Nicaragua. Every one of them has been repaid in full, thus far, allowing us to reinvest the principal. The stories are compelling.

There was María De La Luz Ramírez Sáenz, who runs the Dulcería del Centro in San Juanito, Chihuahua, Mexico—a small sweetshop. Separated from her husband and with five children, Maria wanted to expand her inventory to include piñatas and other items for children's parties. A group of 25 Kiva lenders pooled a loan of $925 through Admic Nacional, a microfinance field partner of Kiva's in Mexico. Maria paid back the loan in three months.

We met Gladys Dede, who runs a general store in the village of Nkurankan, in the Yilo Krobo District of Ghana in West Africa.

A group of 27 Kiva donors lent Gladys $800 through the Kraban Support Foundation to increase her inventory of everyday household goods—an amount she repaid in nine months. One of our newest banking "customers" is Luisa Calero, a resident of San Rafael del Sur in Managua, who is "well-known for the delicious cakes that she makes and sells out of her home." Louisa runs a small bakery, selling cakes and other pastries, and the funds pay for the education of her three children. She requested a loan of $800 to pay for raw materials needed for baking, to be repaid over 17 months.

In each case, the terms of the loans differed and they were administered by different field partners in each country. We look at pictures of the business owners, read their stories, and even meet other lenders through the built-in Kiva social network. There was a clear emotional payoff that exceeded writing a check in response to a piece of direct mail or an email appeal. There was also a sense of putting money at risk (even though repayment rates are very high), a feeling of taking a chance on someone else's future that was quite immersive. As Veronica, who quickly joined the Kiva Facebook group, told me, "When you get involved in a charity, you don't really know what's exactly happening. You might donate money to the Red Cross, but you really don't know where it's going. But when you give through Kiva, you know where it's going— it's something tangible."

New York Times columnist Nicholas Kristof, who writes often about human rights, had a strong experience with Kiva: "For those readers who ask me what they can do to help fight poverty, one option is to sit down at your computer and become a microfinancier. That's what I did recently. From my laptop in New York, I lent $25 each to the owner of a TV repair shop in Afghanistan, a baker in Afghanistan, and a single mother running a clothing shop in the Dominican Republic." Of course, not everyone can visit their business partners a few months later, as Kristof did in Kabul.

On a muddy street in Kabul, Abdul Satar, a bushy-bearded man of 64, was sitting in the window of his bakery selling loaves for 12 cents each.

He was astonished when I introduced myself as his banker, but he allowed me to analyze his business plan by sampling his bread: It was delicious.

"If you give people a chance to make an impact, and you let them see the evidence of their impact, they will respond," says Matt Flannery. "They naturally want to make a difference in the world, they want to respond but mostly they feel helpless. We give them something very tangible and provide feedback."

Scott Heiferman, the visionary serial entrepreneur behind the popular Meetup.com site (a pioneering Web venture that gets people to real-world events through bottom-up online organizing), talked about the phenomenon of risk inherent in the Kiva model:

I think, having played a little bit with DonorsChoose and Kiva, that it's a game. And it's fun. And fun isn't just in data. I personally, you know, am annoyed by the fact that everything in our society and culture has to be in the form of entertainment. . . . But it is very Vegas like. And the reason why people use Facebook is because of the addictiveness. . . . There's a lot that goes into that.

Matt Flannery has his own ideas about the addictive nature of Kiva:

There are a lot of theories. To me, one that makes sense is that it's like collecting, there is a collector mentality to it. It's a little bit like fantasy basketball, where you're collecting people's playing cards, and creating a team. There's an ownership mentality, a collector mentality. People like collecting things that make them feel good, and this is a really easy way to feel good very fast. It's an effortless way to kind of feel better today. For 25 dollars, it gives you a little rush. I think other people do it out of curiosity or a gambling mentality. In some ways, it's almost too secure, the payback rate is too high. Some people want it to be more exciting. People want riskier loans; they want uncertainty.

Kiva has many fans. In my experience, almost everybody who visits the site signs up to make a few loans. It *is* somewhat addictive. And it has spawned specialty blogs like Kivafriends.com (a community for fans of Kiva), a YouTube channel, and several Facebook groups. Admits Flannery: "I'm blown away and shocked and disoriented by it. I was a little pessimistic starting Kiva, to see it work and to see people responding to it. I actually don't understand it, why people are so passionate about it. I mean, Kivafriends—who are these people?"

Still, both Flannery and Charles Best understand that the main strength of their popular and well-hyped organizations lies in the people who use them—the very network their models attracted—and how those people have the power to change the way millions of others support causes around the world. Says Matt Flannery:

One thing I'm excited about is the democratizing of philanthropy. On the source of funds side, a lot of money is clustered in a few people. There is a big disparity between philanthropists with power and the rest of us, but if you can unlock every twenty-five dollars under the mattress, you can change things. I'd love to see more people take risks. As poet-blogger-social entrepreneur Scott Edward Anderson told me in a Twitter message recently: if Kiva and DonorsChoose "can scale, they open up whole new class of socially minded donor-investors." A hundred thousand people with twenty-five dollars each will take risks, but a billion-dollar foundation won't take risks. That's because they have this built-in responsibility to spend the money wisely. We need more venture capital. There is a sense of shame when you make a bad donation, and that's harmful. We need to remove the shame and have some tolerance for failure.

5 | Defined by Causes: The Public Lives of Millennials

At the tail end of the first Internet boom, the iconoclastic entrepreneur Josh Harris, founder of the pioneering online video studio Pseudo, decided to live his life entirely in public. Two months after Pseudo went out of business in 2000 during a wave of dot-com closures that stilled the startup markets on both coasts, Harris set up what *Wired* magazine termed "a 100-day interactive art experiment" in his Manhattan loft, wiring the place entirely with video and sound and streaming the entire thing to a website for anyone to watch. "This wasn't your typical millionaire bachelor pad, mind you, but a lavishly designed webcasting studio, fully outfitted with heat-sensitive cameras to track the occupants' every move" said *Wired*.

"If you're over 18, you can log on to the We Live In Public website for free and watch Josh and Tanya go to the bathroom, watch TV, take showers, sleep together, or do nothing."

■ ■ ■

While the Harris experiment was obviously an early online version of the reality TV explosion that spawned Big Brother and other explorations in always-on human zoological parks, it also anticipated a trend that is far more important, in my view. We Live In Public, for all its hype and drama, was a brilliant experiment in human behavior—one that transcended reality television; Josh Harris's somewhat notorious wired loft life was emblematic of an increasing willingness of consumers to live their lives in public. We Live In Public anticipated the rise of online social networks (indeed, its community of users strongly influenced the "action" in the apartment) and was the bold, performance-art bugle call of *public online identities*—the over-the-top herald of that crucial multimedia unit of measure of social networking: the *humble user profile*.

Everyone under the age of 30 has one, or several (so it seems, anyway). The user profile signals one person's willingness—or desire—to share personal information with other users in a community. On Facebook, the profile is at the center of the entire experience and its ever-changing nature creates an individual's personal newsfeed. That ever-morphing profile can include relationship status, photos, blog posts, videos, comments and notes, music, a growing list of "friends," and yes, causes. Sure, it is an ideal portrait that can be tightly controlled by the user to provide a flattering persona; and since much of the social networking phenomenon revolves around relationships, that is hardly surprising. Still, the sheer amount of personal information can be stunning. I have learned of births, deaths, marriages, engagements, and broken engagements on Facebook through the *mini-feed*, a sort of friend-oriented wire service that loads when you log in. These things used to take a phone call or an email or a chance in-person meeting; for those I am connected to on Facebook, the proverbial "so what have you been up to?" in catching up over coffee is no longer vital.

On Twitter, the short-messaging service so popular with the digerati, the depth of personal disclosure is even more amazing. Limited to 140 characters per post, Twitter is all about information frequency. Users can turn the service into a virtual stream of life, using their mobile phones to post updates throughout the day. Read an interesting article? Flight delayed? Upset stomach? Snowing outside? Just spot somebody famous? Need to reboot your computer? Like that song? Test-drive a new car? Twitter it. Tell the subscribers to your personal feed all about it. Share everything you can. Live life in public.

Science and culture writer Clive Thompson calls this trend *microcelebrity*, the state of being famous to significantly less than millions of people (as with the old mass-media model). Perhaps a thousand people follow your life and your ideas, or a hundred, or a dozen. "Got a Facebook account?" writes Thompson in *Wired*. "A whackload of pictures on Flickr? Odds are there are complete strangers who know about you—and maybe even talk about you. The truth is that people are developing interesting social skills to adapt to microfame. We're learning how to live in front of a crowd." Chances are that if you were born after 1980 you live more of your digital life in public than do older consumers. A landmark study by the Pew Research Center for the People and the Press, published in January 2007, reported that 54% of young adults who responded to their "GenNext" survey had used one or more online social networks; 44% had created a profile, while 38% used the sites daily. Given that the research was conducted in 2006 (just as Facebook became a household name but before its fast-track growth), there is little doubt these percentages have grown.

The group in the Pew study, entitled "Generation Next: How Young People View Their Lives, Futures and Politics," range in age from 18 to 25, comprising life experience ranging from college freshman to young professional and generally seen as coming of age as active media consumers in the years since September 11, 2001. The main survey was conducted in September and October 2006 among 1,501 adults, including 579 people ages 18 to 25. In addition, the report includes extensive generational analysis of Pew Research Center surveys dating back to 1987. "This generation's relationship with technology is truly unique. Young people have adopted new technologies and are using them to both expand their social networks and maintain contact with their families and friends. More than any other generation, Gen Next recognizes the positive aspects of the technology revolution."

■ ■ ■

Quite obviously, this is the most technically savvy generation in American history, but none of us needs an expensive research report to know that. The use of media technology among the millennials is virtually an extension of biological being. Widespread broadband Internet access, cell phones, ubiquitous television, music and video downloads, and networked games all form the always-on, mobile network that is as necessary to modern life as air. But there are some noteworthy numbers in the Pew report, and understanding the attitudes of the millennials is clearly crucial to navigating the future of online social activism.

While all generations (save some of the early Boomers and pre-Boomers) are heavily invested in frequent Internet usage, the quick exchange of personal information dominates the daily life of the youngest consumers: About half of "Generation Next" say they sent or received a text message over the phone in the past day—double the proportion of those aged 26 to 40. This is also a more progressive generation; their attitudes toward religion, race, immigration, war, and sexuality are notably more liberal than are those of older Americans. For instance, "nearly two-thirds of Nexters (63%) believe humans and other living things evolved over time, while only 33% say all living creatures have existed in their present form since the beginning of time." Two-thirds believe an interventionist foreign policy will lead to a greater threat of terrorism against the United States. On matters of tolerance, they are overwhelmingly in favor of interracial dating and strongly accepting of homosexuality. And the majority does not accept traditional roles for women in society. Two-thirds say that an open immigration policy strengthens American society, and 77% argue that the United States should strengthen environmental protection law. Yet the same more-liberal generation is also pro-business, with positive attitudes toward money and the need to make more of it to improve their lives. In short, they are technology-loving, entertainment-obsessed capitalist consumers.

Further, young consumers are as invested in creating an experience online as they are in consuming one—if not more so. Another Pew study from 2007, "Teens and Social Media," from the Pew Internet & American Life Project, found that 64% of online teens engage in content creation on the Internet, a number that continues to grow. Girls lead the way: 35% of teenaged girls blog, compared with 20% of boys, and 54% of wired girls post photos online, compared with 40% of online boys. It is not just about publishing, however; it is about sharing a big part of their lives. Pew researchers found that 47% of online teens have posted photos where others can see them, and 89% of those teens who post photos say that people comment on the images at least "some of the time." In addition, there is a fast-growing group of *supercommunicators* (more often than not, older girls), who use everything at their disposal (cell phones, text messages, blogs, instant messaging, photo-sharing, social networks) to create their ideal selves online and live life in public via the network.

Author and social analyst Allison Fine wrote an important paper in 2008 for the Case Foundation, entitled "Social CitizensBETA—Civic Participation in a Digital Age," a good portion of which dealt with the online behavior of millennials engaged in supporting causes. She sums up that interconnection between technology and ideals that defines the online social activism of the generation:

> They are fascinating and important for what they are growing up with (digital technology); how they work (collaboratively); what they believe (that they can make the world a better place to live); and how they are living their lives (green, connected, passionately, idealistically). . . . Millennials cast a big, wide-open net across their lives, pinging and poking friends on social networking sites, instant messaging and emailing, blogging and posting, uploading and downloading—all instantly and incessantly.

Entrepreneur Jason Paez, an energetic former investment banker in his twenties, created Party4APurpose.com, a free event portal and community whose goal is to list every charitable and purposeful event in the country. The site is also a social network, and clearly aims at younger consumers. "It's a lifestyle pride application, like Facebook Causes," he said. "And no money is given. But it's like they're closing on the proposal that 'I care. This is what I care about. This is who I am. This is who I like to connect with.' They're used to emotionally connecting online through data."

Craig Dyer, who put his Christian missionary organization Bright Hope International on Facebook to appeal to younger activists, believes the millennial generation is inherently tied to causes. "I believe younger people have a desire to be known 'not for what they are paid for, but what they are made for.' They want to be known for the passion they have to help others and the causes they choose to support." According to Allison Fine, it is a group that is "brimming with new approaches and ideas for problem-solving; disposed toward sharing the responsibilities and rewards of effecting change in the world; and equipped with the digital tools and people power to make it happen."

Causes co-founder Joe Green puts it rather pointedly: "This is our generation's chance to prove we don't suck."

■ ■ ■

If demographics are social destiny, then the differences in the group of young Americans born after 1980 compared to previous generations tell an important story. First, this group is quite large, estimated at upward of 80 million Americans. Indeed, there are twice as many millennials as Gen-Xers and already a million more millennials alive than Baby Boomers. The millennial generation is also more ethnically diverse than any identified generation in American history. Between 1976 and 2006, the percentage of young people who are white has steadily fallen from approximately 79% in 1976 to 62% in 2006, according to the Center for Information & Research on Civic Learning & Engagement, and the percentage of young residents who are Latinos grew ten percentage points from 8% in 1976 to 18% in 2006. That diversity has led to greater tolerance among young people than among their forebears: According to same study, 67% of millennials say they have "confronted someone who said something that they considered offensive, such as a racist or other prejudiced comment." That is not just thinking about society's prejudices—it is acting against them. While only 26% said they voted regularly (a number bound to change after the supercharged election of 2008), 36% have volunteered within the last year. And here is a number that the nation's consumer marketers should consider tattooing on some portion of their bodies: 30% told researchers they have boycotted a product in the last year "because of the conditions under which it was made or the values of the company that made it."

That knits perfectly with the results of the 2006 study by cause-marketing agency Cone in cooperation with AMP Insights, "The Millennial Generation: Pro-Social and Empowered to Change the World."

The report found that 61% of Americans born between 1979 and 2001 "feel personally responsible for making a difference in the world," and that 74% said they are more likely to "pay attention to a company's over-all messages when they see that the company has a deep commitment to a cause." Nearly nine out of ten in Cone's survey of young people aged 13 to 25 said that they are "likely or very likely to switch from one brand to another (price and quality being equal) if the second brand is associated with a good cause." And for those entering the workforce, nearly eight out of ten "want to work for a company that cares about how it contributes to society, while more than half would refuse to work for an irresponsible corporation."

Brands that are associated with causes have a leg up on those that are not. I saw this in action during an entirely unscientific bit of research in my own house not long ago. Four teens hovered over the Mac screen in the back of our kitchen, talking about English vocabulary—and provid-ing rice to poor families in developing nations. Video games are, of course, an obsession in our house, which is always crawling with kids. But calling out definitions of words like *diffident* and *abjuration* just for fun when there was no school quiz in the offing seemed a bit different:

"What does *jape* mean?" called out Tim, my 14-year-old nephew.

His cousins, Sean, Kelsey, and Danny, talked it over. "Public speaker?"

"No, I think it's *vault*, right?"

"No, no—go with *jest*—it means *jest*. Click *jest*, Tim."

He did, and more "free rice" was on its way to feed the hungry, at least in the perception of my son and nephews. So, why were they playing?

"It's cool and it makes you smarter and it helps people," said Kelsey.

"Yeah, it's cool," said Sean.

It is cool, indeed. Freerice.com is a vocabulary-testing game that gets harder as you succeed in answering multiple-choice questions about definitions. "For each word you get right," the site promises, "we donate 20 grains of rice through the United Nations World Food Programme to help end hunger." A simple proposition, and it connected with the game-obsessed young people in my house, who watched in amazement as the "grains" added up to a meal—in theory, a bowl of rice for a hungry human being in a country far away from a kitchen in suburban New York. The donations come from corporate sponsors of the site and fund the World Food Programme's anti-hunger programs, feeding refugees from Myanmar who are sheltering in Bangladesh, pregnant women in Cambodia, schoolchildren in Uganda, and Bhutanese refugees in Nepal. And rice is not the only food staple purchased with receipts from the site; rations include vegetable oil, pulses, cereal blends, bread, sugar, and salt. Dig a little deeper, and you can watch video footage of the food being delivered, sign up for email newsletters, and contribute an entire sack of rice for $16.

My kids typically do not get that far. They enjoyed the game, talked about it loudly, and felt conspicuously good about what they were doing, then they went downstairs to play Halo 3, which has no redeeming social value (that I can find, anyway). It was a brief, experience-based exposure to online social activism, one that had only limited depth and education and carried almost no commitment. No money changed hands (unless you count the sponsorship funding) and nobody signed any petitions or agreed to recruit their friends. Yet, there is no question that the cause itself—the feeling that they were not just wasting their time with another online game—clearly held their attention. In a post about Freerice.com, blogger lazylaces summed it this way: "It doesn't sound like a lot, but the more that you play, and particularly the more of you that play, the bigger the donation will be. Head on over, play, and save lives now."

■ ■ ■

This is a very self-aware group as well, very much cognizant of living life so obviously in public. In the Pew study, more than 40% told researchers they have created a personal profile in Facebook, MySpace, or another social network. Yet, 7% of those surveyed believe young people post too much personal information online. While most believe this daily immersion in media technology makes people more efficient and brings people closer together (69% said new technologies make it easier to make friends), they also worry that it makes people lazier and can lead to physical isolation.

The evident self-awareness in the Pew research shows that this super-wired generation—*NextGen, millennials*, or whatever label you would choose—understands not just the technology and new forms of communication, but some of the stakes involved; clearly they are thinking about what it means to human endeavor. Future Leaders in Philanthropy is a grassroots community organized online via a popular blog and Facebook group. FLiP (as it is commonly known) grew from the onPhilanthropy.com site that I produce with editor-in-chief Susan Carey Dempsey. FLiP has about 2,000 people on its network subscribing to feeds, posting comments, taking part in the Facebook group, or showing up at the increasingly popular networking events, mostly in New York. The key aim of the group is to build a network of young people coming into the newly professionalized field of philanthropy as fundraisers, grantmakers, or program officers. Organized by a core group of young professionals that includes my colleagues, Will Schneider, Divine Tabios, Lyndsey Reville, and Elisabeth Anderson, FLiP has used all of the tools of online social activism to build its success—and to get people to show up at real-world events and exchange ideas.

In early 2008, FLiP put together a small focus group over pizza one evening to discuss online causes, Internet activism, and social networks. The group consisted of about ten young professionals, all between the ages of 22 and 28, and included fundraising consultants, nonprofit leaders, a technologist, a social-scene promoter, and a Web publisher. What emerged was a clear consensus among a group of heavy social network users (one that just happened to be oriented toward nonprofit causes) that while online social activism is growing rapidly, it is not yet mature. The plugged-in young professionals also agreed that the CauseWired movement will not define success just by building lists of friends online, but rather by driving people to take action in their everyday lives. Here are some highlights of the discussion, edited slightly for clarity:

WILL: The groups you join in Facebook define who you are—in front of millions of people, it says you are what you stand for.

ANNA: I don't want to be judged by my Facebook profile.

RACHEL: If a friend invites me to a cause, I'm going to join it if they're a friend. I may care more for other causes, the ones I actually focus on.

JANET: At a certain point there gets to be overload, it just gets really over the top. I went through my groups and my causes and it was like "why did I do all that stuff?" I felt bad as well, like I'm sorry I couldn't do more.

INGRID: If you know someone, then it's about the person more than the action, than what [the cause] is actually for.

LYNDSAY: It's incredible how popular [Causes on Facebook] is. But some people say, "that was so 2007." The key questions will be—what was acted on, and will it last?

ANNA: Most real connections [to causes] happen with people; they happen quickly with people you know and have already made a connection with.

DIVINE: Yes, it's that personal connection that drives you to join.

KELVIN: Most money isn't raised online. It's about the social community, the real-world networking. Most money is, in fact, raised in person. The online side is really an organizing tool. It's not necessarily the best way to raise the money, but it's how you're getting your message out.

FONG: Whenever you're aiming to achieve a goal in terms of numbers, there are going to be people who care and people who are apathetic. The really effective campaigns influence real-world behavior, and they're person to person.

PETER: I think we're in the infancy stage of being "CauseWired," the beginning of the learning curve.

FONG: Yeah, there's a huge bandwagon that's growing.

JANET: Part of it is the changing nature of communication in our culture. Podcasting was a breakthrough, and sharing music and YouTubes became another. And you're using them in partnership with other people, so this mentality makes you a lot more aware of what's going on in the world.

ANNA: [The Obama campaign] inspired people not only to organize online but to actually turn out to events. It inspires people to act.

DIVINE: It provides a model for future campaigns.

WILL: The critical step, the one that's sometimes missing, is about the engagement coefficient—how are people moved to take an action?

That last question is crucial. While it is great to build vast lists online, real *change*—the watchword of the millennials—takes action, the breaking of the virtual barrier, and not merely clicking a few links. This is a generation predisposed to believing that action on their part will lead to real change. In their fascinating study of millennials and the changing American political landscape, Morley Winograd and Michael Hais argue that the adoption of new communication technology, along with other factors such as diversity and high self-esteem, creates an opportunity for a political shift away from the stasis of two old political parties battling it out for minor shifts in policy, to a new drive for public service that transcends partisan politics. In *Millennial Makeover: MySpace, YouTube & the Future of American Politics*, they write that "the tectonic plates undergirding America's current political landscape are beginning to shift. The resulting cataclysm will wash away the current politics of polarization and ideological deadlock, putting in place a new landscape of collective purpose and national consensus that involves individuals and communities in solving the nation's problems."

This is heady stuff, and I am tempted to heed veteran progressive policy analyst Micah Sifry's admonition not to "fetishize the millennials." Micah's point is that, being human, the young activists of today will follow the same pattern of pursuing some degree of self-interest as did all the generations that came before—that, and, of course, the fact that there are people over 40 doing important work in social change. When Winograd and Hais state that "Millennials are the largest and most racially diverse generation of Americans ever," it is tempting to add "to date" as a snarky postscript. After all, the Boomers held the same title not so long ago.

But Winograd and Hais do make a compelling argument for a rare confluence of demographic change: ". . . there are now twice as many Millennials as Gen-Xers and already a million more Millennials alive than Baby Boomers," they write, and cite various studies to show that this group is both more socially aware and more self-confident than preceding generations of Americans. That awareness, along with the high cost of higher education, will create the right conditions for a new movement toward national service—clearly the fondest hope Winograd and Hais hold for the millennials. "Above all," they write, "national service will create a bonding and values-reinforcing experience almost as powerful as the GI generation's service in the Armed Forces did three generations ago. In the same way that World War II boot camps helped to break down America's ethnic and racial silos, twenty-first century experiences of working together for a common goal will institutionalize Millennial values of family, responsibility, and diversity as 'American values' for future decades."

■■■

Yet, even without a big national program, the push for public service inherent in the millennials is increasingly evident in the CauseWired sector. At a website called Razoo.com, you will find that NextGen spirit of service very much alive and growing in a way that also emphasizes the public nature of the millennials' online social activism—the willingness to live in public. Founded in 2007, Razoo.com is a "social network for social good" and it encourages recognition for everyday acts of kindness and social relevance. Created by Sebastian Traeger, who also built Christianity.com, Razoo includes philanthropy, but it is based on more than just giving.

"The general purpose of Razoo is to get normal people involved in local and global issues by aggregating ideas, organizations, service and giving opportunities, social entrepreneurs, unique media, and people all in one online ecosystem," says spokesman Scott Overdyke. "The word itself—*razoo*—refers to a New Zealand coin of trivial value. In essence, we're trying to redeem that word by implying that all contributions have value—be they ideas, time, effort, money, or just attention."

Razoo's team is going directly at one of the fiercest criticisms of Facebook-style philanthropy—that it is trivial, a million tiny clicks signifying little. Naysayers complain that hundreds of friends, thousands of cause members, and a fistful of dollars hardly change the philanthropic playing field. That may be true for now. But a new activism, or more accurately, a more vocal, proud, media-savvy activism, will change that landscape in the future. "It is our firm belief that the act of giving and serving is wildly beneficial to both the giver and the receiver and our goal at Razoo is to encourage those small but significant interactions throughout the world," says Overdyke.

"With Razoo, you can join causes that have been posted by other users, or create some causes of your own," writes Mashable.com blogger Kristen Nicole. She continues:

Each cause acts as an individual group that gets its own blog, and has sections for actions users can take, as well as goals that are set for participants. An action could be something like using cold water to wash clothes for living a more green lifestyle, while a goal could be to get ten people to ride their bikes to work. Participating users can contribute by adding resource links, images, videos, blog entries, acts, or goals, making most causes act as wikis for users.

Have you got that? Razoo is a free-form community that allows its own users to decide what gets posted, what the basic topics are, and what forms of media are used—even what "doing good" actually means. The strength is not so much in the deeds and donations described on the site but rather in the sharing of those actions with others. It is a somewhat addictive social networking site that captures all sorts of good works in everyday life, from basic kindnesses like "hug my wife" or basic good works like "take mass transit" to healthy-lifestyle choices like "walk up a flight of stairs." Razoo calls itself a "platform for social change," and it also has a serious cause-recruiting function, encouraging members to get their friends to join causes, as well as some fundraising. What I like about Razoo is that nothing happens in a vacuum; every day, I get a feed that tells me what great things my friends in Razoo are doing and there is the subtle urging to do something good myself.

As Changing Our World interactive fundraising expert Garth Moore says: "Kids don't use email anymore. They text on their cell phones or PDAs; email is for the older folks." He says that this holds important challenges and opportunities for nonprofits and campaigns:

The larger nonprofits are already experimenting with text-based messaging as a possible communication and revenue channel. Just as people can be entertained almost anytime or anywhere with the push of a button (whether it's music, movies, or the Internet), soon they will be able to give anywhere or advocate anywhere. In five years or so, political rallies and disaster relief efforts will be organized through our cell phones.

The idea is to create a way to encourage more action, via the network—a key component to millennial activism. At the invitation-only Wealth & Giving Forum gathering of philanthropic families held in the summer of 2007 at the picturesque Greenbrier resort in West Virginia, a group of students from three North Carolina colleges spoke with insistence and passion about their calling to make philanthropy (*involved* philanthropy, and not just giving) part of their lives. UNC, Duke, and Bennett College have joined together to sponsor a Millennium Village, part of an effort to achieve the UN's ambitious Millennium Development Goals by 2015. The students are raising $1.5 million in the first student-led sponsorship of a Millennium Village (essentially, the adoption of a small village in the developing world) as "a tangible way of demonstrating students' commitment to the international effort to eradicate extreme poverty." An online network that includes a Facebook group links the three campuses and three groups of students, but on-campus events and fundraising drive the actual social activism. *Results* are what is valued, not the mere existence of a network for a cause—so suggested Lennon Flowers, a recent graduate of the University of North Carolina, in her remarks to a room filled with older, experienced philanthropists:

> The reputation of my generation is one of apathy, that we're too numb behind our iPods to care about what's going on in the world. I think there's a lot of passion out there, but passion alone isn't what's valued.

> The idea, she said, is to get things done.

6 | From the Bottom Up: "The Order Is Rapidly Fading"

When I was a political reporter in the Bronx a lifetime or so ago, local Democratic organizations ruled the ballot. In those days, there were two basic factions in the near one-party rule of what was then America's poorest county—the regular organization and the insurgents. One had power; the other wanted it. Both used the same means: armies of volunteers and paid staff, gathering the requisite petition signatures to gain a place on the election ballot. The organization—called the *regulars* in those days—had the upper hand. Their political clubs were bigger and their volunteers usually included a brigade of public employees who used their time off to work for the very bosses who pretty well guaranteed their continued employment and their chance for advancement. These same political activists also contributed to the party coffers, which allowed the organization to pay for the type of advertising efforts that worked in local campaigns— palm cards, fliers, loudspeaker cars, newspaper ads, and the occasional radio spot.

In New York, each borough had its regular organization. In the Bronx, Manhattan, Queens, and Brooklyn, they were Democrats; in Staten Island, they were Republicans. They often got together for the big citywide races, designating candidates after bruising primary campaigns that took real money to buy television advertising. The insurgents, meanwhile, operated around the edges, running their own political clubs and, if they were very well organized, electing some councilmembers, state legislators, and judges of their own. They used the same system of club organization, street signature and campaigning operations, and patronage. Often, they put themselves into position to cut a deal with the regulars and thereby help make a candidate for boroughwide or citywide office.

Thus, there were two tiers of political access: the party insiders and the outsiders who still knew how to run the machinery well enough. In cities all across the country, in suburban districts, and in rural counties, the de facto system has remained very much the same. The two keys to real political power were patronage and money—forever intertwined. Contributions went through the big, organized groups; jobs and candidacies flowed the other way.

Then came the grand disruption: a change in political organizing, still in its infancy but capable of rewriting how we operate this republic. That disruption uses the CauseWired digital tools to displace the entrenched powers, creating new organizing levers for changing public policy and bringing new candidates to the fore. Sometimes, this involves major political campaigns, but sometimes it is just about local issues or putting the pressure on incumbents to change their positions. In all cases, it is about ordinary people plugging in and linking up to create political change.

■ ■ ■

In terms of electing candidates, there is one giant among us—someone who has shown the future path more clearly than anyone else has—a clear beacon of change. His name is Shekar Ramanuja Sidarth.

On August 11, 2006, the 21-year-old Sidarth was in Breaks, Virginia, a small town in Dickinson County, in the heart of the Appalachia region of Virginia in the far-southwestern part of state just below the Kentucky state line. This is coal-mining territory, and home to a regional center celebrating the history of mountain music. When pinstriped columnists and cable talking heads throw around terms like the *heartland* in talking about American politics, Breaks is the kind of traditional place they are talking about. But S.R. Sidarth was about to touch off a very nontraditional political firestorm—one that would have great influence on U.S. politics, and on the way that big-time candidates came to understand how their evolving electorate viewed them.

In the summer of 2006, George Allen faced perhaps his greatest political test since having been elected to the House of Representatives in 1991. The son of famed Washington Redskins coach George Allen, he went on to serve as Governor of Virginia from 1994 to 1998, moving to the Senate in 2000. All the while, Allen had been seen as one of the Republican Party's rising stars, a tobacco-chewing cultural conservative with a sophisticated view of business and technology—and blessed with a big grin and a famous name. Many believed Allen would be in the top tier of candidates for the Republican nomination for President in 2008. Despite his rise, Allen had been dogged by one particularly troubling aspect of his past. The Senator had an affinity for all things Confederate, adorning his office with rebel paraphernalia. He opposed honoring Rev. Martin Luther King, Jr.

with a state holiday and as Governor proclaimed April as Confederate History and Heritage Month and called the Civil War "a four-year struggle for independence and sovereign rights." Allen had earned protests from civil rights groups like the NAACP. But the Confederate flag—once proudly adorning his jacket lapel and featured in the background of his television advertising during his gubernatorial run—had disappeared from Allen's public life when he took the microphone before 100 or so supporters at the rally in Breaks.

Close your eyes and you can probably picture the video. There is Allen in an open-necked blue shirt, sleeves rolled up against the heat, a wireless microphone in his hand. He is standing in what looks like a picnic ground in a park, with trees in the background. The standard stump speech, until the Senator looks directly at the camera and points:

> This fellow here, over here with the yellow shirt, Macaca, or whatever his name is. He's with my opponent. He's following us around everywhere. And it's just great. We're going to places all over Virginia, and he's having it on film and it's great to have you here and you show it to your opponent because he's never been there and probably will never come. [. . .] Let's give a welcome to Macaca, here. Welcome to America and the real world of Virginia!

To say that Allen's remarks came at an inopportune time is an understatement. First, there was Sidarth, there to record them and quickly load them onto YouTube and other sites. The electorate of Virginia was also changing, as more independents and Democrats moved into the expanding Washington, D.C., suburbs in the northern part of the state; the Commonwealth was turning from solid red to a more nebulous shade of purple. Finally, Allen's opponent was James Webb.

James Henry "Jim" Webb had been a registered Republican until the early 1990s. Born in 1946, Webb is a graduate of the U.S. Naval Academy and served in the Marines in the Vietnam War. He is the author of the nonfiction book, *Born Fighting: How the Scots-Irish Shaped America*, as well as six well-written novels. Though initially a Republican because of national security issues, Webb drifted toward economic populism and libertarian issues, and gradually came to see the Republicans as threatening to both. "I agree with Andrew Jackson and William Jennings Bryan," he said of his conversion. "The wealth of a society isn't measured at the top, but at the bottom." Webb served as Secretary of the Navy under Republican President Ronald Reagan but resigned in protest of cutbacks in the fleet. By the summer of 2006, when he ran against George Allen, Webb had become a strong critic of the war in Iraq, arguing, "I don't think Ronald Reagan would have ever done that, and I don't think Bush's father would have done it." While he campaigned, he wore combat boots with his tailored suits—the boots left behind by son Jimmy, a Marine deployed in Iraq.

Webb's evolving political views fit Virginia's, but the insurgent also had another trick up his sleeve: He believed in the power of technology, and invested his campaign resources in developing a network of supporters. Webb's campaign was one of the "Fighting Dems" campaigns of 2006, a loose coalition of Democratic congressional candidates that took advantage of a national network of bloggers and supporters centered around sites like the DailyKos. When Sidarth's video file arrived at Webb headquarters, it did not stay local for long.

Aided by the Fighting Dems network (an online fundraising consortium), Democratic blogs, and the Webb campaign itself, Sidarth's video exploded across the Internet, not just in Virginia but nationally. Hundreds of thousands of people watched Senator Allen in action on YouTube, the video-sharing network founded only a year earlier by Steve Chen, 28, and Chad Hurley, 29, two veterans of PayPal, another Silicon Valley startup that had revolutionized online payments a few years earlier. A few months after the Allen "macaca" incident, they sold YouTube for $1.65 billion to Google, and the site became the leading video service on the Internet, and to this day remains heavily used for causes—political, nonprofit, and social. But back in the sweltering Virginia summer of 2006, the fast-moving video of a popular incumbent Senator mouthing what most believed was a racial slur at a young man with a digital camera was a real phenomenon—something new on the political scene, something even the cigar-smoking backroom veterans suspected was changing the game they had grown up on.

Allen tried to play defense, coming up with several explanations for his use of the word *macaca* and what he meant by "the real world of Virginia," but he seemed to dig himself in deeper as his campaign tried to tamp down the story. Said the *Washington Post*:

> Despite a quick apology Monday, criticism poured in about Allen's use of the word "Macaca" to address a volunteer for the campaign of his Democratic opponent, James Webb, and also about another Allen comment, "Welcome to America." Democrats, left-wing bloggers, and civil rights groups called him "insensitive" and "racist," while some conservatives called him "foolish" and "mean."

Allen's double-digit lead evaporated and he became a symbol of a major politician who simply did not understand the new world of networked politics, where information traveled much faster than spin. The liberal-leaning general-interest culture site Salon.com named Sidarth its person of the year for 2006, and in the accompanying article, journalist Michael Scherer captured the moment:

> It must be said that the young man, Shekar Ramanuja Sidarth, is not much of a cameraman. In the macaca footage, his hand shakes, though he manages to hold Allen in the frame as the senator points him out, an Indian-American in a crowd of whites. But in the weeks that follow, Sidarth does not shy from the spotlight that surrounds him. He undergoes a transformation of sorts, appearing on CNN and the

network news, giving long interviews to the pen-and-paper press. He becomes a symbol of politics in the twenty-first century, a brave new world in which any video clip can be broadcast instantly everywhere and any 20-year-old with a camera can change the world. He builds a legacy out of happenstance.

Weeks after Allen's blunder, Sidarth finds himself writing an entrance essay for a class at the University of Virginia, where he is a senior. The class is called Campaigns and Elections, and it has about four applicants for every spot. "I get all these large, elaborate essays about the meaning of politics and why they are going to be president," says Larry Sabato, the professor. Sidarth writes only three words. "I am macaca." Sabato lets him in. "When you have the right stuff, you don't need to brag," the teacher explains. "A simple declarative sentence will do."

The "macaca moment" has been called a watershed in American politics, but what is often left out is the role of the network in Webb's eventual victory over Allen. Totally wired Democrats, many of them veterans of the insurgent campaign of Howard Dean in 2004, had created a virtual patchwork quilt of supporters numbering in the tens of millions across the country. On large, multiblogger sites like DailyKos, MyDD, Talking Points Memo, and FireDogLake, along with thousands of single-writer blogs, news traveled outside the mainstream press, and often much faster. The Allen video rode that network, and then the big television networks noticed. As conservative columnist Andrew Sullivan wrote for the London *Sunday Times* in 2007, the "macaca moment" was the difference between victory and defeat: "Hand-held videocams in any citizen's hands gave thousands of complete nobodies the power to record and expose and engage politicians in real time to devastating effect."

Two years later, Democrats Barack Obama and Hillary Clinton both used viral videos for positive messages about their campaigns. Obama supporters struck gold with a music video produced by Bob Dylan's son Jesse and Black Eyed Peas frontman Will.i.am that put a typically inspirational Obama "Yes We Can" speech to music, mashed up in quick cuts to singing voiceovers from celebrities ranging from R&B singer John Legend and actress Scarlett Johansson, to rapper Eminem. The video served to remind voters of Obama's youth-oriented campaign and his vague but optimistic message. Earlier in the cycle, the Clinton campaign ran a clever video (also a hit on YouTube) that parodied the final episode of the just-ended HBO series, *The Sopranos*. The clip starred Bill and Hillary Clinton in a suburban diner, and was aimed at humanizing the powerful former First Lady in advance of a bruising primary season.

This was positive branding: using clever, polished media to project a good image of the candidate, and social media tools to distribute those tools. However, as Elvis Costello preached, accidents will happen, and several videos made the rounds in 2008 that, while not fatal in the macaca sense, nonetheless caught major candidates by surprise and influenced the race. When Bill Clinton likened Barack Obama's lead in the South Carolina primary to that of Jesse Jackson a generation earlier, Obama supporters cried foul, accusing the former president of trying to make the contest a choice over race. The snippet of Clinton shaking his finger at reporters was a hit on YouTube, though its short length destroyed any context in the president's remarks. Videos of Obama's longtime Chicago pastor, the Rev. Jeremiah Wright, using vitriolic language went viral online just as the mainstream media ran the angriest of them repeatedly on the nightly political gabfests. Video of Senator John McCain's remarks at a town hall meeting in New Hampshire, when he said that maintaining a U.S. military presence in Iraq for a hundred years "would be fine with me," became among the most-watched videos featuring the Republican nominee.

Two months later, as voters readied for the crucial Pennsylvania primary, a blogger named Mayhill Fowler recorded some audio of Senator Obama at a fundraiser in San Francisco that was closed to the regular press. Fowler was an Obama supporter who had contributed the maximum personal total of $2,300, and was granted access as an insider. She was also a correspondent for a new website called OffTheBus, a citizens' journalism project created by New York University professor Jay Rosen and blog entrepreneur Arianna Huffington to cover the 2008 campaign. The founders believed that "participants in political life had a right to report on what they saw and heard themselves, not as journalists claiming no attachments but as citizens with attachments who were relinquishing none of their rights. We talked about it, but we never anticipated anything this big, or wave-like," wrote Rosen on his popular media blog, PressThink.

Fowler's audio file captured Senator Obama's remarks before a group of well-heeled Democratic donors on the West Coast, just as he was locked in a battle with Senator Clinton for less-than-wealthy working votes in a major swing state. Much of his talk was pretty standard stump language for the eloquent candidate, until Obama tried to explain the cultural gap between more liberal and affluent Democrats and their white, blue-collar counterparts:

> You go into some of these small towns in Pennsylvania, and like a lot of small towns in the Midwest, the jobs have been gone now for 25 years and nothing's replaced them. And they fell through the Clinton Administration, and the Bush Administration, and each successive administration has said that somehow these communities are gonna regenerate and they have not. And it's not surprising then they get bitter, they cling to guns or religion or antipathy to people who aren't like them or anti-immigrant sentiment or anti-trade sentiment as a way to explain their frustrations.

Fowler knew she had something powerful on her tape recorder, and that her subsequent blog post would set off alarm bells. "I was thinking to myself, 'Oh my God, he is confirming to my fellow Californians the worst stereotypes they have of small-town America.' I was just dismayed," she told the *L.A. Times*. She held off for several days, torn between her feelings for Senator Obama and her instinct as a blogger. Eventually, the blogger won out and her post drew 250,000 page views and more than 5,000 comments in 48 hours, making national news and forcing the Obama campaign to explain their candidate's remarks. Mayhill Fowler was a citizen journalist with a nose for the controversial. Late in the campaign, she captured President Clinton lambasting a *Vanity Fair* writer in colorful language for its unflattering portrait of his life after the White House and role in the Clinton campaign.

■ ■ ■

In many ways, Mayhill Fowler was the direct descendent of S.R. Sidarth—a new type of citizen journalist, deployed as part of a virtual semiprofessional media army that could be counted on to capture every stumble on the campaign trail. But in one way she was different: Fowler was a supporter of the Obama campaign, she believed in the cause, and yet she did not follow the traditional top-down strictures of modern media campaigns. In short, she freelanced. She owned the copy, she controlled the message, she arranged for distribution via the vast network of people who get their political news online, and she decided what was newsworthy. Fowler's scoop was an extreme example of the potential pitfalls political campaigns face when they free up their messages in the new open-source landscape of CauseWired activism. The great irony is that it damaged—for a time—the message of a national campaign whose willingness to trust its online activists opened a new chapter in American political history.

By the middle of 2008, Barack Obama's campaign for president boasted more than 8,000 Web-based affinity groups, 850,000 online volunteers, and 1,276,000 donors. As the *Washington Post* noted,

Obama has shattered fundraising records and challenged ideas about the way presidential bids are financed. While past campaigns have relied largely on support from small circles of wealthy and well-connected patrons, Obama has received contributions from more than 1 million donors. He raised $91 million in the first two months of 2008 alone, most of it in small amounts over the Internet.

Obama's online success, likened to a "classic Internet startup" operation by the *New York Times*, combined two seemingly opposing core strategies: a tightly controlled and well-organized website with simple messaging and the slickest branding of any campaign in history, and an architecture for distribution that basically told supporters, "Here is what we have got, now show us what you can do with it." For all the money the Obama campaign spent on media in the 2008 cycle (perhaps the largest total media buy in history), it was that army of digital volunteers that made every dollar spent on branding and communications peel into two or three dollars in actual outreach to real voters. At the center of this effort was a clever platform designed to make even the slightest of supporters feel at home; My.BarackObama.com was a virtual organizing center that combined blogs, outreach groups, virtual volunteering, fundraising, and a series of tools designed to give each Obama activist the media or the network needed to recruit other supporters.

From the start, the campaign was agnostic about platforms, and the content and organizing tools available on My.BarackObama.com migrated almost anywhere a digital conversation could take place. You could easily take your support for Obama on the virtual road; to your own social networks at Facebook, LinkedIn, and MySpace; by sharing media Flickr and YouTube; by voting up top stories at Digg.com; or by participating in social networks targeted toward various demographic groups, like Eons (Baby Boomers), BlackPlanet (African Americans), Faithbase (churchgoers), AsianAve.com (Asian Americans), and MiGente.com (Latinos). And everywhere you went, the ubiquitous Obama brand followed, centered on hagiographic photos and a campaign insignia that was one part Tolkien's "one true ring," and another part corporate Middle America margarine logo.

On My.BarackObama.com, you could sign up for an Obama campaign event, volunteer to travel to primary states and knock on doors, or make telephone calls with a handy database tool that provided both a script and a valid phone number for each bit of outreach. You could download widgets that broadcast news stories about the Obama campaign or scrolled his biography. You could send campaign text messages on your phone, or even download one of several approved "Obama ring tones." Every now and then, you would be asked for money. "We've tried to bring two principles to this campaign," Joe Rospars, Obama's new media director, told *The Atlantic*. He said:

> One is lowering the barriers to entry and making it as easy as possible for folks who come to our website. The other is raising the expectation of what it means to be a supporter. It's not enough to have a bumper sticker. We want you to give five dollars, make some calls, host an event. If you look at the messages we send to people over time, there's a presumption that they will organize.

Obama's opponents for the Democratic nomination also rolled out decent online efforts, but the combination of demographics (Obama was strongly favored by millennials) and the strategy behind his "Obama everywhere" campaign, allowed the Illinois Senator to dominate much of the online action. Obama's strength in online organizing showed up everywhere. By late March, as his lead in delegates over Hillary Clinton grew, the numbers were pretty plain, according to techPresident.com, the website started by the Personal Democracy Forum to track the impact of media technology on the 2008 race. Obama had 499,811 Facebook friends to Clinton's 111,567; he boasted 273,665 MySpace friends to Clinton's 182,695. Then there were the statistics that track, for lack of a better word, online "buzz" by counting links about a candidate or official videos downloaded: Obama enjoyed 17.6 million links or downloads per day, compared to 6.5 million for Clinton.

While blog mentions were roughly even according to weblog tracking service Technorati.com, showing the historic level of interest in both candidates in the Democratic race, in terms of *audience share* for each of the campaign's official sites it was no contest at all. Obama led Clinton 61 to 39. That kind of media penetration made a real difference. "The main thing that stands out is his willingness to invest heavily in staffing the online social network hubs," said techPresident co-founder Micah Sifry, "and his heavy usage of long-form video. The latter in particular has worked very well for his campaign—you can find hundreds of Obama videos on YouTube, all made by the campaign, many of which are mini-documentaries that run five, ten minutes or longer, and a number that are fine-tuned for state-level field organizing and training." Those videos were particularly helpful with a traditional task of top-down political campaigns: controlling the message. Even when Senator Obama had a bad news week during the campaign, he could count on a video-friendly online audience that was as big as the cable news networks'.

What about the Republicans? While John McCain did use some online tools to help fuel his comeback from also-ran to nominee in less than nine months, the CauseWired candidate of the right was a little-known Republican Congressman from Texas, a nontelegenic libertarian named Ron Paul. For many, Paul represented a contradiction to those who believe a totally wired, socially networked population will change politics and how we elect candidates. The libertarian Republican was a true gadfly in the GOP race—contesting the legitimacy of the Iraq war while calling for the virtual end to the large federal government as we know it—and he mobilized an army of young supporters around issues of personal freedom. In some ways, Paul's campaign mimicked Howard Dean's more substantive run from the left four years earlier, especially in the degree to which the central campaign staff essentially ceded almost all control to a network of activists. Like Dean '04, Paul '08 ran a lean operation that not only signed up donors, but empowered actors to take the lead for the campaign.

Yet Paul was openly mocked in debates by the other "major" candidates for the Republican nomination, despite the fact that in the first half of the race, Paul raised more money online that any candidate in either party, keying huge online efforts on Guy Fawkes Night and the anniversary of the Boston Tea Party to highlight his antigovernment theme of rebellion. The latter was "arguably the largest single-day fundraising haul in U.S. political history" up to that time, according to Politico.com. Though he never overcame his long-shot status, Ron Paul was one of only two candidates to raise $20 million in the final quarter of 2007—Barack Obama and Hillary Clinton were the others. Paul was decidedly an outsider in the GOP race, hated by the establishment and infamously dropped from a Fox television Republican debate, even as his poll numbers crept into double digits in some states—and even as he won most open online polls, including the "MySpace primary" on the GOP side.

As was Howard Dean four years earlier, Ron Paul was quite obviously teaching a stagnant political organization—in this case, the Republican Party—about the power of online social organizing. Joe Trippi, the tech-savvy media consultant who ran the Dean campaign's online operation, summed up those early efforts: "We were the Wright brothers, we showed you could fly. We barely got off the ground but we got it done." Scott Heiferman put it differently: "The cat is out of the bag. The people have it in their brains that they can organize themselves."

That thought is at the core of CauseWired political activism. Republican blogger Alexander Brunk lamented, as Obama sealed the Democratic nomination, "Their side is full of activists, and ours is full of pundits." Taking action was at the core of Democrats' success online as they evolved from the Dean campaign, to the breakthrough fundraising and organizing juggernaut of the 2006 Congressional elections, to Barack Obama's historic campaign for president. The left rode a not-so-subtle shift in demographics (as was described in the last chapter) and consciously empowered a new generation of supporters to take action, no matter what the platform. "I would venture to say that the reason for [Obama's] continued success," said new media analyst Tristan Louis, "in the face of any existing model is also based on the realization that he, as a candidate, can make himself available in any media form."

If Ron Paul's organizing and online fundraising were a hint at how the Republican party might change in coming years—led by pioneering GOP organizers such as Patrick Ruffini—no clues from second-tier candidates were necessary for the Democrats. Change arrived like a sledgehammer on a condemned building. As the titanic Clinton–Obama race rolled through the first half of 2008, it was clear that no one would ever run for president again like they did before 2008. Veteran political columnist Ron Brownstein captured the seismic nature of the shift in *The National Journal*:

In scope and sweep, tactics and scale, the marathon struggle between Barack Obama and Hillary Rodham Clinton has triggered such a vast evolutionary leap in the way candidates pursue the presidency that it is likely to be remembered as the first true 21st-century campaign. On virtually every front, the two candidates' efforts dwarf those of all previous primary contenders—not to mention presumptive GOP nominee John McCain. It's easy to miss the magnitude of the change amid the ferocity of the Democratic competition. But largely because of their success at organizing supporters through the Internet, Clinton and, especially, Obama are reaching new heights in raising money, recruiting volunteers, hiring staff, buying television ads, contacting voters, and generating turnout. They are producing changes in degree from prior primary campaigns so large that they amount to changes in kind.

■ ■ ■

Political campaigns remain staged demonstrations of media and messaging, massive set pieces with a singular goal: electing a candidate. At the national level, they masquerade as "movements" in this cynic's view. They are like Rolling Stones tours—a massive temporary corporation staffed from Keith Richards down to the lowliest laborer, set up to tour the nation and take its money for a set period of time, which is then broken down, packed up, and moved off the stage for few years. While electing a candidate is an important cause in itself, to some—especially partisans angry at the other side—the ultimate goal in politics (along with power) is changing policy. Watching the massive social media operations in 2008, with their unprecedented list-building and constituent relations, the obvious question becomes: "What happens now?"

The stakes for actual policy are pretty high—and not just for the winners. Even after Senator Clinton conceded the Democratic nomination to Senator Obama after the closest, longest primary battle in political history, she retained a huge list of online supporters ready to take on policy battles. And Clinton didn't hesitate to use that online army, either—leveraging her votes and policy arguments in areas like security legislation and women's rights by appealing to millions of die-hard supporters who remained close to the former candidate through the Internet. As the 2008 finalists lined up for their November show-down, it was clear that Clinton emerged from the race a bit battered perhaps but also a stronger, more independent political presence on the national scene. Much of that strength—and most of the promise of building an ongoing movement from her presidential run—resulted from her online organizing. It may have been second-best to Obama, but it was also second-best in terms of size in electoral history, yielding a potentially potent army of wired supporters. The policy potential of Obama's vast online audience may even be greater.

"When one imagines how Obama's political army, presumably intact, might be mobilized to lobby for major legislation with just a few keystrokes, it becomes possible, for a moment at least, to imagine that he might change the political culture of Washington simply by overwhelming it," wrote political analyst Marc Ambinder in the *Atlantic Monthly*. He went on:

> What Obama seems to promise is, at its outer limits, a participatory democracy in which the opportunities for participation have been radically expanded. He proposes creating a public, Google-like database of every federal dollar spent. He aims to post every piece of non-emergency legislation online for five days before he signs it so that Americans can comment. A White House blog—also with comments— would be a near certainty. Overseeing this new apparatus would be a chief technology officer.

Mark Glaser, who writes the popular MediaShift blog for PBS (and who co-wrote the proto-blog Media Grok for the *Industry Standard* back in the 1990s with me and Jason Chervokas), developed a list of "open-source" ideas for the next president to consider in bringing policy closer to the people. He proposes moderated wikis for major policy initiatives, live online chats to complement press briefings, a transparent schedule, and a Google map of political contributions. I like this suggestion best:

> Create an online community of trusted advisers. Why not tap the wisdom of crowds and invite people with knowledge of critical subjects (energy, Middle East history, religion, etc.) to join up into online communities? These people would have to pass a certain threshold to join and be accepted, but they could give more outside opinions to subjects that are often misunderstood by politicians and political operatives. While lobbyists and special interests might join up, at least the others that join will make it a more level playing field for advice.

To some degree, that online community of advisers already exists. However, it is not trusted per se, and it is not vetted except by hard-won community building, trial and error, and a taste for rhetorical battle. Lost, to some degree, in the partisan wrangling of the Bush years and the bitter 2008 campaign is the fact that the so-called *netroots* effort, primarily a phenomenon of the left, developed a growing influence over public policy. For every "Flightsuit McChimpy" post blasting the Bush Administration, for every puerile "John McSame" post about Senator McCain, for every lame "Hitlery" or "Obambi" reference in battling Democratic blogs, there percolated a growing maturity on legislative matters and executive policy, on both the state and national levels. Indeed, when Obama reneged on a campaign promise to filibuster a bill providing immunity for telecommunications companies engaged in controversial domestic spying, his own supporters on MyBo took direct action. They created "President Obama, Please Get FISA Right," which quickly grew to be the largest group on the candidate's own site. The single issue opposition didn't stand outside the candidate's offices waving placards; instead, it organized quickly, using Obama's own community organizing methodology. And it seemed that the splinter group of Obama supporters had entirely suffused their actions with the philosophy of another famous Chicago organizer, Saul Alinsky, who began his career organizing workers in the Second City's fetid stockyards. His motto—"Agitate, Aggravate, Educate, Organize"—fits the online involvement in policy on the left perfectly.

Yet, it is a relatively quiet development that has been effectively masked by the more brass-knuckled contest-oriented bloggers—by the language of the political horserace still dominated by talking heads on cable television. It is clear, however, that given the growth of causes among the wired populace, the desire for real change is quite evident.

■ ■ ■

Over the past few years, a growing cadre of bloggers has created a force in progressive politics. On blogs such as Digby's Hullabaloo, Jane Hamsher's and Christy Hardin Smith's FireDogLake, and Glenn Greenwald's blog at Salon.com—as well as in the non-horserace-oriented posts on group blogs such as MyDD, Talking Points Memo, OpenLeft, The Moderate Voice, and TalkLeft—there is a real sense that the netroots effort has created a growing and viable channel for holding legislators' feet to the fire and for influencing policy. In the debates over the Iraq war, the torture of U.S. detainees, immigration reform, same-sex marriage, stem-cell research, tax policy, privacy and telecommunications, and poverty and the middle-class squeeze, bloggers and regular commentators on the blogs have gained some measure of sway in the larger public debate. And while that influence may be growing, one crucial element is already here: the core idea that regular citizens can and should be engaged in lobbying politicians, in pushing for legislation, and in advocating for policy—and not just at moments of crisis, but all the time.

"Democracy forces us to accept that idiots and fools (i.e., people who disagree with us) should be allowed to vote . . . or to blog," says David Perlmutter in *Blog Wars*, his study of the political impact of bloggers. And that is just the point. Idiots and fools were always the opposing forces on the sharp and critical blog of New Yorker Steve Gilliard, a gifted liberal writer whose death in 2007 at the age of 42 left a real gap in the growing leftwing blogosphere. Gilliard was caustic and honest, holding forth several times daily on politics and history, race relations (he was black) and culture, and less serious subjects like music and television and food. To me, one of the great convergences of actual policy and blogging came about when Steve's fingers crossed his keyboard during the 2005 transit strike in New York City.

Just before Christmas, the Transit Workers Union walked out, shutting down the city's vast public transportation system and leaving its millions of daily riders stranded. The old print media immediately sided with its readership: the stranded commuters, and by extension, Mayor Michael Bloomberg and the transit chiefs. Both the politicians and the media missed a larger story that Steve reported brilliantly: the union's very real safety concerns, and how the burgeoning city economy was leaving the workers far behind. Gilliard's lone voice gathered steam, however, and it was clear by the end—when the union got a new deal—that his network had exerted its influence in the process. One of Gilliard's frequent themes was the assault on the entrenched powers of organized politics and policy by outsiders who knew how to use technology. The last thing the powers that be want to deal with, said Steve, "is an Ohio housewife who wants a voice in national politics. They want to tell her what to think, not to listen to her ideas. She isn't a member of the club, no matter how smart she is."

Electing candidates is just part of the story; indeed, it becomes too easy to focus on the horserace aspect, the polls, and the money raised. "Ultimately, you cannot change our politics until you engage regular people in a meaningful conversation about the policy that determines the quality of their lives," says Andrea Batista Schlesinger, executive director of the Drum Major Institute for Public Policy (DMI), a nonpartisan, progressive think-tank based in New York. I am privileged to serve on DMI's board, and to have taken some small role in the reinvention of the Drum Major Institute, which began life as a support mechanism for the work of Rev. Martin Luther King, Jr. in the 1960s. Much of DMI's evolution took place online, in public, often amidst fierce policy debate; yet it stood apart from most of the partisan bickering.

DMI recognized Steve Gilliard's clarion call to move beyond the established (and entrenched) policy elites (to "route around," as the early Internet architects used to say) and take policy debate directly to a young and hungry audience on the Web. So every report and whitepaper made its debut online, and every bit of research invited argument from any citizen willing to type. When DMI released scorecards on how state and federal legislators voted on a host of crucial legislative initiatives benefiting the middle class, those scorecards appeared on the Web. They also appeared in search results for every single legislator on Google, thanks to a sly and innovative keyword purchase by DMI. The organization's blog became the hub for everything that affected the policy initiatives the group supported, and DMI launched mini-sites such as Mayor.tv and TheMiddleClass.org to highlight key issues. Video on those sites was, of course, available for anyone to post on any blog or Facebook profile. We set up a "Netroots Advisory Council" to encourage bloggers to write about policy.

In short, this was not your father's policy shop. DMI became a fast-moving leader in progressive policy and a growing influence among legislators, not just because of the quality of its research, but because those public-sensitive politicians knew damn well that DMI could attract a virtual crowd like no other small think-tank. Thanks to my board member status, I had an inside view of this reinvention. Andrea says, "We figured out early on that we could harness the potential of the Web to do not just politics, but policy." What stands out is the willingness to take a risk (and fail publicly) and the open nature of the effort: This was not preaching policy from some white-glove liberal institution swathed in polished limestone and oak. It was public policy sausage-making in a ground-level shop with a huge plate glass window and an open door to the street.

■ ■ ■

Government itself remains largely another matter, though there are signs of open-source improvements. In Great Britain, a movement to open government itself parallels the netroots effort to influence it. My friend and blogging doppelganger, Tom Watson, Member of Parliament for West Bromwich East (Birmingham), was appointed in the spring of 2008 by Prime Minister Gordon Brown to the Cabinet Office and given the task of coordinating the transformation of British government in the digital age. In a much-quoted speech in the House of Commons, Watson pointed out that one in ten British citizens has emailed 10 Downing Street.

The next step, he said, "is to enable e-petitioners to connect with each other around particular issues and to link up with policy debates both on and off Government webspace."

Watson neatly encapsulated the coming change in the way government deals with information:

> The challenge is for elected representatives to follow their customers and electors into this brave new world. Five years ago, I set up a political blog. At the time, it was seen as a radical act. People couldn't believe that I had opened myself up to such scrutiny and occasional daily abuse. But the blog broke down the walls between legislators and electors in a way that interested me. So I persevered. Today I'm no longer a pioneer. There are thousands of political bloggers. And politicians can no longer set to default broadcast mode. They have to engage. Some have said that the Power of Information agenda is a geek manifesto. It's not. It's about making people's lives and their communities better.

That is undoubtedly true. While there is a temptation among those who track causes and online fundraising to separate political organizing from philanthropy, I think that is a mistake. It is wishing for a division that the audience simply will not tolerate going forward. It is like hoping that a print classified operation will continue to grow during the age of Craigslist. Young people do not separate their causes into neat little boxes labeled POLITICS and CHARITY. They simply respond to what moves them, what their friends recommend, and what they believe might change the world. This chapter cannot possibly capture the massive changes in politics that information technology has wrought, but it is important to include a sense of just how quickly the landscape is changing. It is no accident that our nonprofit clients at Changing Our World are asking about websites like Barack Obama's. As Dylan said, "The order is rapidly fading."

"Until very recently," wrote Steve Gilliard in the last months of his life, "there was a lot of concern about the engagement of the American people in politics. They didn't vote, they weren't interested in politics. But technology can liberate and strengthen people because they can work together without the endless debate which occurs in meetings. It also allows for goal-centered activism."

7

Spare the Paperwork: The Quick Rise of Flash Causes

The Santa Ana winds become hotter and drier as they push west from the deserts through the winding canyons of Southern California. The temperature climbs, the winds roar through the valleys, and the perfect natural tinderbox is ready for ignition. In late October 2007, the winds caught a spark and fueled one of the worst wildfire seasons in the populated history of the region. Two-dozen pockets of raging fire, heat, and ash burned from the Mexican border up to north of Los Angeles. In San Diego County, just four years after a blaze that killed 15 people and singed more than 200,000 acres, ten residents died and more than 300,000 acres burned. The images were frightening—homeowners watching their property burn, firefighters gamely battling the winds and the roar of the flames, and thousands of local residents camped out on the home field of the San Diego Chargers.

Sitting in his home in the University Town Center neighborhood of San Diego, Web entrepreneur Nate Ritter was watching the horrifying broadcasts on television, worrying about his community, and wondering what to do. "I started to blog, and I ended up finding too much information to blog—it went so fast—so I ended up using Twitter because it was so quick, short, to the point, just facts, and I could post a zillion times, so it was really fast," Ritter told the NetSquared technology blog later. As fast as he got the information about the fires—from television, from the radio, from websites and blogs—Ritter was firing out *tweets*, those short messages limited to 140 characters or less that have made Twitter.com one of the fastest-growing micropublishing tools on the Net.

Soon, Ritter was posting almost around the clock, providing a virtual wire service or hotline for more than 350 followers—people who were either scared or curious about the news and wanted a central point of information, one feed created by a human being with many sources. In may ways, Ritter's Twitter work in the San Diego fires took the place of local government and nonprofit work, or at least supplemented it in important ways. Getting good information to people who desperately needed it became a cause, something worth time and resources and energy.

But there was no nonprofit organization behind the work Ritter did. Government did not support it. There was no formal structure involved. One man's passion to provide information in an emergency drove the enterprise, and created an instant burst of community activism—or, as I like to call it, a *flash cause*.

■ ■ ■

Flash causes have always been part of the landscape in a democracy, where speech is bedrock freedom. A terrible accident spurs residents to push local government for a new traffic signal. A controversial war overseas causes protest at home. A firefighter dies in the line of duty and funds are raised. The local ecology is threatened, and residents quickly get a petition drive started. These causes flash into existence on the back of human emotion, and from the drive not to accept the hand that fate has dealt, but rather to change it. In some ways, we are conditioned to believe—even the cynics among us—that we really can fight city hall or that big corporation. And, by gosh, we love a fighter.

It is in our DNA to battle back, to organize, to push for change when something stirs us. Josh Ritter took matters into his own hands during the California wildfires, but he used a new set of tools: blogs, short message systems, feeds, and online video. He signed up a new kind of participant in a new type of relationship—highly motivated but almost entirely virtual. It is easy, in some ways, to see the effects of media technology on savvy nonprofit organizations or hungry politicians and political movements. It is almost impossible to track these flash causes online, and yet they pop up as quickly as wildfire in a San Diego canyon. Some of them flash and burn out as quickly as they came, and others catch on and spread. To my way of thinking, they are among the most interesting phenomena in the growth of online causes.

In many respects, this book of 200 pages or so attempts to bring order to a phenomenon that defies order in almost all forms, and to capture this movement in a permanent medium. Even as these words go into a word processor (to visit your mind months or years after their commitment to bytes), new causes are forming, gathering people to their cases, and either growing and succeeding or withering into digital ghosts. The movement of causes beyond the regulations governing 501(c)3 tax-exempt organizations, beyond political parties, beyond political action committees, beyond unions and fraternal organizations, and beyond governments and

associations is essentially without limit; in some respects, it is a vast phenomenon for physics to ponder—the transfer of trillions and trillions of
electronic impulses from millions of brains to millions of wired networks
around the world. These causes almost always originate with an individual, or a small group. They leverage the do-it-yourself nature of the online
network and the ideal among connected consumers that they have the
power not only to say what want, but to create what they need to get that
message across. Tapscott and Williams have high hopes for this CauseWired
creative class: "For individuals and small producers, this may be the birth of
a new era, perhaps even a golden one, on par with the Italian renaissance
or the rise of Athenian democracy."

This phenomenon cannot be ordered neatly; it cannot be dia-
grammed or put into a spreadsheet. As you read this, a college student
somewhere in the United States has become angry at some social problem, some injustice, some wrong that needs righting. In the time it
takes to write this paragraph, she has fired off a message to her closest
online contacts. By the time this page is complete, they have created a
movement somewhere. Perhaps it is very thin at first: a Facebook cause,
a couple of blog posts, perhaps a Twitter stream or some text messages.
Somebody finds an outrageous video, and that makes the rounds. More
posts are written. Tags are created and other college kids in other schools
around the country stumble on the cause via Google or Technorati—or
better yet, because some friend of a friend invited them in via MySpace
or Razoo. Perhaps there is a tax-exempt organization that works in this
area, so money can be raised. Maybe it is an issue for government: We
need to get those emails to Congress, and those online petitions going,
and perhaps some political fundraising for a candidate who has taken up
the cause.

Now things are really percolating. There are thousands of "friends"
who, at a minimum, proudly wear the badge of this cause on their profiles or blogs. The really savvy Members of Congress have heard about

it, and some of the A-list bloggers have begun to post about it. The tag for the cause hits some of the leaderboards that search blogs, and it rises in Facebook Causes. Thousands of people begin to use Digg and other social-news tools to raise the profile of stories related to the cause. By this time, our original student is working around the clock. Her grades have slipped slightly, but she is changing the world. Then she gets a ping from a reporter—a newspaper wants the story, perhaps for the print edition, but who cares? Newspapers have become 24-hour news bureaus with reporters blogging stories when they happen. What our cause leader needs is the legitimization of the story, the cause that excited her and made her take action. The newspaper gives her that and one other vital asset: a link. Now that "legitimate" media link is sent throughout the piecemeal cause network. Television comes calling—a cable station wants to do a segment. That is good news. But the great news is that the station puts all its video online. Our student goes through makeup and nails her standup, and the B-roll surrounding her talking points looks very good. Her buddy with the mad video skills captures it all, and by that night, her video moment is on thousands of Facebook profiles and blogs, and is rising on the YouTube charts. She gets a call from a U.S. Senator.

Is this an ideal scenario? There is no question about it. Many causes go nowhere after the initial burst of interest and energy. But others raise money, get attention, and change policy. The CauseWired phenomenon is intrinsically democratic. It puts the tools of attention, and fundraising, and action into the hands of any citizen who cares enough to use them. This breaks down some of the barriers to entry that organizers traditionally have had—the need for funds to rent a hall, run phone banks, fire off large direct-mail drops, buy television or radio time, or travel around giving speeches. But it also removes that first weeding out of the serious, committed organizers from the spur-of-the-moment short-term activists. Spend any time with Facebook Causes and you realize that, for most, the experience is a slight one. Your friend asks you to join a cause. If you are slightly interested, you do. You never give any money to that cause and chances are you ignore the messages the cause generates, chalking it up to "Facebook spam" as the price of being popular.

This is the great evolutionary tank of Facebook Causes, and, in many respects, all online causes. In the sediment lie the untold numbers of tiny organisms that never evolve into anything but a cluster of a few friends who decided for few days or a few hours to try to bring attention to an issue or support research into a disease that killed somebody's grandmother. Then they move on, and these tiny bursts of light flicker out—well intentioned, perhaps born of actual passion, but not sustained. It is a marketplace, to be sure. And most of the startups stay small and die off quickly.

However, this activity makes the causes that really do catch on that much more compelling. As participants in the vast, swelling multitude that lives on wired social networks, online consumers know they are being bombarded with messages on a dizzying, constant basis. So when one breaks through, respect for the effort—for the sheer numbers—can create an instant brand, a cause that lives well beyond that initial burst of social consciousness.

So you are not a registered 501(c)3 tax-exempt organization. You are not a formally organized association or a lobbying group or political campaign. Perhaps you are not an incorporated entity at all. New groups organizing online are eschewing traditional labels and structures, creating themselves for short-lived but powerful campaigns, and then morphing into other types of causes and campaigns. This is a strong antibureaucracy movement—one that prizes transparency and speed and despises old rules and additional costs. These flash causes have changed the definition of charity and volunteerism, and they are an important microtrend.

■ ■ ■

Take the tragic story of Nataline Sarkisyan, a California native whose death at age 17 became a flash cause almost overnight and whose very name came to represent economic injustice during the 2008 presidential election. A leukemia patient who sought a liver transplant, Nataline, died in Los Angeles on December 20, 2007, taken off life support just as her insurance company reversed itself and agreed to pay for the transplant, according to the *Los Angeles Times*. Her family had mobilized supporters with the help of Armenian groups and Eve Gittelson, the health policy writer known as "nyceve," whose posts appear on the progressive blog, DailyKos. The day after her death, Gittelson posted to DailyKos, where she had managed a campaign to get the insurer, Cigna, to change its mind. "Though she is gone, an immense piece of her proud legacy will be that through her untimely death, she gave us a glimpse of our collective strength. Yesterday was a great day for people-powered politics."

But the cause was just beginning. Her case moved beyond one family's desperate struggle to save a young life and became a cause for thousands of people who discovered her case on the Internet—on blogs, in Facebook, on YouTube, and in their Twitter feeds. Though I occasionally read DailyKos, I had missed Eve Gittelson's post and I found out about Nataline from Jason Calacanis, a well-known digital entrepreneur and an old friend from our Silicon Alley days in the 1990s. Jason posted on his blog and into his Twitter stream (I do not remember which I saw first), and like many others, I was immediately struck by the story.

A leukemia patient, Nataline, needed a new liver after her treatment for the blood disorder caused serious complications. The family hired a lawyer and organized friends to pressure Cigna to change its mind. Cigna appears to have reversed its decision to deny the transplant after about 150 teenagers and nurses protested outside its Glendale office, according to ABC News. But it was too late, and the story only picked up steam. After the teen's death, family attorney Mark Geragos said that Cigna "maliciously killed her" and asked for criminal charges against Cigna HealthCare; the company vigorously denied any wrongdoing.

I had read nothing of this until this headline showed up in my feeds: "CIGNA kills Nataline Sarkisyan." Wow, Jason's headline certainly got my attention and, as it did for thousands of others, the full story pulled at the heartstrings and stoked a sense of anger and outrage. Calacanis is more than your average blogger. A born promoter, who created a series of successful Internet properties during a decade-long career that began when he crossed the river from Brooklyn as a young lad with a certain attitude toward those who might get in his way, he wrote, "15-billion-dollar market cap . . . almost 20B in revenue . . . you can't afford a transplant?!" Then he posted the names and titles of Cigna's top executives, asking his considerable readership to go after them directly. And as the CEO of the startup Mahalo, a socially wired search engine with results created by human editors instead of algorithms, he directed the creation of a section dedicated to the case. The page was filled with links to mainstream media stories and blog posts about Nataline, but it led with a moving video that was created and posted on YouTube by Nataline's brother.

Nataline Sarkisyan, who was already a cause before her death, became a national headline. An hour or so after I read Jason's post, I checked in on Facebook to deal with the usual requests to test my movie knowledge, poke somebody back, or rate a new band. And there was an invitation to join a new group—CIGNA is Sicko—with 80 new members. Meanwhile, the YouTube video has been seen more than 15,000 times. Even as a memorial service was held in California, the cause kept growing. Many blogs picked it up. I knew immediately that as the Democratic candidates prepared to kick off the 2008 race in Iowa, it was likely that her case would become part of the important national health insurance debate.

John Edwards, as it turns out, was the candidate who made Nataline Sarkisyan's case his own. Just after Iowa, where he finished second to Barack Obama, I noticed that one name jumped into his stump speech when he got to health care: *Nataline Sarkisyan*. Indeed, in conceding Iowa, Edwards led with the cause in his speech—which was part concession (to Obama), part victory (over Clinton), and part pledge (to keep on campaigning)—as he continued the call for universal health care:

And we are so proud of this cause. But I want all of us to remember tonight while we're having all these political celebrations, that just a few weeks ago in America, Nataline Sarkisyan, a 17-year-old girl . . . needed a liver transplant, and [her] insurance company decided they wouldn't pay for her liver transplant operation.

Finally, her nurses spoke up on her behalf. Her doctors spoke up on her behalf. Ultimately, the American people spoke up on her behalf by marching and picketing in front of her health insurance carrier.

And, finally, the insurance carrier caved in and agreed to pay for her operation. And when they notified the family just a few hours later, she died. She lost her life. Why? Why?

Afterward, the Sarkisyan family campaigned with Edwards in New Hampshire. The Sarkisyan story unfolded just as I was gathering material for this book, and its pattern was familiar—passionate people who organized to change something, but outside of the usual organizational channels. Pure passion drove the cause, and the cause used any technological means at its disposal.

■ ■ ■

As it happens, I saw this flash-cause pattern from the inside just a couple of years ago, when I was one of a small group of activists who helped rile a community of online users to take action. Sometimes it starts with an op-ed column and a whole bunch of bloggers. On September 29, 2004, *New York Times* commentator Nicholas Kristof wrote a column headlined "Sentenced to Be Raped," and introduced the world to an amazing young woman from a rural village in Pakistan who quickly became a personal hero to me, and a symbol of strength and perseverance against forces of repression and violence in a very dangerous corner of the world. The story of Mukhtaran Bibi was searing:

The plight of women in developing countries isn't addressed much in the West, and it certainly isn't a hot topic in the presidential campaign. But it's a life-and-death matter in villages like Meerwala, a 12-hour drive southeast from Islamabad.

In June 2002, the police say, members of a high-status tribe sexually abused one of Ms. Mukhtaran's brothers and then covered up their crime by falsely accusing him of having an affair with a high-status woman. The village's tribal council determined that the suitable punishment for the supposed affair was for high-status men to rape one of the boy's sisters, so the council sentenced Ms. Mukhtaran to be gang-raped.

As members of the high-status tribe danced in joy, four men stripped her naked and took turns raping her. Then they forced her to walk home naked in front of 300 villagers.

The column served to introduce the story of Mukhtaran Bibi to Americans, and it was picked up on several blogs, including mine. At the time, the battle between Massachusetts Senator John Kerry and incumbent President George W. Bush raged on, centering around the Bush Administration's war in Iraq—which had stalled after its initial toppling of Saddam Hussein—and the country's general reaction to the attacks of September 11, 2001. The Muslim world was radicalized versus the United States, and national security was the top issue in the campaign that fall. As Kristof noted at the conclusion of his column, Mukhtaran Bibi's decision to use the court settlement she received for prosecuting her case to open schools and increase tolerance ran counter to some of what Americans were hearing in that campaign: "We in the West," he wrote, "could help chip away at that oppression, with health and literacy programs and by simply speaking out against it, just as we once stood up against slavery and totalitarianism."

I found that story quite compelling and put up a short post on my blog, which was then only nine months old:

We wring our hands over the election, over the stock market, and we talk proudly about freedom from the safety of our abundant shores.

But Mukhtaran Bibi is fighting the real battle. She is a real hero for our times. Read the story. Think about what we can do to help.

And that was that, one of many posts related to something I had read elsewhere that I post every month. I provided the address for checks to be sent, gave a few more links in comments, and discussed the case with my readers. Then I moved on.

About 10 months later, Kristof broke some troubling news about the Mukhtaran Bibi case: Invited to speak in New York about human rights, the Pakistani leader was instead placed under house arrest by the regime of President Pervez Musharraf. In effect, her heroism had become an embarrassment to Pakistan's military and she was prevented from traveling from fear "that she might malign Pakistan's image," according to the government. "Excuse me," wrote Kristof, "but Ms. Mukhtaran, a symbol of courage and altruism, is the best hope for Pakistan's image. The threat to Pakistan's image comes from President Musharraf for all this thuggish behavior."

The story enraged me. Here was my personal hero, a woman who had turned hatred into hope—and not just some imagined concept of hope, but actual schools for the sons and daughters of her attackers—herself under attack by a regime that our own government supported. At that moment, the story of Mukhtaran Bibi became a flash cause for me—and the Internet was the perfect accomplice.

I began posting right away, beginning with Kristof's column and links to sites like the Asian-American Network Against Abuse of Human Rights (which had invited Mukhtaran Bibi to speak), Mercy Corps (a nonprofit that provided funds to assist her in Pakistan), and a group of students led by organizer Declan Hill at Oxford in the UK. I had never personally met any of these people, including Nick Kristof, but we corresponded via email and almost immediately formed a virtual coalition with points of strength in the United States, Britain, and Pakistan. In a break from the traditional old-media style of columnists—and their "I write, you read" proposition—Kristof took an active role, providing updates for bloggers, commenting, and posting links on his *Times* bulletin board for fundraising and activism. He was the bulwark around which the virtual network was able to organize.

We organized very quickly. Looking back, my behavior during those couple of weeks in June and July 2005 was singularly boorish, but also effective. I used a technique of "calling out" major bloggers I knew by using their names as tags in the popular social linking sites Technorati and del.icio.us, knowing full well that bloggers check their incoming links and mentions on an almost-hourly basis. Luckily, the story I was selling was so compelling that almost no one took offense at my bullying tactics. The bloggers responded: More than 100 wrote their own posts and included the Mukhtaran Bibi tags. I then created a post, updated constantly for two weeks, that included every blog link on the story. This brought traffic to the blogs (always the best currency for bloggers) and also increased search engine activity for the cause. Many of us included in our posts the names and email addresses of Pakistani officials, particularly the diplomatic corps residing in the United States and Britain. On June 15, I began a post on the ongoing story this way:

> In less than four days, you've mobilized a small army on behalf of Mukhtaran Bibi, my personal hero and a symbol of courage to many millions. I'll continue to update the main post below, but I wanted to comment briefly on the speed and effectiveness of the small corner of the media world that connects to this tiny Weblog.
>
> It's incredibly powerful, and I'm not sure I realized that until this morning. Since last night you (and yes, it's you, not me) have gotten links and coverage on more than ~~30 40 65 80~~ 100 blogs. We can do more; we can get it into the talking head slipstream, and onto some larger blogs and sites. So please, take this story and run with it—to me, the outcome of Mukhtaran Bibi's story says everything about what we really believe about freedom.

The posts within this coalition of bloggers numbered in the hundreds, and the comments in the many thousands. They included well-known bloggers and commentators like James Wolcott of *Vanity Fair*, tech guru Robert Scoble, Markos Moulitsas of the DailyKos, new-media maven Jeff Jarvis, and political analyst Ezra Klein. They also included many of my blogging buddies, folks such as Lance Mannion, Shakespeare's Sister, Joe Gandelman, Pamela Parker, Lindsay Beyerstein, Matt Gold, Steve Gilliard, Steve Bowbrick, and others, including my longtime collaborator, Jason Chervokas, and my brother-in-law, Ralph DeMarco. I posted updates to the well-trafficked Huffington Post group blog. The web of links spun outward, beyond anything I could reasonably track. But I could feel the momentum and the power of all those voices. The Pakistani government received an onslaught of email. Local fundraisers were held. This wide-ranging coalition helped to support Kristof's contention at the *Times* that Mukhtaran Bibi's case was a major international story, and it supported the underfunded grassroots organizations working to shine a light on the repressive, misogynistic practices of her society. In Britain particularly, the press took up the case, and newspapers such as the *Independent* and the *Guardian* carried stories that embarrassed the Pakistani government. The U.S. State Department got involved (to the credit of Secretary Rice, because most of the heat was coming from the left side of the blogosphere), adding official pressure on the Musharraf government. Then, I posted an update:

This just in: the Pakistani government says Ms. Bibi has been released! Let's hope this is true and she can complete her travel plans. I know that many, many people used the email addresses posted here and on the other sites—it made a difference, folks: shining a light sometimes can. But please keep blogging this story, now and in the future.

Yet, the situation was far from clear. Kristof posted an item saying Mukhtaran Bibi still had not been given back her passport by the Pakistani government. Amnesty International weighed in with a strong protest, and the State Department issued a formal, public appeal to the Musharraf government. More bloggers got involved, and I posted this sentiment in the heat of the cause:

> But even as Musharraf travels in his Presidential jet, the word is spreading. Even as he defends his abysmal record, the word is spreading. Like wildfire, the immoral detention of Mukhtaran Bibi has taken on a media-based life of its own. Musharraf's thugs can take her passport, threaten her lawyers, and place her under house arrest, but in a wired world, ever more connected and free to write, to post, to speak, word is spreading. We're routing around President Musharraf and the military of Pakistan. And Mukhtar Mai's words are spreading.

The blogger campaign for Mukhtaran Bibi was a success, but it was an instant campaign of sorts, and not a permanent organization or coalition. In the *Columbia Journalism Review* that summer, columnist Samantha Henig wrote about the episode and I think she captured some of that flash-cause momentum, and the techniques in use:

> In Psych 101, we learned that when there is an emergency, it's not enough to yell "Somebody please get help!" Humans, with our tendency to shy away from danger or responsibility, will simply ignore the call to action, opting for a sort of "Well, that guy over there will probably do something" mentality. The best method, then, is to single someone out, point at him, look him in the eye, and firmly instruct, "You, in the green shirt—call 9-1-1. Now!"
>
> Tom Watson used exactly that tactic in his plea Tuesday that bloggers worldwide join him to publicize the kidnapping of Mukhtaran Bibi by the Pakistani government. And, just as a psychology professor might have predicted, he has gotten a response.

Watson refers readers to his older posts chronicling the terrible treatment of Mukhtaran Bibi before adding a heartfelt touch: "It sounds quaint and facile and boyish, but Mukhtaran Bibi is my hero—a small, willful package of courage and steel in the face of group torture and violence by the weak-souled, God-hating cowards who would make her a victim."

And then, the call to action. Watson asks bloggers to help draw attention to the issue by linking to his post and to Nicholas Kristof's latest column in the *New York Times* about Mukhtaran Bibi, or by writing a piece of their own about her strife. But he does not just issue a blanket request; he singles out 24 bloggers who should get involved. And just to tack on a little peer pressure, he crosses off their names once they do their part for the Mukhtaran cause. So far, 11 from Watson's list have responded, and the message has spread through the blogosphere.

In the end, hundreds of bloggers responded. And this was before the age of formal social networks, when transmitting the call for a cause became such a simple matter. The story of Mukhtaran Bibi, who eventually won her release and today travels freely to speak about human rights, was the compelling force behind the flash cause that I helped to ignite online. Her heroism spurred people to take action: to write, to email, to give money, and to post links.

Before the commercial Internet's dawning, such a fast-moving cause over the story of one woman in a small village in rural Pakistan would never have been sparked. The ease of communications today made it possible; each decision to support the cause—whether via a blog posting or an email to a government official—became easier to implement. Ten minutes for an email, 20 minutes for a blog posting, 30 seconds to add a link—the time commitment involved was exceptionally light. This allowed wider participation and stronger distribution of the message.

■ ■ ■

Early in 2008, Facebook became the staging ground for another spontaneous flash cause on the international scene, this time involving a protest in South America. The story's genesis is long and complex, but the cause itself was almost instantaneous. Some brief background is in order.

Fuerzas Armadas Revolucionarias de Colombia (FARC)—Ejército del Pueblo (the Revolutionary Armed Forces of Colombia—People's Army) is considered a terrorist organization by the Colombian government, and was established in 1964 as the military wing of the country's communist party. According to the BBC, the organization is in decline in Colombia, but still has more than 6,000 members and is active in the cocaine trade that has troubled the South American nation for decades. As a series of kidnappings in 2007 brought controversial Venezuelan President Hugo Chavez into mediation efforts to secure the release of rebel-held hostages, Chavez outraged Colombians by referring to FARC as "a real army," and not a terrorist group. Many Colombians are tired of more than 40 years of civil unrest and a state of civil war in part of the country. They strongly oppose FARC, and some favor a negotiated peace and a demilitarization of Colombia.

In January 2008, the cause exploded across Facebook, and its impact was felt in street protests around the world. On MediaShift, Mark Glaser's innovative community exploring digital media on the PBS website, blogger Jennifer Woodard Maderazo picked up the story. A social-media skeptic who wrote that Facebook "seems like a place for sending fake toys and cocktails to friends, but not very useful for the more profound issues we deal with as a society," Maderazo was nonetheless impressed by the FARC cause. "Oscar Morales created a Facebook group called 'Un Millon de Voces Contra las FARC' ("One Million Voices against the FARC") as a way to take what many Colombians were feeling about the situation and express it online," she wrote.

From a mere 20 invites to other Facebook friends, the group quickly signed up 20,000 members. But the organizers worried that their online movement would end there: "We thought we'd just end up like other groups on Facebook," organizer Felipe Echeverri told Maderazo. "Someone creates it and it just sits there. So we created the 'Un Millon' application, and all of the group members started putting the logo on their Facebook profiles, and sending out invitations to their friends. This helped refine the idea and make the group grow."

The group built an application on Facebook and also launched the website ColombiaSoyYo ("I am Colombia"), and soon membership reached 116,000 members. "By this point," wrote Maderazo, "the initiative had extended beyond Colombia, and the group had already assembled organizers for marches in 160 cities around the world. The true test would be the day of the march. Would the online momentum translate into a successful offline protest?"

On February 4, 2008, the online organizing paid off. What started as a flash cause within a small group of people fed up with a long and deadly civil war became a worldwide movement. As Maderazo put it: "The world watched as people around the globe took to the streets to show the FARC that enough was enough." Spain's EFE news service put the numbers at more than 10 million people. Hundreds of demonstrators gathered outside the United Nations in New York, where protester Salvador Zapata, a restaurant worker in Edgewater, New Jersey, held a bright-blue poster: "FARC STOP THIS DIRTY AND FRACTIOUS WAR AGAINST THE PEOPLE," it read. The *New York Times* gave credit to the Facebook group, which won the support of the Colombian government as well as much of the Spanish-speaking world.

"The Colombian people were lethargic, with an almost cynical indifference to the problems of violence," said Óscar Montes, 33, a civil engineer in Barranquilla who helped organize the marches on Facebook. "At this time the FARC can say whatever they want," he said in a telephone interview. "But they will not have legitimacy."

■ ■ ■

Flash causes are everywhere in the network of networks. They are political, social, and charitable. They can benefit or destroy a brand. The flash cause that media analyst Jeff Jarvis launched against Dell in 2005 after his computer malfunctioned is justly famous for its negative impact on a consumer brand that fails to meet a networked crowd's expectations. Jarvis's "Dell Hell" posts forced the company to change its customer service practices, and to monitor blogs and social networks—a move quietly adopted by other consumer brand companies worried about the easy reach of the blogosphere and the Facebook/MySpace audience.

The common denominators of flash causes are passion and the lack of a formal infrastructure. To some degree, they just happen. They may not have formal leadership; they may not boast any organizing structure. They just come together out of passion and necessity—and online, they can come together quickly. Sometimes, using the power of the network, they can change the world.

8 | Heralds of Change: Giving Goes Open Source

Matthew Arnold called Oxford the city of dreaming spires, a reference to the timeless beauty of the harmonious architecture of the colleges spread across the landscape—but also to the centrality of thought that Oxford expresses for all of Britain. Every year, at the annual Skoll World Forum, those dreaming spires take on another meaning as leaders in social entrepreneurship from around the world gather at the University of Oxford's Said Business School.

The forum is the brainchild of Jeffrey Skoll, a young entrepreneur who became a billionaire in the moment of eBay's initial public offering in 1998. The Canadian-born Skoll was the online auction giant's second employee and its first president. In the years since his eBay billions made him one of the Internet industry's richest men, Skoll has turned most of his attention to social causes. He has funded feature films such as Al Gore's Oscar-winning *An Inconvenient Truth*, and, through the work of the Skoll Foundation, has been an ambitious funder in the growing field of social entrepreneurship and the convener of the annual forum amid the gates and walls of Oxford. Along with Pierre Omidyar, eBay's original founder, Skoll has attempted to turn the very marketplace-democracy that powers the best online businesses into a force for social change. Indeed, through his foundation and the Skoll Centre at Oxford, Skoll has emerged as the leading light of the social entrepreneurship movement, which began as early as the 1980s, when technically savvy entrepreneurial types such as Ashoka founder Bill Drayton and Grameen Bank founder Muhammad Yunus first sought to bring their brand of disruptive change to the world's problems.

At the World Forum I attended in the warm British spring of 2007, Skoll spoke under the dome of Christopher Wren's seventeenth-century Sheldonian hall at Oxford's town center and remarked candidly on "a changing time for philanthropy." He suggested that while much of the focus of the past several years is on bringing business practices to philanthropy, buzzwords like *philanthropreneurs* may miss the point: It is not just about a change in the nature of philanthropy, "but a movement from institutions to individuals." Individuals, he suggested, can move faster and take more chances: "Wherever you find humanity at its worst in the world, you'll find a social entrepreneur working for change."

Indeed, there is considerable glamour attached to social causes. While social entrepreneurship often involves starting small and leveraging scant resources to create change, whether in environmental science, feeding the poor, or facing down disease, any movement like this needs star power, and at Skoll that incandescence is provided by people like rock star Peter Gabriel, Google.org chief Larry Brilliant, and Queen Rania Al-Abdullah of Jordan. Each year, the social entrepreneurs bring with them stories of human struggle from the field, ideas about innovation in programming and finance, and seemingly boundless optimism about fomenting social change. They also bring some very real-world concerns to the "dreaming spires" of social entrepreneurship. At the various panels and convocations, they worry aloud about funding and sustainability, attracting talent, and working with governments. Many dare to puzzle about the concept of *social entrepreneurship* itself—whether it can grow and thrive beyond its current buzzword status, whether it can truly change the seemingly hidebound worlds of foundations and established philanthropy.

Time and again in the Skoll sessions, committed social entrepreneurs talk about how hard it is to raise funds (donations, capital, "investments") for innovative ideas that do not fit into what foundations and philanthropists believe about funding projects. Outside of the self-funding ventures in microenterprise, the money it takes to fire up major movements such as tackling global warming, eradicating poverty in Africa and South Asia, preserving delicate environments, and empowering poor women generally comes from fundraising. Jacqueline Novogratz, CEO of the Acumen Fund, admits that fundraising remains central—that social enterprises "always came back, somewhat reluctantly, to philanthropy—to finding a few big supporters." Nothing I have heard here changes that formula, particularly for startups; entrepreneurs have always had to battle, to scratch, to promise their firstborn to get the capital they need to launch something. For social entrepreneurs, that means major donors. Said Novogratz: "Look, we need philanthropic money still."

■ ■ ■

Indeed, American philanthropy now surpasses $300 billion per year, or roughly the size of the entire economy of Norway. Yet, its relationship to the U.S. economy is stable, logging in year after year at just under 2% of the nation's gross domestic product. For all the headlines around massive philanthropic commitments tied to billionaire names like Buffett and Gates, for all of the attention philanthropy and social investments receive in the halls of the World Economic Forum and the Clinton Global Initiative, and for all the marketing and media that have made social causes a central force in our consumer economy, philanthropy has not grown. Every great idea for change needs funding, and every social entrepreneur must compete for capital.

The competition would seem to favor online markets for capital. Just as eBay expanded and democratized the market for used consumer goods from Pez dispensers to vintage Corvettes, so, too, might a wired marketplace connecting millions of people and hundreds of thousands of causes expand and democratize philanthropy. While that marketplace has yet to develop (this book covers several attempts at that market), it is clear that something in what we have thought of as *philanthropy* is changing. The maturation of the social entrepreneurship movement, coupled with the emergence of new online models and a willingness to blur the lines between traditional charity and social causes, has created a fertile field for change. When Google, the leading online company in the world and a powerful force at the center of human communications, announced that its "philanthropic" commitment would not be a traditional foundation but rather a for-profit hybrid known as Google.org, my colleague, Dr. Susan Raymond, one of the world's leading philanthropy analysts, knew it was time to ask some bigger questions. In her onPhilanthropy column, she wrote:

> In centuries past, these were fairly straightforward definitions. Philanthropy was charity, the donation of private dollars to private organizations and individuals caring for social problems for which no private organization had a sufficient commercial interest that motivated action and for which no government agency wished to raise taxes. Orphanages. Soup kitchens. Homeless shelters. In the past several decades, the blurring began and definitions began to erode.

Clearly, continued Dr. Raymond, "The End of Definitions is upon us. This is a good thing. Change reflects the adjustment of institutions and intellects to the realities of life. As Abraham Lincoln observed, 'The dogmas of the quiet past are inadequate to the stormy present.'" That stormy present is made all the more changeable in the world of philanthropy by the unparalleled growth of private wealth in the United States in the past quarter century—wealth that has prompted the kind of personal philanthropic investment and involvement that personified the age of Andrew Carnegie. The United States is an increasingly wealthy country, but even those with massive, fast fortunes won in the IPO wars or the hedge funds respond to leadership when it comes to causes; not only do billionaires put on their pants in the same fashion as you and I, they are also moved to give by the same motivations. An 18-year-old college freshman urging her friends to "Save Darfur" by joining her Facebook group is employing the same tactic as Bill Gates when he urges other captains of industry to fight malaria or improve American high schools. It is good old peer pressure, used for a noble cause. When *Forbes* released its annual list of the 400 richest Americans two years ago, a mere nine-figure net worth no longer cut the mustard: The list was made up entirely of billionaires. It is true, the economists confirm, that the rich really are getting richer—and they are getting richer faster. As the ranks of the wealthy swell (there are more than eight million millionaires now in America), the ways in which they take advantage of their wealth are changing. The surge in luxury goods, the myriad travel opportunities, the lifestyles, and real estate are all part of it. But so is philanthropy.

■ ■ ■

Americans are hearing that message. Even before billionaire investor Warren Buffett announced that he would give the bulk of his fortune to the Gates Foundation, before Bill Gates stepped down as day-to-day

CEO of Microsoft to manage his philanthropy full-time, before former president Bill Clinton launched his billion-dollar Clinton Global Initiative, the trend lines were clear. Not only has total philanthropy increased (to almost $300 billion in 2006, according to Giving USA's annual data, and well over that now), but wealthy Americans are becoming increasingly involved and sophisticated in their giving. Two years ago, *Barron's* reported that over the previous six years, the number of family foundations nation-wide increased by more than 60% and were expected to increase to more than 33,000. Part of it is pure opportunity. In a society where philanthropy is expected—and America is the most philanthropic society on Earth—the market of donor opportunities is ever expanding. Every day in this country brings 115 new nonprofits, not including religious organizations. There are more than a million registered 501(c)3 organizations. They are spring-ing up faster than would-be stars on *American Idol*, and they have every bit as much of a chance at permanence and scale. It takes permanence and scale to change the world.

On the opposite side, there has never been a larger, wider, more diverse donor pool. And that is just the rich; the rest of us are also giving more, just in smaller increments. Consider the wealth available to today's nonprofit causes. The number of households with $5 million or more in investable assets (excluding the family home) rose by 26% to a record 930,000, according to a study by Spectrem Group. An analysis of income-tax data by the Congressional Budget Office released in 2006 found that the top 1% of households own nearly twice as much of the nation's cor-porate wealth as they did just 15 years ago. Another study by the Center on Budget and Policy Priorities and the Economic Policy Institute found that the income gap between the poorest fifth and the richest fifth of Americans has grown rapidly (some would say alarmingly) in the last quarter century. Within the top fifth of families, the study found that the wealthiest families enjoyed the highest income growth over the past two decades. In the 11 states that are large enough to permit this calculation, the incomes of the top 5% of families rose between 66 and 132% during this period. For the bottom fifth of families in those states, income growth ranged from 11 to 24%.

Think of the numbers for a moment: hundreds of billionaires, almost nine million millionaires, tens of thousands of incorporated family foundations, all trying to be like Bill or Warren or Lance. You get the idea; it is a lot of giving power concentrated in one growing, but still narrow, segment of our society of 300 million strong.

There is a danger, however, that what used to be compulsory in supporting the needs of society becomes purely voluntary. The private sector is expected to supplement the public sector in providing crucial services to millions. Yet, this growing reliance on philanthropy is hardly democratic. As any philanthropist will tell you, not only is their giving aspirational—it is darned personal as well. That does not change at the top of the food chain. The big-time philanthropists wear their causes just as publicly in the major international forums of the day (Davos, the Clinton Global Initiative, the Skoll World Forum, the Milken Global Forum) as any kid does on Facebook or MySpace. Yet, if you are not one of the nation's nine million millionaires, how do *you* create any impact? How do you know your money is well-given?

■ ■ ■

In the first months of 2008, no word carried more promise among Americans, and more weight in the media, than *change*. The very center of Barack Obama's cleverly constructed "insurgency" against the old-line Democrats of his own party (but assisted by a brilliant phalanx of image-makers, the Chicago Democratic organization, and a vast partnership of talented marketers), *change* was a vague, center-left, semi-activist movement of symbols and basketball-arena crowds. It was also a real challenge to a small group of social entrepreneurs who aimed to use modern media technology and the desire of a younger generation of Americans to conduct public affairs their own way. The latter group was certainly fascinated by the Obama phenomenon, but its own reach for the elusive DNA of change ran much deeper than the impermanence of a political campaign.

On the Web, the change-oriented centers of social entrepreneurship include Kiva.org, DonorsChoose, ChangingThePresent, Causes, and Razoo—as well as the fortunately named Change.org, whose origins predated the change craze of 2008 by almost three years. In the summer of 2005, Stanford graduate Ben Rattray conceived of an open social network that would allow nonprofits to bring the power of online networks to their causes.

"The genesis of my interest was in this debate group senior year on social issues," says Rattray, a garrulous, engaging entrepreneur clearly driven by his vision for the project. "We were talking about what was going on in the world, both domestically and internationally. At the last session I had this amazing conversation, and the question basically was 'what's next, what have you done?' and we hadn't done, frankly, a damned thing."

Rattray nursed his initial idea for two years, and with a friend from Stanford, Mark Dimas, and the support of a founding team of Darren Haas, Rajiv Gupta, and Adam Cheyer, launched Change.org in February 2007:

Obviously, we all care about the world's problems but there was this chasm between the desire for change and practical access to the means for change. When I was in school, social networks still hadn't been applied to philanthropy. There were real concrete problems for giving, volunteering, taking action. The traditional means are very impersonal, you have no idea where your money's going, no idea what the impact is. Truthfully, your $25 doesn't matter.

Rattray tapped into a growing problem for nonprofit organizations as well. There was a growing sense that old-style direct marketing, including telephone calls and printed material, had reached its fundraising limits, and would decline as the population aged. Younger Americans, and to be honest, anybody who ran his or her life on the Internet, paid no attention to direct mail and screened out telephone fundraisers. Rattray was not being an angry iconoclast at all when he told me, "I had literally never given money to charity; it wasn't that I didn't care, but I was inhibited by personal psychological barriers. I didn't sense my impact."

In some ways, Change.org tapped into the very emotions woven into the basic blues chords and easy lyrics of John Maher's 2006 hit song, "Waiting on the World to Change," a rather soft-spoken generational call for a new direction. The song has a strong sense of coming change, but it is also somewhat passive in tone. There is no angry mob storming the gates, and it is not 1968, either. The hint in the lyrics is that the system needs to be changed, and then an eager generation will follow. Rattray's Change.org was launched in early 2007 with as much hoopla as any of the wired social ventures of the era, including a positive story in TechCrunch, perhaps the most widely read blog in the world of new media, which bestowed what might be the ultimate Silicon Valley compliment when it said, "Change.org doesn't reek of smugness."

Indeed it does not; Change.org is earnest and straightforward in its goals, even as its ultimate success in the marketplace of fundraising and social activism remains (like those of its CauseWired cousins) entirely uncertain. Ease of use is critical to the site's design and method. Thirty seconds after agreeing to the log-in via a Facebook application, I became a member of Change.org, an online community and social venture that "aims to transform social activism by serving as the central platform that connects like-minded people, whatever their interests, and enables them to exchange information, share ideas, and collectively act to address the issues they care about." Membership completed, I was immediately faced with eight choices:

1. Eliminate Child Labor Worldwide
2. Protect Endangered Habitats

3. Promote Fair Trade
4. Save Darfur
5. Stop AIDS in Africa
6. End Homelessness
7. Stop Global Warming
8. Empower Women

Now, anyone might reasonably want to accomplish all eight, and just as reasonably conclude that none of the eight goals was possible to achieve through website participation or online social networking. But the clarity of the choice was appealing; unlike the case with many online charity portals, I was not faced with yet another search through the Internal Revenue Service database of registered 501(c)3 organizations, or with an endless group of choices in a world of infinite causes. Earlier online giving portals such as Network for Good, and dot-com names like Google and PayPal, that offer charitable contributions have admirable platforms for nonprofit transactions across the entire spectrum.

Blogger Sonny Cloward of NPowerNY, a nonprofit that provides technology consulting and services to other nonprofits, challenged Change.org in an initial review in 2007 on the blog of NTEN, the Nonprofit Technology Network:

The premise is pretty straightforward—connect people with one another and organizations to push forward common causes (i.e., changes). I perused the site, thought it was a great idea, didn't dig very deeply, felt a moment of kumbaya with my fellow do-gooders, and then quickly forgot about it. And based on Change.org's Alexa traffic rankings, I wasn't alone. So, is Change.org just another fly-by-night project of some well-meaning people with a good concept—just badly planned and executed—awaiting a slow descent into the dead pool?

Rattray argues that good online fundraising requires four assets: awareness, engagement, activism, and recurrence. "And there are very little of the last two," he says. According to Rattray,

[Success is] all about deep engagement—a lot of these viral campaigns, it's not just getting them to join, it's about deeply engaging them in the issues. One of the limitations thus far in spreading the word about things is that you're not spreading authentic stories. The causes are massive and important, but there's a huge spread between what you're seeing on television and reality. There is no internalization of the issues. You know, we all care, but there was this chasm between the desire for change and practical access.

To Rattray, it is about bringing existing nonprofits up to speed and introducing them to a new donor audience:

A lot of the excitement [in Web 2.0] is all about disintermediation, you know, all we need to do is give people the tools and there will be action. I think that dismissing organizations is a fault—when you consider the impact of individuals, it pales in comparison to what nonprofits actually accomplish.

The goal, he says, is to "transform how nonprofit organizations engage with individuals, to improve the giving experience for thousands and thousands of people."

■ ■ ■

Since Netscape popularized the Web browser in 1994, nonprofits have looked to an online donor pool as a source of increased revenue. Yet, the growth of Internet philanthropy has been nothing like the explosive power of the commercial Web itself. In short, it has been rather slow and steady; and it has certainly been no panacea, nothing like the obvious revolution in national political campaigns. The greatest growth has accompanied disastrous news stories: the attacks of September 11 and natural disasters such as Hurricane Katrina and the South Asian tsunami. Those surges have often been about convenience and immediacy. Donors' instincts tell them a fast online contribution may be the only way to "help now."

Organic growth in online giving is obvious to those working in the field. Colleges and universities increasingly ask young alums to make their pledges online. Health-care institutions and single-disease foundations are finding large Internet audiences for their donor appeals. Environmental groups understand completely that their future in direct marketing is among the young, wired activist base that has made going green part of our popular culture. And religious organizations are increasingly using online outreach to raise money from the faithful and spread their message. Estimates of online giving in the United States range from $6 to $8 billion. This is small in the overall scale of American philanthropy, but growing every year. Furthermore, savvy development professionals understand that good online outreach through websites, blogs, newsletters, social networks, widgets, text messages, and other digital tools helps organizations to build their brands as worthy causes—and usually at a price that is significantly lower than direct mail or traditional media.

Nonprofits are changing slowly, and adding more resources to direct communication with smaller donors. Vinay Bhagat, founder of the online fundraising and donor management platform Convio, sees a trend toward more individualized donor stewardship at the bottom of the pyramid:

> There is very little meaningful focus on treating a donor or prospect like a valued customer. That would entail communicating more than soliciting; learning what is important to constituents; and treating each constituent as an individual. Nonprofits typically reserve such levels of

treatment for high-value donors and prospects because it is expensive and resource-intensive.

While Kiva and DonorsChoose are the most-cited new models for philanthropy online, many forward-looking nonprofits (including some with long histories) are taking advantage of the idea of direct donor involvement below the millionaire line. Oxfam, more than 60 years old with a long history of fighting poverty, quietly created Projects Direct in 2007 to experiment with direct funding of fieldwork by mid-level philanthropists. Oxfam, which was founded in 1942 as the Oxford Committee for Famine Relief to support England's National Famine Relief Committee during World War II, is now a confederation of 13 organizations working together with more than 3,000 partners in more than 100 countries to find lasting solutions to poverty and injustice with a budget of around $700 million a year. Oxfam is a global charity brand, one of the world's best-known nonprofit causes, and raises much of its funding from public contributions. However, the desire to allow donors to "invest directly" led to an online catalogue for choosing projects to fund, with funding goals in the low six figures.

The proposition is straightforward:

> Each year we will present a number of projects in communities we are working in, that vary by geography and by theme. You will be able to browse the information online and get a good feel for the context to the issue, how we plan to tackle it, and what sorts of changes we might expect to see in the life of individuals in the community.

Some of the projects during a recent visit include increasing sustainable agriculture to enable poor rural farmers in Honduras, improving working conditions for cotton farmers in India, and improving the climate for small business in Sudan. Participants receive as many as a dozen updates on the project per year from a personal case officer. They are also guaranteed that 100% of their funds will go the project. Sarah Thomas of Projects Direct's Programme Partnerships team told the UK/Philanthropy website: "We wanted to do better at developing long-term relationships with new and existing supporters that meet their giving goals, as well as make a difference to poverty and suffering in the world. The idea is that together, we can deliver change."

Another mature nonprofit organization founded during World War II, Heifer International, is already an online pioneer, using its innovative virtual catalogue of livestock and plants to encourage gifts relieving global hunger and poverty. In 2007, its grantmaking Heifer Foundation affiliate combined social networking with the idea of virtual charitable portfolios in the Kiva mold to create Hope Equity, an online community that allows donors to invest in a variety of funds by region or by cause. With the look and feel of a traditional stock portfolio, Hope Equity creates an online "portfolio of giving," investing in endowments that support ending hunger and poverty while caring for the Earth. This online model offers a type of investment that Heifer calls *micro-endowments*. In the program, Hope Equity invests the donations and makes a percentage available to the donor's selected causes each year. This allows for the original contribution to remain untouched, continuing to grow in perpetuity. Donors who commit to a certain level of giving can create their own funds for causes such as HIV/AIDS, environmental issues, and hunger in Africa, and funds for countries including Kenya, Mozambique, and Afghanistan.

Greg Spradlin, vice president for Hope Equity, says that the investment approach favors an open approach to information. Just as everyday investors revolutionized financial reporting, modern charitable donors and investors may well change philanthropy. The online portfolio, so common in the consumer brokerage world, is beginning to gain favor among donors who crave information. "One of the things people respond to is the non-competitive approach, the fact that it's not tied to any religion or any political party, the open source nature of it," says Spradlin. "We have investors with a broad spectrum of beliefs, but it doesn't matter because we're not tied to one way of thinking—and they love the idea that it is open source."

Those investors range from young software entrepreneurs in Seattle to an 85-year-old woman who "just wants to know the money's being used the way she wants it being used." Spradlin believes that the formal nature of philanthropy is rapidly changing, and that personal involvement and a desire for information, metrics, and results is at the core of that change—as well as a societal movement toward causes as a defining factor in how people view themselves:

> I really believe we are on the tipping point of change in philanthropy, based on what we are seeing and hearing from donors—and we deal very personally with people—giving and causes are part of their family, part of them. We created this to meet a need because we believe people are going to change the way they give, and they favor the integrative approach, not just "it's that time of year again, I'll write a check." Giving is a daily choice and causes are part of people's lives, whether it's the Red campaign or what coffee we drink. I don't think it's going to be a fad thing; I don't think it's going to fade. People are making it part of their lifestyle choices on a daily basis. You have to be socially conscious. In today's work, we don't have the choice to be isolated any more.

In some ways, HopeEquity.com is a capital market for philanthropy, in much the same way Kiva.org and DonorsChoose are. It is part of what Carla Dearing, president of GivingNet (formerly the Community Foundations of America), calls "the Schwabification of philanthropy," with greater direct access to the mission of nonprofits, and the greater expectation of transparent reporting as well. As Daniel Rabuzzi, CEO of

Peter Drucker's Leader to Leader Institute, wrote in onPhilanthropy.com in 2004: "Capital markets for the social sector is an idea whose time has come." Yet, as pioneering venture philanthropist Mario Morino has said repeatedly, historically there have been no markets for philanthropic capital. That is just beginning to change, and the open nature of online communications and data-sharing is fueling what may be a fast evolution. "If new wealth creates new philanthropy, then what does new philanthropy create?" asked Morino and Bill Shore of Community Wealth Ventures in a paper entitled "High-Engagement Philanthropy: A Bridge to a More Effective Social Sector":

> It creates dialogue, in public and private, reflecting vigorous, animated soul-searching on how such precious new resources can be best put to use to improve schools, health care, and the other delivery systems for basic human needs. And, hopefully, it leads to transformational change.

■ ■ ■

There are two trend lines heading for a collision. On one hand, people are ever more conscious of philanthropy and its role in commerce and society; on the other, these people are talking to each other more than ever before. Allan Benamer, IT director at Coalition for the Homeless in New York and the blogger behind the aptly named "Confessions of a Nonprofit IT Director," argues that the notion of consumer philanthropy has a small, point-of-sale consumer quotient as well:

> Let's take that whole notion of "consumer philanthropy" and put that back in the Economy 2.0 space. Wouldn't it be possible to move the hardest social services cases in the nonprofit sector over to the Web? And wouldn't it take just a little more thinking to get people to donate to those cases, in effect, becoming a consumer philanthropist?

We're basically applying the network effect to donations and ending up with another shading on the notion of consumer philanthropy. It's not so much big-money philanthropy but online retail philanthropy.

Benamer has a point, of course. As the Web experience grows ever more personal and less about big portals and media brands, so, too, does the giving experience, especially for the net-native demographic. Even as consumers are inspired by the big names and big cause-marketing campaigns, their day-to-day online world may well expand to include philanthropy. Is this a tipping point, or an inflection point? You pick the economic cliché.

My partner in onPhilanthropy.com, editor-in-chief Susan Carey Dempsey, has reported from the frontlines of philanthropic change these past eight years:

Everyone is intrigued by the phenomenon of online social networking, which is making an impact on the micro-level in nonprofit fundraising as well as grass-roots political activism. Yet, the implications of these millions of tiny interactions have the nonprofit community intrigued, encouraged, and, with good reason, shaking in their boots. Clearly, the rules that have governed the donor–grantee relationship over the last few centuries of American philanthropy increasingly will not apply; those rules of engagement are still being rewritten.

As that relationship changes, fewer decisions will be made entirely by the nonprofit professionals, and some degree of influence will devolve on the vast pool of donors, much as investors ultimately control the destiny of a public company. "The basic premises of seeking diverse input, trying some design methodologies such as rapid prototyping, and drawing from multiple disciplines are strategic approaches to solving social problems that are starting to gain some traction," wrote philanthropy analyst Lucy Bernholz in her 2008 essay, "Is Philanthropy Going Open Source?"

The concepts, she said, are exciting, but "they also raise some questions for philanthropy. Where are the lines between public and private when it comes to ideas for the public good? Can or should someone be able to own a policy innovation? Protect a service delivery process? Are all socially positive ideas public?"

■ ■ ■

When a massive earthquake ripped through the Sichuan province of China in May 2008, one of the centers of that new social capital market swung into action. GlobalGiving, an organization founded in 2002 to "unleash the potential of people around the world to make positive change happen," instantly created two special projects to assist victims of the powerful earthquake, which killed more than 29,000 people and destroyed three million homes. GlobalGiving's model is to partner with existing organizations and to make reporting on the efficacy of its supporters' philanthropy central to its mission. The Washington, D.C.–based nonprofit has funneled more than $6 million to 900 projects around the world, providing what the *Washington Post* called "foreign aid at the speed of light."

At the center of the GlobalGiving value proposition for donors is the chance to make small contributions in the same highly vetted and researched manner that large philanthropies make their commitments. For $25, a small-time donor can count on GlobalGiving's rigorous due diligence process, which measures the effectiveness of each nonprofit partner in its program on several variables, including expense ratios and social impact. So, when the earthquake hit China, GlobalGiving donors could turn to one of the organization's partner projects, knowing that the philanthropic homework already had been filed away. GlobalGiving launched the Half the Sky Children's Earthquake Relief Fund to provide "emergency shelter, food, and medical care for children orphaned or separated from their families, also temporary or long-term foster care or, if needed, temporary institutional care" through its trusted partner, the Half the Sky Foundation.

The project was posted on May 13, 2008, and within three days, GlobalGiving had received $173,582 from 1,483 donations toward an overall goal of half a million dollars. The project's page on GlobalGiving.com featured profiles of donors, a Google map showing the area affected by the earthquake, updates from the field, and a widget (a bit of code that creates a small ad-like promotional box) that bloggers and members of social networks could add to their pages elsewhere to spur donations. For a small amount of money, a donor at GlobalGiving was given access to tools and information that were once the province of big foundations and well-heeled philanthropists.

"The most significant trend we've seen is the increasing desire of donors to know where their money is going and how it's used," Donna Callejon, GlobalGiving's chief operating officer, told *Forbes*. "It used to be that you needed to give a lot of money to get that kind of reporting back." Indeed, major donors increasingly demand proof of impact: More than 58% of high-net-worth individuals say they would give more to charity if they could determine their gift's impact, according to a 2006 survey of Americans earning more than $200,000 a year by the Center on Philanthropy at Indiana University. But new markets are offering that opportunity to smaller donors as well. GlobalGiving guarantees that 90% of funds raised will go to the field, and even offers a money-back guarantee—donors unsatisfied with the result of their gift may request a voucher that can be used on other projects.

■ ■ ■

Susan Davis, founding chairperson of the Grameen Foundation and CEO of BRAC-USA, the American fundraising arm of the Bangladeshi microfinance agency, spoke about the shift in the winds of philanthropy at the Hilton Humanitarian Symposium in New York in 2007. "I believe a change is coming between palliative philanthropy and what I call *jujitsu philanthropy*," she said. *Palliative philanthropy* is "about saving lives and it's based on compassion and a sense of social justice." But "jujitsu philanthropy is all about finding the point of highest leverage to effect systems change."

The CauseWired phenomenon may well have its greatest impact in the sector that is traditionally the slowest to change. In the past 50 years, only two new nonprofits have entered the ranks of the nation's largest organizations. Otherwise, the top charities remain the same, year after year. Even in the most charitable country on Earth, giving remains stagnant as a factor of our national wealth. But "Facebook philanthropy"—along with Carla Dearing's *Schwabification* and the growth of philanthropic markets for change—is redefining what it means to give, how people view charity and social involvement, and what causes will ultimately succeed in the new philanthropic landscape. Why are nonprofits literally racing to adopt social networks and to integrate them into their overall communications efforts? In an interview at NetSquared, Eric Mattson, co-author of the recent study, "Blogging for the Hearts of Donors," about social media usage by the 200 largest charities in the United States, talked about cost and implementation:

I think it fits their pocketbook piece of the equation. When you can go and get a free blog, and you don't need to spend $100,000 on it, well gosh, that really fits with the attention to the bottom-line and limited funding that a lot of these start-ups have. I also think that these are wonderful tools for engaging a passionate core.

Mattson and Nora Barnes, Ph.D., of the University of Massachusetts Dartmouth Center for Marketing Research, conducted a nationwide telephone survey of nonprofits named by *Forbes* to its list of the 200 largest U.S. charities for 2006, and found very fast adoption of so-called Web 2.0 technology by larger American organizations. They wrote:

This research proves conclusively that charitable organizations are outpacing the business world in their use of social media. Seventy-five percent of the charitable organizations studied are using some form of social media including blogs, podcasts, message boards, social networking, video blogging, and wikis. More than a third of the organizations are blogging. Forty-six percent of those studied report social media is very important to their fundraising strategy.

■ ■ ■

Making data available to everyday philanthropists, so that I can see that my $25 is invested with nearly the same care and efficiency as Warren Buffett's billions, is what this movement is all about. As Dennis Whittle, chief executive and co-founder of GlobalGiving, puts it: "eBay revolutionized shopping, and the iPod revolutionized music. Now the Internet is revolutionizing part of philanthropy."

9 | Aspiration and Activism: Armies of Online Leaders

There is an inherent irony in the CauseWired movement: It is incredibly individualistic, and yet *leadership* is still an operative quality, and a real change-maker. People follow other people, whether they are national candidates for president or just talented bloggers with a knack for stirring the pot. Not every online participant is an equal, not every activist succeeds, not every fundraiser raises money, and not every networker gets her friends deeply involved in a cause. For the bottom of the pyramid, "involvement" is a few clicks and a few bucks, perhaps some intense guilt-satisfaction, maybe a few emails or comments, and that is all. While causes spread like wildfire across the Internet, leadership grows more slowly. It takes time. It requires investment. But that is where the payoff is.

In an article in *Wired* magazine that turned into a best-selling business book, journalist Chris Anderson identified a phenomenon among online retailers such as Amazon.com and iTunes that he christened the *long tail*. The term reflects the shape a sales chart takes when considering the range of revenue from big hits to older inventory; online, retailers can keep an almost-endless inventory supply on hand, especially if their products are digital or if they rely on a network of suppliers rather than their own warehouses. While the blockbusters rack up massive sales over a short period of time, the myriad smaller-selling products create a long tail of revenue that is very much worth encouraging, especially as costs of production are already sunk.

The long-tail theory has since been applied to an endless array of online media, from blog networks to digital music and video sites. The entire business model of search giant Google, for instance, is built on the long tail; the company makes money on paid placement amid search results based on algorithms. On one end of the graph are the big websites that get a huge share of Internet traffic. On the right side of the almost-horizontal axis are millions and millions of obscure Web pages that nonetheless add up to a vast income for Google. Indeed, the reason for its existence is to find these results on the long tail. Anderson signals a new open era of digital distribution in his definition of the long tail: "The Long Tail is about the economics of abundance—what happens when the bottlenecks that stand between supply and demand in our culture start to disappear and everything becomes available to everyone." Or as one Amazon employee put it: "We sold more books today that didn't sell at all yesterday than we sold today of all the books that did sell yesterday."

In online social activism, the vast inventory is not made up of digital music tracks or out-of-print books. It consists of people: those who take action, those who lead, those who follow, those who lend their voices, those who link, those who blog, and those who "friend" other people (to use the strange verbiage of Facebook and MySpace). And the long-tail equation is not quite as simple when the inventory lives and breathes. Indeed, I am tempted to turn Anderson's description of abundance on its end, and to portray the long tail of social activism as one of scarcity, and the inherent need to make the most of leaders. One might think of the CauseWired power law graph as laid out with intense leadership on one end and passive participation on the other—both yielding results over time. But in the online retail shop of social activism, the doors simply would not open without the leaders. As prominent digital social critic Clay Shirky notes, the long-tail pattern "doesn't apply just to goods, though, but to social interactions as well. Real-world distributions are only an approximation of this formula, but the imbalance it creates appears in an astonishing number of places in large social systems." Traditional fundraisers in the nonprofit world refer to this imbalance as the *80/20 rule*, plotting their campaigns on the assumption (born of hard experience) that 20% of their prospects will provide 80% of the campaign's funds. In online causes, the rule generally holds, and leadership clearly matters.

CauseWired hierarchy relies on a few leaders—usually someone to get things started, and a leadership cadre that is small enough to maintain continued communication and unity of purpose. In his book, *We-think: The Power of Mass Creativity*, management consultant Charles Leadbeater describes the phenomenon:

> Creative communities have a social structure. As we have seen, a relatively small, committed core group tends to do most of the heavy lifting: the discussion moderators in Slashdot; the original inhabitants of Second Life. These are the Web 2.0 aristocracy: people who, because they have been around longer and done more work, tend to get listened to more. There is nothing unusual in this. Most innovative projects, whether inside a company, a theatre group, or a

laboratory, start with intense collaboration among a small group who share a particular passion or want to address a common problem, as did the worm researchers who gathered around Sydney Brenner at Cambridge. Often, however, such communities can become closed and inward looking. To be dynamic, they have to open out to a wider world of more diverse contributors who add their knowledge or challenge conventional wisdom.

■ ■ ■

When Barack Obama's strategists first sketched out their plan for online support for the Illinois Senator's presidential run, they placed much of their emphasis on building a regiment of leaders—an empowered group of activists that then went on to create the larger army of donors and volunteers that changed how American politics is organized in 2007 and 2008. "We decided that we didn't want to train volunteers, we want to train organizers—folks who can fend for themselves," Temo Figueroa, the campaign's field director, told *Rolling Stone*. The Obama organization built on what Howard Dean's campaign accomplished in 2004, but took it in a whole new direction with a much wider scale and deeper use of new online social networking tools and sites. Where Dean's online campaign was intense and somewhat insular, Obama's Internet operations were broad and well-scripted. It was clear watching the rollout of MyBarackObama.com (MyBo) that there was someone in charge of the message, and that the corps of leadership was well trained in how to use it. So successful was the campaign's use of online activism, that it widely became viewed as something of a revolution in national politics. *Rolling Stone's* Tim Dickinson proclaimed: "Obama campaign has shattered the top-down, command-and-control, broadcast-TV model that has dominated American politics since the early 1960s."

Yet, there was one top-down quality that remained, in my view: leadership. The Obama online juggernaut was well organized and ran beautifully, but it was hardly an organic phenomenon, a gorgeous field of waving grassroots fronds sown only by the nutrients of hope and change. Indeed, Obama 2008 was a top-down organization, built on message discipline and strong branding. It was built on leadership as well—from the candidate and his staff, and from his highest levels of volunteer coordinators and field captains. From the start, it had one goal: to get people to take action, not just by giving money but by doing something offline. "We wanted to make sure we learned from Howard Dean's campaign," deputy campaign manager Steve Hildebrand told *Rolling Stone*. "We didn't make the assumption that people signing up on our website meant that they were going to help the candidate or even vote for him. From the beginning, we had an initiative to take our online force offline."

MyBarackObama.com did not just organize clicks. It got people to organizing events, to rallies, to caucuses, and to primaries. And, as every fundraiser (volunteer or professional) reading this knows, that strategy was simply using leadership to create action and employing new social networking tools to do so. It is the same principle behind a local capital campaign committee trying to put a new wing on the hospital. It is why people like Warren Buffett and Bill Gates inspire philanthropy as well as practice it.

■ ■ ■

In December 2007, the foundation created by America Online founder Steve Case and his wife Jean launched an online program aimed at inspiring everyday people to adopt wired causes, and motivating nonprofit organizations to begin to take advantage of the burgeoning social Internet. Through the first-ever America's Giving Challenge and Causes Giving Challenge, the Case Foundation staked $750,000 in a series of fundraising contests that ran from mid-December through the following January. The foundation's leading partners were Facebook and its Cause application created by Project Agape, and *Parade*, the glossy Sunday newspaper supplement with its massive weekly circulation of 32 million people.

The rules were pretty simple. More than 2,500 organizations were represented by causes created during the Challenge. The Causes Giving Challenge awarded $50,000 to the cause with the most unique donors, $25,000 to the second- and third-place causes, and $10,000 to the next ten causes. Throughout the Challenge, Causes on Facebook awarded daily winners $1,000 for having the most unique donations in a single day. Any Facebook user could participate by using the Causes application to promote his cause through direct user-to-user messages, and feature it on his profile. In the end, a total of 32,886 donations accounted for $571,686 in donations supporting 747 different organizations—an average gift of $17.38. The *Parade* portion, which brought in contributions via the magazine's website, accounted for another $1.2 million from 48,711 donors, for an average donation of about $24, slightly higher. These online fund-raisers used widgets (bits of code users could pass around and put on their blogs to urge donations and involvement) and relied on charity donation sites such as Network for Good and GlobalGiving to process gifts.*

Jean Case, the foundation's chief executive, observed: "Thousands of people embraced new technologies, built new online communities, and proved that simple daily actions and small donations can inspire others and tap into their energy and passion to make a difference." I would argue that the manner in which the causes were supported on Facebook and through blog-based widgets and other tools on the *Parade* side of the ledger may count for more in the end than the money that was raised, because getting those contributions involved creating and activating a social network, a group of people who in the process probably learned a bit more

---

*An important disclosure is necessary: The Case Foundation is a client of Changing Our World, Inc., the consulting firm where I work, and the company has been involved in some of the online causes work of the foundation, although none of the information in this book comes from that relationship.

about the causes they were supporting—a group that may well be more open to real activism in the future than names on an email list. Further, I would suggest that the online social activism portion of the program best served one of the key goals of the Case commitment—priming the pump of activism with leadership.

Raising that money online took real leadership. Take one of the top eight finishers in the Parade.com challenge as an example. Route Out of Poverty for Cambodian Children, a grassroots project of the Sharing Foundation, garnered 1,650 donations totaling $41,673, and won a $50,000 grant from the Case Foundation for finishing in the top four among international causes. I know a little more about the foundation's work in Cambodia, and the Route Out of Poverty program, which teaches Khmer to 100 children of illiterate farmers, and English to over 500 students seeking to move beyond subsistence farming. I know that thousands of Cambodian children grow up illiterate, with very few educational options. I also know that the Sharing Foundation's Khmer literacy school helps farm children learn their native alphabet and numbers well enough to attend elementary school. I know that this English Language Program offers village students from 8 to 18 the opportunity to learn Cambodia's language of commerce, allowing them to obtain jobs in tourism and word processing. But I know this not because of a website, or a Facebook profile, or a cool blog widget, or a well-publicized giving challenge. I know all of this because of Beth Kanter.

GlobalGiving tracked 1,650 donations to Route Out of Poverty for Cambodian Children—and one of them was mine. I made the list because of Beth, a Boston-based consultant who is one of the Web's most ardent champions of online social activism. In addition to her blogging, coaching work, and consulting, Beth is passionate about the Southeast Asian nation of Cambodia. A few years ago, she adopted two Khmer children, and is quite passionate about helping them to know about their homeland and celebrate their culture. Beth writes about Khmer culture and technology at the Cambodia4kids blog and maintains a website with the same name that provides information for U.S. teachers and parents. Her Typing to Learn Khmer blog is where she practices her very basic Khmer language skills using Khmer Unicode. She has covered the Cambodian blogosphere as an author for Global Voices Online, a project of the Berkman Center for Internet and Law at Harvard University.

In addition to her many accomplishments, Beth is something of a *nudge*, which in the kinder version of the Yiddish translation means "someone who pushes you, sometimes to the point of annoyance." When I asked Beth for some information related to this book, she very kindly held her hand out, digital palm up. A member of the board of the Sharing Foundation, she was passionately committed to ensuring that its Cambodian cause made the top four finishers in the Case Foundation contest. An inquiring journalist who was merely an online acquaintance simply did not qualify for a free pass. Every time I asked a question, Beth would shoot back some version of: "The deadline's coming; did you make your gift yet?"

Beth bugged a lot of people, posted to her blog, and urged others to post the widget—a small graphic showing Cambodian children with the current giving levels of the campaign. I finally made a small gift, and posted the widget to my own blog. Other people asked me about it and I told them what I knew. Some of them went on to make donations. Now we are all savvy about the small foundation changing the lives of poor Cambodian children. Beth's leadership brought in needed funds, but it also created real awareness and a network of potential supporters for the future.

And there was a small reward, in addition to Beth's hearty thanks. In March, two months after the Case challenges ended, Dr. Nancy Hendrie, president of the Sharing Foundation, sent Beth a video that she posted to her blog and sent around to the donors. Only ten seconds long, it nonetheless connects a frenzied online giving contest with real-world recipients. It shows dozens of small children sitting on the porch of the

Roteang Orphanage. Prompted by an adult voice off camera, the smiling children shout a few words as loudly as their voices allow: "Thank you! American! Challenge! *Yaaaay!*"

But as Beth said in a comment on the CauseWired.com blog not long ago, "You know, I'm not sure I agree about the term *leadership*—there's something else." She may well be right. This is not a one-to-many phenomenon. It is more of a *some-to-s'more* development.

■ ■ ■

During the New Year's break between 2006 and 2007, I started noodling on a small group blogging project. I have always found New Year's dull and depressing, and usually try to use the time off to dig into something new while avoiding Times Square and the international celebration of the turning of a calendar page; in 2004, I kicked off my personal blog and, as 2007 bled into 2008, I worked on this book. But that year, I was thinking about culture. In the world of online causes, hunger and disease and issues of war and peace tend to get the headlines. They deserve it, because they motivate people to ask their friends for money. The site I cobbled together on the open blogging platform Wordpress that frozen New Year's week was not a traditional cause. It would save no lives, raise no money, change no one's world. But newcritics.com (a group blogging community that now has about 50 contributing writers) held some lessons in online group dynamics.

Newcritics really began after a dinner at the Algonquin Hotel roundtable in New York in the fall of 2006. The dinner brought together some political bloggers and activists to celebrate the Congressional victories by Democrats that year, taking back the House and Senate. But as we sat around that table, a funny thing happened: We did not talk about politics very much. We talked about TV shows, and novels, and actors. I wanted to continue that conversation, but the odds of recreating that roundtable these days were pretty slim. From the start, the "cause" in building newcritics was the creation of a nonpolitical, moderately congenial circle of bloggers to share reviews and analysis of what I called *upper-middlebrow* culture, a term that prompted a friend to quip: "That's the area I wax every month." The blog used Wordpress, a popular open-source publishing platform that allowed intense customization. Once I had a simple layout, I began inviting bloggers to come on board, and that is when the fun started.

At the start, a core group of about dozen bloggers whom I either knew in the real world or had online relationships with created the basis for newcritics—with interesting and iconoclastic posts about music, television, movies, books, and theater. The discussions were a lot of fun—endlessly poring over the Rolling Stones catalogue, creating lists of the all-time best television sitcoms, recalling great actors of the 1930s and 1940s, live-blogging the Oscars. That core group in turn brought in more users by cross-posting to their own personal blogs. And as users came on as regular commentators, I invited them to become contributing writers. Newcritics never grew too large; as editor, I kept at least a modest relationship with all the bloggers. We posted hundreds of articles and thousands of comments. The discourse was polite and light, if a bit ephemeral. Newcritics was a nice little blog with no particular ambition.

Then we met in person, and the nice little blog (a fun project for all) became something a little more important to those involved. The catalyst, in our case, was Ellen O'Neill, a talented writer who also worked at the Paley Center for Media (formerly the Museum of Television & Radio) in midtown Manhattan. First on her apartment rooftop and then at the Paley Center, M.A. Peel (her blogger name) organized gatherings that brought our diverse group together over some cultural chitchat and appropriate libations. On some level, the gatherings felt like meetings of superheroes in the League of Justice Hall. Sure, some of us use our real names, but the pen names are better. Lance Mannion and Tony Alva could be 1970s crime shows starring James Garner and Mike Connors. Blue Girl and the

Self-Styled Siren are like characters out of a Dashiell Hammett novel. We also had The Shamus, The Viscount LaCarte, Neddie Jingo, Trickster, and Gotham Gal—all miniature personal brands in the social network.

Something changed when we took a loose collection of bloggers and met in person. Newcritics was noninfluential. It was nonprofitable. Indeed, by any standards of the day it was nonsuccessful. Yet, we reveled in the minor glory but sweet karmic profit of the small group blog. Why? Because we liked each other. That was obvious in the courteous style of our site, and in the ongoing conversation each week. We were also genuinely interested in what we each had to say about media—about film, television, music, theater, and books. And in our busy, disparate lives, a place to turn for some polite and middlebrow conversation over a glass of wine or a cup of coffee was a very nice thing indeed. Newcritics was an experiment, not a business. It was an experiment in satisfying part of our inner lives. The external parts are packed enough, but I argued that many of us did not devote enough time to our own enjoyment of art, of beauty, of sight and sound and words. The newcritics bloggers had vastly different experiences in life, but we all loved those things—that is the common thread—an old movie, a new drama, a single song. And the blogging experiment gave us just enough breathing room to explore our inner selves through discussion, and through connecting with others.

Most of the newcritics bloggers were old enough to remember the days when everyone was most certainly not a critic—at least not a critic with any audience outside their own kitchen or the office watercooler. Some of us had been professional critics of a sort; my longtime collabo-rator, Jason Chervokas, and I were digital media critics for the *New York Times*, for example. Many of the bloggers had written elsewhere. Yet, we write for each other, without being paid. Newcritics was indicative of the semiprofessional passion that really drives online social discourse, from political sites to group financial blogs. The gathering itself was the real cause. In this cause, we all loved art and media—movies, television, music, and books—and despite our busy lives we congregated to review and discuss them, fairly seriously and with good humor at a little website that worked most of the time.

I cannot get too serious about newcritics, which remains a small-scale experiment among friends, but there are three key lessons in the experience that remain important to the CauseWired movement:

1. *Online organizing requires a hierarchy*. I was the creator and force behind newcritics, small as it was. Although dozens of bloggers and thousands of commentators joined the discussion, whenever I dropped out for any substantial period of time, the discourse waned. Other writers took limited leadership roles (especially around the events), but it was clear that sustaining newcritics over time was primarily my job.

2. *Moving from online to in-person cemented the cause*. Before we began planning our real-world gatherings, newcritics was a nice little blog. After we met in person, it became a community. From there, it gained a quality of permanence in people's lives.

3. *Small but well-connected can be more effective than huge and widely disbursed*. We kept newcritics small, not necessarily in a conscious way, but because it simply worked better. Within the larger group blog, there were smaller circles of bloggers who worked together and organized themselves: the big-time movie fans, the literature majors, the classic rock obsessives. These smaller groups kept the place vibrant; newcritics with a thousand bloggers and a million readers might well have become a business, but it would not be the same cause.

The point is that some structure is necessary in successfully organizing an online cause; pure groupthink rarely leads to accomplishment. Wikipedia, after all, has its founders and its high-performing core of volunteer editors; the rest of us dabble. Explains Charles Leadbeater in *We-think*:

Social creativity is not a free-for-all; it is highly structured. Although the lines between expert and amateur, audience and performer, user and producer may be blurred, those with more standing in the community, based on the history and quality of their contribution, form something like a tightly networked craft aristocracy.

■■■

The nonprofit sector, I think, will always struggle with this issue of creative control even as peer-to-peer fundraising networks grow. Marnie Webb is vice president of knowledge services at CompuMentor, a nonprofit that has brought technology to other nonprofits for more than two decades, and runs both TechSoup and the NetSquared Community of online practitioners for causes and organizations. Marnie blogs on social change at her popular ext337 blog and is a leading voice in the ongoing discussion of the use of social media for nonprofit causes. Her concern is providing guidance to nonprofit organizations, and she set out a simple series of four rules to help them take advantage of social networks and online activism in a way that emphasizes that *some-to-s'more* ethic for organizing:

1. *Find your people.* Do not just dive into a social network because it is taking up space in your inbox or traditional media. Dive in because that is where your people are—the people who care about your issues (whether they agree with you or not). Use a variety of search tools (Technorati, Google Blog Search, Icerocket, as well as more traditional search services like Google, Yahoo!, Microsoft Live, and Wikipedia) to find out where people are having real honest discussions and then make your social media investment there.
2. *Think about how to make social media accounts.* Let the people in your organization make social media accounts on your behalf. Give them guidelines. Make sure they know what is for sharing

and what needs to stay internal. Make sure that you are following what is going on and leave comments. Engage. But let people make accounts naturally. You might want to have organizational accounts for a variety of reasons, but people do not necessarily feel the same level of ownership over those accounts as they do over their own. Let them create their own and pull the best of what they create and share into the organization's story.

3. *Give people a way to share your story.* This does not necessarily mean widgets or Facebook applications or anything involving cut-and-paste or APIs. It means telling your story. Honestly, get the voices of the people you care about, the people working on the change and those impacted by it, on your site. Get photos, get voice recordings, and get small film clips. Use services like Flickr and YouTube to host the media and use the tools they make available to pull that content back onto your site. Tag richly; write descriptions.

4. *Invest in conversations.* Do not just ask for money. Do not just ask people to spread the word. Invest in conversations. Leave thoughtful comments on photos, profile pages, and blog posts—genuinely engage. This investment will bring new people to you and, I firmly believe, will bring people to you who do not already agree with you. That, after all, is a big part of the reason for organizing.

That last point may be the most important, and in some ways it provides the explicit answer to Beth Kanter's idea of "something else." You can encourage a conversation, but you cannot force it to occur. Some degree of online social activism—or peer-to-peer fundraising for nonprofits—has to be organic. In other words, an organization or a candidate or the founder of a cause has to cede some control to the community of users. It is not a top-down formula. As Geoff Livingston writes in his book, *Now Is Gone*, "Since social media is inherently two-way, a controlling entity that enters the community will be met with anger, distrust, and either rebellion or deaf ears by key stakeholders." Yet, the phenomenon is aspirational: Giving encourages giving, involvement encourages involvement, and leadership encourages more leadership. In our media-soaked consumer economy, prominent examples of involvement and leadership provide the kindling for many causes.

■ ■ ■

Michael J. Fox looked out across the ballroom at the Beverly Hilton and began to talk about what motivates the creation of a cause. In the audience were hundreds of chief executives from dozens of business sectors, scores of economists, many philanthropic leaders, and a large media presence—all gathered at the annual confab of philanthropist and social investor Michael Milken. "Think the World Economic Forum in Davos, Switzerland, without the skiing and antiglobalization protesters and with better shopping" is the way the *Los Angeles Times* describes the Milken Institute Global Conference, held each year in Beverly Hills. In the same ballroom where Frank Sinatra and his cronies Janet Leigh, Tony Curtis, Judy Garland, and Mort Sahl once celebrated the nomination of John F. Kennedy with a small crowd of 2,800 paying guests, Milken and his friends from the worlds of finance, government, media, and philanthropy kick around the world's biggest issues for three days each spring. In the past few years, the top philanthropists have shared the stage with celebrities, and philanthropy has filled an increasing portion of the agenda. At the 2007 conference, the actor discussed his Michael J. Fox Foundation, created to help advance Parkinsons disease research through embryonic stem-cell studies.

"I always tell people that I didn't volunteer for this job, I was recruited," he said in that famous voice, now relegated to animation voiceovers due to the progress of his disease. "You can have a passion, but things don't just fall out of the sky. It really is a matter of making it happen."

At the same Milken Forum, veteran actor Kirk Douglas spoke openly
about his slow recovery from a stroke and what staying active in the service of his foundation and its cause—providing playgrounds for inner-city
youth in Los Angeles—has done for him:

A stroke is a very difficult thing. You get depressed. Do you know
what my wife told me when I was laying there moaning about my
condition? She said, "Get your ass out of bed and go see the speech
therapist." And what I found was this: The cure for depression is to
think of others, to do for others. You can always find something to be
grateful for.

Modern philanthropy is inherently a consumer marketplace, and in
the upscale reaches where mall-hoppers and Chevy drivers do not venture,
it is as aspirational as anything else. As *Women's Wear Daily* said in a special
report on luxury consumer goods and causes: "[Upscale] companies are
mining a new cultural mind-set and giving consumers a chance to feel
virtuous about an upscale product they purchase." To put it another way:
Bill Gates alone is a phenomenon. Bill Gates and Warren Buffett together
constitute a trend—and this is one trendy crowd. Coupled with moguls
like Gates, Buffett, Sir Richard Branson, and the founders of online pow-
erhouses like Google and eBay, stars like Bono, Oprah, Lance Armstrong,
Tiger Woods, and Brad Pitt add a consumer-friendly, front-page brand of
philanthropy—stylistically a cross between the sidewalks of Beverly Hills
and the lobby of the Ford Foundation. As with all luxury consumer brands,
this surge in upscale philanthropy has one clear message: "Be like us." Or, to
be more precise: "Give . . . and be like us."

That social pressure has always brought the well-heeled to the black-tie
banquets in droves. In New York, where I have spent my life, big-time
philanthropy is entirely blended with the social register; everyone flips to
the Style section of the *Times* on Sunday to see whom society photographer

Bill Cunningham has snapped at the previous week's galas and cocktail soirees. In a city of boldface names, those who give in public are recognized in public, and there is a healthy competitive force at play that spurs one mogul to compete with another.

More than a decade after the game "Six Degrees of Kevin Bacon" made the rounds of college campuses and lived on to be a shorthand term for the small-world phenomenon, the actor decided to put that whimsical notoriety to good use. Teaming with Network for Good, the online donations site originally created by America Online, Bacon created SixDegrees.org to promote "social networking with a social conscience." The site promotes charity "badges," small interactive boxes featuring nonprofit causes that anyone can add to their blog or social network profile. To date, the effort has raised more than $2.2 million through its network of virtual volunteers for causes ranging from fighting disease to supporting a local animal shelter.

Naturally, Bacon started with his own social network, and that star power added to the spread of the application. His friends included Kyra Sedgwick, Tyra Banks, Nicole Kidman, Robert Duvall, Rosie O'Donnell, and Jessica Simpson, and each star hand-picked a cause to raise money and attention for. The site was launched amid celebrity hoopla at the Sundance Film Festival, and underwear manufacturer Hanes made grants of $10,000 each to the most successful noncelebrity causes. "SixDegrees.org is about using the idea that we are all connected to accomplish something good," said Bacon at the launch, adding that he hoped the site "will soon be something more than a game or a gimmick. It will also be a force for good, by bringing a social conscience to social networking."

Craig Dyer, who is using Facebook to build support for the Christian missionary organization Bright Hope International, said that increasing celebrity involvement in causes has a direct effect on young activists and would-be philanthropists:

Overall, I believe younger people are being influenced by increased media coverage of people like Bono, Angelina, and Oprah and their humanitarian efforts—more so than older generations. So many of them grew up in relative comfort and security. These days, young people don't have to worry so much about their own comfort and security, so they can afford to focus more on global needs. Overall, younger people have so much more of the world brought to them through their television sets, the Internet, music videos, etc. The world has become a smaller, more accessible place due to the media and technology, and therefore, the needs of people around the world have gained greater exposure.

Dyer is right about the influence of popular media, which is indeed dominated by celebrities of all stripes and importance. Combine a fully wired, always-on lifestyle with the aspiration that goes along with any degree of celebrity worship, and you may get a recipe for action. Fame or media exposure need not be a central ingredient; passion, however, is vital.

The essence of group dynamics in online causes is creating other leaders, a battalion of activists who go out and recruit others to the cause. As Leslie Crutchfield and Heather McLeod Grant write in *Forces for Good*:

Once people have had a positive experience with an organization and are convinced of its impact, they are much more likely to act as an ambassador on behalf of the cause. In all the groups we studied, we found this phenomenon time and again. When we interviewed board members, staff, program participants, alumni, and even volunteers, they all had their own story of conversion to tell. They ranged from people in entry-level positions to the most prestigious board members. Whether the nonprofits call these individuals evangelists, ambassadors, champions, or even guardian angels, all of them have figured out how to leverage powerful relationships for greater impact.

That "more accessible place," however, is also crucial—because it allows the truly passionate to get out and front and try to organize others. In the end, though we may have equal access to information, and equal opportunity to get involved, we are not all equal in the CauseWired world. Some people build and work and lead; and other people—thankfully—follow.

10 | Distributing the CauseWired Future

In the late spring of 2008, Peter Deitz is swirling in the familiar and frantic minuet of the driven entrepreneur. A soft-spoken but intense 29-year-old Canadian, Deitz has created Social Actions, a "mash-up" of 19 different social action platforms. The startup, which consists of Deitz and any resources he can cadge from volunteers and supporters, is neither funded nor yet incorporated, either as a nonprofit or as a company. It exists only as a project, and that is partly because its founder just has not had time yet to think through the ultimate decision on its structure—and partly because its ultimate structure will depend on how Social Actions evolves.

So far, so good: Deitz has taken the data supplied by a wide range of platforms, from Kiva and DonorsChoose to Change.org and GlobalGiving, and created a rudimentary but workable meta search engine that allows

179

users to look for opportunities to donate or get involved across the sites in his directory. Deitz is building Social Actions as an open platform; indeed, it may turn out to be less about a search box on his website than the open-source API (application programming interface), which will eventually allow developers to plug in Social Actions content on any website. The idea is to increase the number of people participating in all of the campaigns and projects by creating a virtual marketplace for online peer-to-peer activism—one that does not require allegiance to any one website.

Deitz has been traveling to promote his idea (New York, Stockholm, California) and he is working on the elevator pitch. "It's like Google for social actionable opportunities," he says. That is pretty good for a one-liner, but Deitz's thinking on the matter runs deeper than cadging the name of the hottest Internet startup ever and applying it to the sector he is working in. To my way of thinking, the work Peter Deitz was exploring early in 2008 is a clear road sign of where online social activism is headed, and it carried both the broad opportunity in its slowly crystallizing business plan and the potential barriers to widespread societal success.

What Social Actions did first was clearly to delineate an emerging sector—a burgeoning group of startup entities (nonprofits and companies) and a growing cadre of leaders, the founding entrepreneurs of what will grow into a permanent portion of the causes firmament.

In some small ways, Social Actions reminded me of the very early days of the commercial Internet, of the advent of Netscape Navigator and the various guides that sprung up around it to provide the trailblazer's marks on the digital trees of the virgin online forest. Social Actions itself may go the way of pioneering but semi-forgotten early 1990s guideposts like WWW Wanderer, Aliweb, or Webcrawler, or it may blossom into Yahoo, the early directory that became a true central gathering spot for the explosion of the popular Web.

I am not sure it matters to Peter Deitz, whose intense concentration seems wholly focused on making it work. Indeed, his long-form elevator pitch reveals deep ambition:

Social Actions is attempting to make it easier for people to participate in online social change, or peer-to-peer social change. Its goal is to make it easier for people to do something when the spirit moves them to go and do something.

There is a deceptive simplicity to that goal, however. Each of the platforms that Deitz's algorithm hooks into has its own business model, its own techniques for empowering citizen activism, its own immediate metrics (fundraising, list-building, friend-convincing, karma-tracking, etc.), its own financial models, and its own set of constituents and partners. Social Actions is looking to tease the common thread of peer-to-peer activity from each of the sites and provide a way for a wider group of potential users to wade in without necessarily choosing one platform over another for all of eternity. This has its challenges: Some of the activist sites might not appreciate being lumped in with others. After all, some of their business plans actually stipulate becoming the central point for, say, microphilanthropy or socially networked activism. In other words, they want to be the Google of online social actions.

In their very names, you can sense the ambition (some would say the romanticism) that pervades the sector: the very palpable feeling that in this time and place groups of networked activists will indeed change the world. In addition to the Swahili-monikered Kiva and the emphatic Change.org and DonorsChoose, there are BringLight, ChangingthePresent, FirstGiving, Fundable, GiveMeaning, GlobalGiving, and MicroGiving. There are the more exotic Razoo and Zazengo, the action-oriented Helpalot, PledgeBank, and DemocracyinAction, and the more obtuse SixDegrees, ThePoint, PincGiving, and Care2. Together, they represent dozens of entrepreneurs, social activists, and technologists working in small teams—and millions of users.

So much of the language is kept in common. Zazengo, for instance, was created by social entrepreneur Vicky Saunders, who asked the question: "What if we could build a common platform that could be shared across communities that allowed for individualized branding that was free for these exceptional nonprofits?" It is based on bringing together sponsors with activists to create projects and campaigns using an array of digital tools. In this, it is a close cousin of Change.org and ChangingthePresent. However, it also shares some essential DNA with sites such as Razoo and Change.org, which emphasize team-driven actions and social identities of participants in the network, and perhaps a little farther out on the genetic chart, a startup such as PledgeBank, which, as the founders say, "is based on a psychological bet. We believe that if a person possesses a slight desire to do something, and then we help connect them to a bunch of people who also want to do the same thing, then that first person is much more likely to act."

A site such as PincGiving is dedicated to "personalized giving through either fundraising pledge pages or direct donations," and relates clearly to FirstGiving, which aims to "make it possible for everyone to raise more money online faster and more easily for the causes that are important to them." There is also a line, perhaps once removed, to Helpalot.org, founded by Dutch graduate student Julius Huijnk. The site boldly states: "We want to put a name and face to every project in the world." The microfinance-oriented startup Kiva, with its notion of direct lending, relates to Microgiving.com, which is "dedicated to direct online person-to-person giving from the heart to those in need," and clearly to DonorsChoose. Group action suffuses many of the startups and is the main focus of The Point, which "helps groups of people, large or small, coordinate action and solve the problems they share," as well as Fundable.com, which allows groups of people to "pool funds to make purchases or raise money."

Among these sites and others, including Causes on Facebook, there is overlap in mission and some competition for consumer attention. It is a developing marketplace, though much of it remains nonprofit. Social Actions, says Deitz, is "treating this whole phenomenon as a sector—and the sector itself is beginning to realize that it exists." His embryonic solution is aimed at eventually assisting a broader swath of the general public to understand what social action platforms actually offer:

> Right now, to participate you have to visit each website separately. The systems are so siloed, there are already five or six Facebook applications that allow you to connect to social actions. I want to facilitate a search across the whole space and sector—in collaboration with the platforms themselves—and for the platforms to see value in taking down those walls. You know, you can't use Google this way—you can only use Google to find nonactionable, static web pages, and there is very little likelihood what you get will allow an action right away. And most actions are by individuals, not organizations.

To some degree, the parallel with the mid-1990s holds. In those days, many old-school media companies invested heavily in massive Internet *portals*, thusly labeled because of their inherent benefit to the big "gatekeepers" who would extract financial value by allowing access to vast oceans of their "content." However, the open nature of the online network eventually bypassed the big portals, and rewarded both techniques and startups that encouraged individualistic activity. Classified ads migrated to Craigslist. Google became the largest portal the world has ever known without an ownership relationship to the content it connected users to. Sharing music and video replaced the old bricks-and-mortar record store mentality, and hits were made by open source rather than A&R people. Photos migrated from dusty albums on the shelf to Flickr.com. Blogs competed with old-line news operations. Social networks became the way to share most of a person's life in public.

"There's a parallel between what happened with journalism and what's happening with user-generated activism right now," says Deitz. "It's a new way of thinking, and it's very citizen-centric. The older established organizations should be thinking about how their programs and communications will be articulated through these grassroots networks."

Are large-scale nonprofits sitting in the same position that the big media companies occupied in the early 1990s? Is there an inherent threat to the old model of philanthropy, or to the old ways of social organizing and politicking? That remains to be seen, of course. I suspect that, very much like the naysayers who dismissed the emergence of the consumer-oriented Internet as the "CB Radio of the nineties," so, too, will many underestimate the power of online social activism as it begins to change the social commons. In what we commonly call *philanthropy* (that is, the formal transfer of assets to recognized charities), the change will be hard-set, indeed. In an article in the *Stanford Social Innovation Review*, Deitz neatly covered the demands that online donors will make on the philanthropic sector in coming years. "As legions of digital natives start to self-identify as citizen philanthropists, they should be given online tools that permit them to do more than donate to an existing organization or recruit friends to a cause," he wrote. "Instead, micro-philanthropists should be as respected as large-scale philanthropists. They should be treated in a way that implies that they can address the root causes of a problem and spread the knowledge required to resolve similar problems." He argued that certain "corrective actions" could be facilitated by the social action platforms:

- Creating feedback mechanisms where individuals and beneficiaries of nonprofit programs can immediately inform the program staff as to whether a service is having the desired effect
- Pioneering innovative models for philanthropy where individuals can coalesce into collective grantmaking bodies that fund community-level social-change projects
- Building a tax-deductible open marketplace for funding outstanding individuals and informal projects
- Using constituent and donor pressure to bring about new forms of collaboration among nonprofit groups and foundations

■ ■ ■

The collective nature of social action platforms, those already in use and those yet to be developed, is at the center of the CauseWired movement. Fueled by information that is freely available, groups of individuals coalesce around causes like charged particles in an atom. In Chapter 7, we saw how a worldwide network of outraged individuals used blogs and email and links to pressure the Pakistani government to release civil rights leader Mukhtaran Bibi. Much of this book is dedicated to reporting on the efforts of Americans to create online platforms for social change, but the development of a CauseWired sector is really an international trend. In the past few years, it is being powered by increasing access to the digital network through the world, but most particularly in developing nations. In a speech to the United Nations less than two years ago, *Fortune* magazine senior editor David Kirkpatrick focused on one particular area of growth:

[L]et's be clear about the technology that is already having the greatest impact—the cell phone. As soon as a person possesses one they acquire a window into the entire world. More than 80 percent of the world's population, calculates Motorola, already lives in an area covered by wireless networks. There are an estimated 1.5 billion cell phones now in use in the developing world. That figure will go to at least three billion over the next five years. In India alone, five million new customers sign up for cell phones every week. People are starting to talk about owning a cell phone as a basic human right.

As the work of organizations such as Foko Madagascar (described in Chapter 3) makes clear, there is a growing shift in international causes from a purely aid-based charitable formula to an information-rich collaboration toward development goals; the advance of microfinance has surely fueled the trend. However, the growth in citizen journalism, in live reporting from the field, has also played a part.

Amra Tareen is a native of Pakistan by way of Australia and a postgradu-
ate degree in the United States. A former venture capitalist in the technology
sector, Tareen launched allvoices.com in 2008 to "create a global community
that shares news, videos, images, and opinions tied to events and people." Like
most social entrepreneurs, Tareen's story starts with a personal experience
(in this case, a cause) and continues in trying to solve a problem.

"Why allvoices?," she wrote. "Last year I volunteered with Relief
International's livelihoods team in Mansera, Pakistan, to setup micro-credits
programs for the most vulnerable women, the widows, and orphans of the
2005 earthquake in Pakistan. I was on the ground for a short period of
time, in Mansera and Balakot, but it was an experience that inspired me.
The women and people 'on the ground' were very resilient, they had strong
belief that they will be okay regardless of what happens."

That experience led her to explore ways of telling stories, of empowering
people to relate what they are witnessing:

I wanted to share my experience with the rest of the world, to see
what was really going on, on the ground. There was so much to tell,
but how could I communicate? I had pictures of the devastation and
destruction, I had stories of heroism, I felt the compassion of people
who were good and generous to the core, even though they had
nothing. How do I get this message out? Do I send an email to CNN?
Do I write a blog that no will ever find? . . . This inspired me to start a
company that would let people no matter where they were to write
about what they knew about an event, upload photos and videos, and
write their stories and views and share with the rest of the world.

At allvoices.com, those stories are combined with news reports from
media organizations, as well as links to blog posts, photos and videos
from a wide variety of sources. That way, the stories from the field—so
compelling in their immediacy—could gain an informed audience:

We quickly realized that in addition to sharing, every voice needs a context, so that other people can understand why a person has a particular point of view. We at allvoices believe that you don't need to be an avid blogger or be an expert to share your experiences with the rest of the world.

The signature image on the site's homepage is an interactive map with a series of stars highlighting the latest posts from contributors. The site is very much in beta and has limited contributions from the field, but you can see where it may develop. There are reports from the field in central China, the Congo, northern Pakistan, France, and San Francisco. Reports are accepted by cell phone as well via Web postings, and they are entirely unedited. Many report on disasters, wars, famine, and injustice—the raw material of some the CauseWired social platforms. Amra Tareen is trying to close the gap between the field and the consumer of information from the field. Ultimately, this is the same gap that growing social action platforms such as Kiva and DonorsChoose are trying to close, bringing the actual work closer to those who support it and making the cause integral to its funders and cadre of volunteers and activists. Yet, if there is a soft underbelly to the CauseWired movement, a flaw in the closing of that gap, it clearly lies in the open question of whether more information actually leads to greater involvement—and to real activism.

■ ■ ■

In December 2006, *Time* turned a mirror on the DIY consumer culture of the Internet and its growing social networks, literally pasting reflective paper on its cover for the annual Person of the Year issue. Yes, it was all of us—obsessed with ourselves and our personal brands. However, I thought the cover missed its mark, not only because it was a hokey way to play up digital consumerism, but because the Person of the Year for 2006 was so clearly Warren Buffett. Six months earlier, I sat in a midtown ballroom and watched as the world's most famous investor gave away most of his billions to the Bill and Melinda Gates Foundation.

His biggest-in-history divestiture of personal wealth—and related comments about inheritance and the growing gap between rich and poor—did not make the cut. In a year of big-philanthropy headlines, the big gifts came up short in the eyes of the news magazine editors. I thought this was a huge mistake on *Time*'s part—a missed opportunity to call attention to what is clearly a growing national phenomenon. The "mirror" cover highlighting so-called "users" of information—empowered consumers in control of media and distribution in a networked world—seemed a lesser choice in comparison, especially in the world of philanthropy and social activism. Because the actual numbers are small compared to the Buffett or Gates billions, it may be too easy to dismiss the impact of distributed networks and social computing on giving. We have all lived through the hype of platform after platform and system after system. How are you going to touch the kind of money that changes hands at Davos or the Clinton Global Initiative with a few widgets and blogs, videos and podcasts? Honestly, it is not possible—at least right now. I think it is important to keep that limitation in mind even as we celebrate the involvement of millions of people in online causes. The big money still matters; and in our celebrity-obsessed, media-soaked society, big public commitments matter as well.

This era of consumer philanthropy sometimes masks the importance of those big commitments—and the vitality of true citizen action. In some ways, the staged world of reality television provides a stark contrast to what online social activist platforms are attempting to accomplish. Idol Gives Back was the massively popular *American Idol*'s attempt to turn some of its success to cause marketing—while burnishing its own image as a socially aware production at the same time. The Emmy Award–winning ABC reality television series, *Extreme Makeover: Home Edition*, is devoted to "rebuilding families' homes when the family is in need of new hope." Yet, when families are faced with disease or loss or disaster, does the overwhelming emphasis on creating a luxurious domicile with all the latest in home technology really provide any sort of solution to the underlying cause of their crisis? Or does it merely create the impeccably produced *image* of assistance, leaving viewers at home feeling better about the American Dream?

Consider Oprah's Big Give, a highly glossed version of philanthropy and activism featuring contestants who participate in a series of challenges in order to become America's "greatest unknown philanthropist." The winner gets a million dollars—half to keep and half to give away. Even the entertainment press was impressed with this version of "philanthropy." The *Hollywood Reporter* called it "a profoundly hyperkinetic and unwieldy adventure in product placement, in Oprah-as-Messiah hype and, ultimately, in what's so utterly fake and insidious about 'reality' television itself." Philanthropy analyst Phil Cubeta wrote on his popular blog, The Gift Hub: "Again, we have the reality-show, vote-them-off-the-island mentality. The winning do-gooder gets the bundle; losers get humiliated. This is America, folks."

Just as those reality shows and their brand of philanthropy can seem shallow, there are valid questions about the depth of peer-to-peer causes, Internet philanthropy, and online social activism. After all, the lowest common denominator—the smallest point of entry—is the humble click. A friend invites you to "join a cause." You read a few lines of text, and click once to join. Andrea Batista Schlesinger, executive director of the Drum Major Institute for Public Policy (a liberal think-tank based in New York), has used the Web to sign on activists and spread the word about DMI's policy work. She is at work on her own study of political activism among young Americans, and she believes that the "vote-them-off-the-island mentality" clearly challenges real involvement:

> I worry that young people are navigating their democracy increasingly as consumers. . . . Consumers select. They pick. They do not make.

They do not transform. We need a generation of young people who want to ask the core questions of their democracy and challenge the institutions of that democracy—including corporate America. I worry that the consumers of [social networks] will be less inclined to engage in government and less inclined to take on corporate America because they approach both as consumers.

Robert Tolmach also sees some danger in overemphasizing the quick, consumer choice aspect of online social activism. Tolmach is the creator of ChangingthePresent.org, an online philanthropy platform that presents a "taxonomy" of well-researched causes for users to choose from. "Social networking can be used to raise awareness for causes, like the monks in Burma, or brand awareness—it's Obama's 'yes we can,'" says Tolmach, whose background as an architect and investment banker informs his new social enterprise. He continues:

And people sign up. But the search is really for a deeper understanding. If you ask them "what is Obama's health care plan?," or "what's going on in Burma?," or "do you know that a billion people have no safe drinking water?," I doubt you'll get an answer.

ChangingthePresent is a nonprofit and is guided by a board of more than 125 advisers from all fields in social activism, from environmentalism to health care to international development. It aims to better educate consumers about where their money goes and how it can fund change, and emphasizes "meaningful" gifts and social networking through online gift cards, fundraising drives, and gift registries. In Tolmach's view,

For every major sector of the economy, there is a marketplace, a place not just to spend money but to create relationships, from iTunes to the local shopping mall, to the lists of music at lastFM or the stocks on the New York Stock Exchange and the auctions at eBay. But every other market is more open than the philanthropic market, and you can see this online. If I need a new cell phone or a digital camera, I can Google them and instantly be comparing prices and features. But if I'm worried about the 600 children who will die today from malnutrition, there is no way to work the market to find the best solution to that problem.

To Tolmach, the idea of knowledgeable giving is as important as the actual money raised for causes. "The question is not whether you can get them to give, but can you get them to give more intelligently. You get a picture of a baby seal in the mail and you give a hundred dollars. That's not a way to allocate a precious resource."

But are informed consumers enough? Should supporters of online social causes be considered consumers at all? "Changing the world isn't a hobby," says Andrea Batista Schlesinger:

It isn't a sport. It doesn't belong in the same category as sharing music files and photos from your last camping trip. My fear is that the CauseWired sector institutionalizes the business of social change, and with that comes a loss in urgency, in personalization, in the senses of personal empowerment and sacrifice that are typically associated with lending yourself to a movement for social and economic justice. Ultimately, I think young people need to engage in their own physical communities in order to truly experience citizenship.

When I ask her about it, my 16-year-old in-house millennial confirms Andrea's concern: "We're not really a political generation," says Veronica. "We do think we can change things, but we show our support more than really doing things."

■ ■ ■

Nor is the pure "wisdom of the crowds" ethic so prized in modern Web development likely to create world-changing movements. Existing non-profits, governments, the corporate world, and other well-organized—and, yes, hierarchical—organizations are still better positioned in many cases to make a real difference in areas like health care, education, international development, political choice, and ecology. As Ben Rattray of Change.org argues in Chapter 8, "dismissing organizations is a fault." As we saw with the Obama campaign in Chapter 6, a top-down message can be combined with an army of relatively empowered digital volunteers to create something like a movement.

Sometimes, the rare organization that appears to be driven entirely by a sort of digital collectivism (such as Wikipedia) creates unreasonable expectations for a kind of pure online democracy (*cyberlibertarianism*, as we used to say in the 1990s) that cannot live up to its promise. Computer scientist, composer, visual artist, and author Jaron Lanier wrote about this exception that proves the rule in an insightful 2006 essay, entitled "Digital Maoism":

> [T]he problem is in the way the Wikipedia has come to be regarded and used; how it's been elevated to such importance so quickly. And that is part of the larger pattern of the appeal of a new online collectivism that is nothing less than a resurgence of the idea that the collective is all-wise, that it is desirable to have influence concentrated in a bottleneck that can channel the collective with the most verity and force. This is different from representative democracy, or meritocracy. This idea has had dreadful consequences when thrust upon us from the extreme Right or the extreme Left in various historical periods. The fact that it's now being re-introduced today by prominent technologists and futurists, people who in many cases I know and like, doesn't make it any less dangerous.

> The beauty of the Internet is that it connects people. The value is in the other people. If we start to believe that the Internet itself is

an entity that has something to say, we're devaluing those people and making ourselves into idiots.

The downside to pure digital democracy is obvious, even to proponents of online collaboration. As we saw in Chapter 2, the loose idea of causes is linking tens of thousands of people on Facebook and other social networks, leveraging the growing sense that pure choice and intellectual freedom are ever-approaching perfections to our connected lifestyle. Yet, no less than Charles Leadbeater, author of the influential *We-think: The Power of Mass Creativity*, throws out warning flags:

> Many people are deeply uncertain about whether the world the Web is creating will leave us feeling more in control of our lives or less. On the one hand, the Web is the source of our most ambitious hopes for spreading democracy, knowledge, and creativity. It ought in principle to give us untold capacity for solving shared problems by allowing us to combine the knowledge and insights of millions of people, creating a collective intelligence on a scale never before possible.
>
> But the Web is also the source of some of our most lurid fears: It has already become a tool for stalkers, paedophiles, terrorists, and criminals to organize shadow networks for shadowy purposes beyond our control. The Web's extreme openness, its capacity to allow anyone to connect to virtually anyone one else, generates untold possibilities for collaboration. It also leaves us vulnerable to worms, viruses, and a mass of petty intrusions. The more connected we are the richer we should be because we should be able to connect with people far and wide, to combine their ideas, talents, and resources in ways that should expand everyone's prosperity. But the more connected we are, the easier it is for small groups to cause enormous disruptions, by spreading viruses, real or virtual.

There is also simply too much: too many causes, too many links, too many email solicitations, too many widgets, too much video, too many instant messages and text messages, too many podcasts and photos—heck, too damned many friends. The daily slog through the digital world has become very much like an evening stroll through Times Square—an assault on your attention and a maddening battle to get through the crowds to your destination. All the while, a big screen overhead screams, "watch me!" The digital media inundation that has swept the western world makes it tougher to build true support for causes. As Ben Rattray says, we may simply be asked to care too much, organize too much, and give too often:

> The most effective way to get people engaged is to have a friend invite them, but if you have a huge influx of invitations and nothing is compelling, you don't gain much. . . . You can only care about a certain number of things—there are too many solicitations, they're not that effective, and people are so accustomed to joining causes that it just seems trivial. It doesn't seem to have real, substantive engagement. Sometimes the organizations involved aren't even that active or aware. The danger is saturation and people taking many minor actions, but if the saturation is the invitation itself—if that defines saturation—then it's not compelling and leads people more easily to dismiss the cause.

Impressive as the rise of online social activism is, there are clearly some red flags and warning signs to observe as we consider the CauseWired movement. First, activism and involvement may be as slight as a single click. Real change will come from true investment of time and resources, which even the best online social platforms do not necessarily produce. Second, a slight involvement does not create true knowledge or a depth of understanding, which are vital to long-term involvement and commitment to a cause. Third, the group of young people so poised to embrace the CauseWired movement is also a group with other things on its collective mind. Inundated with media and communications in an increasingly attention–overloaded existence, it may be ill prepared to get involved in the kind of sustained manner that builds organizations, political campaigns, and successful causes. Finally, the crowd is not always right: The cause with the most clicks is not necessarily the one you should support with your time and money.

■ ■ ■

"Self-organizing groups have always changed the world," says Scott Heiferman. "You might think that it's all up to a charismatic leader or a Martin Luther King. But, in fact, it's the thousands of small groups around the country that created the civil rights movement, and the women's rights movement was about thousands of small groups."

Those small groups have always held power, limited only by reach and funding and motivation. Imagine hundreds of thousands, or even millions, of small groups. Some of those groups are two people. Some contain millions. Some raise money. Some distribute video. Some build lists of activists and supporters. Some knock on doors, virtual and otherwise. All are connected and wired and driven by the causes they are organized to support. This is not some imagined vision of a futuristic digital nirvana. This is *now*.

However, it still feels early to me, and that is a good thing. What I call the *CauseWired sector* is still being defined. It includes online social activism, nonprofit fundraising, wired social entrepreneurship, political organizing, flash causes, and digital philanthropy. It overlaps the larger worlds of organized charity and nonprofits, of politics and policy organizing, of consumer brands and marketing, even as it changes them. It rides the demographic trends of the younger, superwired polity. The exact size of this sector is not yet known, but it includes the millions who have used social networks to raise money, to push for votes, or to bring attention to some cause, big or small, that will make the world a better place. Today, some of the platforms that we think of as pioneers of online social activism are still evolving. The models will almost certainly change; and it is wise to consider how even the largest online success stories adjusted their business models as they went along.

This new sector relies on open access to information, on the new consumers' expectations of transparency in transactions, and on the new activists' insistence on transparency in political campaigns and government. Donors at even the smallest level of commitment are gaining access to information about the successes or failures of the initiatives they support—and, on occasion, direct access to the people they seek to help. This not only lowers boundary walls, it destroys them. It encourages an abandonment of the kind of top-down paternalism that has institutionalized much of mainstream philanthropy. Further, the CauseWired sector thrives on experimentation and risk; it encourages the flow of capital to projects that carry the fantastic promise of world-changing success, as well as the possibility of failure. We need that. Risk and reward drive innovation, and some towers simply need to come down.

Will online social activism unleash a golden age for causes—for philanthropy, for activism, for citizen engagement? Perhaps; some of it is still gimmickry and fast marketing. Yet, as I hope you have gleaned from this book, the CauseWired movement is also changing lives and inspiring a generation of wired social entrepreneurs to reach for something better.

■ ■ ■

Without making this too personal, my little girl was only 2 years old when the Internet became a consumer marketplace in 1994. She was a preschooler when online commerce exploded and we all moved vast portions of our lives online. While I have been frustrated by the fits and starts of online philanthropy, Veronica does not even consider it. To her generation, it simply does not matter. They live online, their causes are online; there is no separation between real and virtual. If you want to know where philanthropy and activism and politics are going, watch what they are doing. After all, as novelist William Gibson said: "The future is already here; it's just not evenly distributed."

Websites

There are many websites cited in this book, but there are some other useful sites that are not specifically mentioned. This section is intended as a handy guide to readers who want to explore on their own some of the sites, blogs, and networks that inspired this book without having to pore through the chapter notes. It is by no means exhaustive, but should allow readers to begin exploring the CauseWired world on their own.

Social Activism Sites & Platforms

Allvoices

www.allvoices.com

BetterPlace

www.betterplace.org

BringLight

www.bringlight.com

Care2

www.care2.org

Causes on Facebook

apps.facebook.com/causes/giving

Change.org

www.change.org

ChangingthePresent

www.changingthepresent.org

ChipIn
> www.chipin.com

Convio
> www.convio.org

DemocracyinAction
> www.democracyinaction.org

DonorsChoose
> www.donorschoose.org

Firstgiving
> www.firstgiving.com

freecycle
> www.freecycle.org

Fundable
> www.fundable.org

GiveForward
> www.giveforward.org

GiveMeaning
> www.givemeaning.org

Global Giving
> www.globalgiving.com

Helpalot
> www.helpalot.org

JustGiving
> www.justgiving.com

justmeans
> www.justmeans.com

Karmadu
> www.karmadu.com

Kiva
> www.kiva.org

Knowmore.org
> www.knowmore.org

Make The Difference Network
>www.mtdn.com

MicroGiving
>www.microgiving.org

Network for Good
>www.networkforgood.org

PincGiving
>www.pincgiving.com

PledgeBank
>www.pledgebank.org

Razoo
>www.razoo.com

Social Actions
>www.socialactions.org

SixDegrees
>www.sixdegrees.org

SocialVibe
>www.socialvibe.com

TakingItGlobal
>www.takingitglobal.org

ThePoint
>www.thepoint.com

Zazengo
>www.zazengo.com

Assorted Blogs

Allison Fine
>afine2.wordpress.com

Beth's Blog: How Nonprofits Can Use Social Media
>beth.typepad.com

Bring Light
>www.bringlight.com

BuzzFeed

 www.buzzfeed.com

CauseWired

 www.causewired.com

Confessions of a Nonprofit IT Director

 www.nonprofittechblog.org

Clay Shirky

 www.clayshirky.com

ext337

 www.ext337.org

Future Leaders in Philanthropy

 flip.typepad.com

GiftHub

 www.gifthub.org

The Green Skeptic

 www.greenskeptic.blogspot.com

Howard Greenstein

 howardgreenstein.com

Nate Ritter

 blog.perfectspace.com

newcritics

 www.newcritics.com

onPhilanthropy.com

 www.onphilanthropy.com

Philanthropy 2173

 philanthropy.blogspot.com

PhilanthroMedia

 www.philanthromedia.org

SocialEdge

 www.socialedge.org

Sustainablog

 www.sustainablog.org

Tactical Philanthropy

    tacticalphilanthropy.typepad.com

techPresident

    www.techpresident.com

Tom Watson: My Dirty Life & Times

    tomwatson.typepad.com

Tom Watson MP

    www.tom-watson.co.uk

Organizations

Ashoka

    www.ashoka.org

Case Foundation

    www.casefoundation.org

Changing Our World

    www.changingourworld.com

Clinton Global Initiative

    www.clintonglobalinitiative.org

Drum Major Institute for Public Policy

    www.drummajorinstitute.org

The Milken Institute

    www.milkeninstitute.org

NetSquared

    www.netsquared.org

NTEN

    www.nten.org

Personal Democracy Forum

    www.personaldemocracy.com

The Pew Internet & American Life Project

    www.pewinternet.org

Skoll Foundation

    www.skollfoundation.org

TechSoup

www.techsoup.org

Venture Philanthropy Partners

www.vppartners.org

Web 2.0 and Social Networks

Craigslist

www.craigslist.org

del.icio.us

del.icio.us

Digg

www.digg.com

Eons

www.eons.com

Facebook

www.facebook.com

Flickr

www.flickr.com

FriendFeed

www.friendfeed.com

Friendster

www.friendster.com

Idealist

www.idealist.org

lastFM

www.lastfm.com

LinkedIn

www.linkedin.com

Mahalo

www.mahalo.com

MySpace

www.myspace.com

Pandora

      www.pandora.com

Technorati

      www.technorati.com

Twitter

      www.twitter.com

Typepad

      www.typepad.com

Wikipedia

      www.wikipedia.org

Wordpress

      www.wordpress.org

YouTube

      www.youtube.com

Further Reading

The works of several authors are cited in the text, but other important books also influenced the author and deserve to be mentioned. This list, while not a complete guide, is intended to provide a jumping-off point for readers who might be inclined to dig deeper.

Banker to the Poor: Micro-Lending and the Battle Against World Poverty
>   Muhammad Yunus and Alan Jolis (PublicAffairs, June 1, 1999)

Blogwars: The New Political Battleground
>   David D. Perlmutter (Oxford University Press, March 7, 2008)

Code and Other Laws of Cyberspace
>   Lawrence Lessig (Basic Books, July 13, 2000)

Crashing the Gate: Netroots, Grassroots, and the Rise of People-Powered Politics
>   Jerome Armstrong and Markos Moulitsas Zuniga (Chelsea Green Publishing Company, 2006)

Darknet: Hollywood's War Against the Digital Generation
>   J.D. Lasica (Wiley, 2005)

Forces for Good
>   Leslie R. Crutchfield and Heather McLeod Grant (Jossey-Bass, October 19, 2007)

The Future of Philanthropy: Economics, Ethics, and Management
>   Susan U. Raymond (Wiley, March 22, 2004)

207

Giving: How Each of Us Can Change the World
> Bill Clinton (Knopf, September 4, 2007)

Here Comes Everybody: The Power of Organizing without Organizations
> Clay Shirky (Penguin Press, 2008)

How to Change the World: Social Entrepreneurs and the Power of New Ideas, Updated Edition
> David Bornstein (Oxford University Press, September 17, 2007)

The Long Tail: Why the Future of Business Is Selling Less of More
> Chris Anderson (Hyperion, July 11, 2006)

Mapping the New World of American Philanthropy: Causes and Consequences of the Transfer of Wealth
> Susan U. Raymond and Mary Beth Martin (Wiley, April 13, 2007)

Millennial Makeover: MySpace, YouTube and the Future of American Politics
> Morley Winograd and Michael Hais (Rutgers University Press, 2008)

Millennials Rising: The Next Great Generation
> Neil Howe and William Strauss (Vintage, September 5, 2000)

Momentum: Igniting Social Change in the Connected Age
> Allison Fine (Jossey-Bass, September 29, 2006)

Naked Conversations: How Blogs Are Changing the Way Businesses Talk with Customers
> Robert Scoble and Shel Israel (Wiley, January 2006)

The New Philanthropists
> Charles Handy (Random House UK, October 31, 2006)

Now Is Gone: A Primer on New Media for Executives and Entrepreneurs
> Geoff Livingston (Bartleby Press, November 12, 2007)

Revolutionary Wealth: How It Will Be Created and How It Will Change Our Lives
> Alvin Toffler and Heidi Toffler (Doubleday Business, June 12, 2007)

Richistan: A Journey through the American Wealth Boom and the Lives of the New Rich
> Robert Frank (Crown, June 5, 2007)

Social Entrepreneurship: New Models of Sustainable Social Change
>   Alex Nicholls (Oxford University Press, 2006)

The Pirate's Dilemma: How Youth Culture Is Reinventing Capitalism
>   Matt Mason (Free Press, January 8, 2008)

The Wealth of Networks: How Social Production Transforms Markets and Freedom
>   Yochai Benkler (Yale University Press, May 16, 2006)

We the Media: Grassroots Journalism By the People, For the People
>   Dan Gillmor (O'Reilly Media, January 24, 2006)

We-think: The Power of Mass Creativity
>   Charles Leadbeater (Profile Books, Ltd., February 2008)

Wikinomics: How Mass Collaboration Changes Everything
>   Don Tapscott and Anthony Williams (Portfolio Hardcover, December 28, 2006)

The Wisdom of Crowds
>   James Surowiecki (Anchor, August 16, 2005)

Notes

As is true of the blogs and social networks that have inspired it, this book makes a liberal use of direct quotes. Wherever possible, I have included a url so that readers can further explore the ideas of scores of fine writers, bloggers, and analysts. Bear in mind, however, that many online addresses do not last forever and that some of these links may no longer work by the time this book goes to press.

Chapter 1

DailyKos diarist, "Hunter," "Left Behind," DailyKos.com (September 2, 2005), www.dailykos.com/storyonly/2005/9/2/31040/36581.

"Thousands of Blogs Cover Hurricane Katrina's Impact," BloggersBlog.com (August 31, 2005), www.bloggersblog.com/cgi-bin/bloggersblog.pl?bblog=831051.

Web 2.0, Wikipedia (last modified on March 30, 2008), http://en.wikipedia.org/wiki/Web_2.

Tom Watson, "Just One Photograph," My Dirty Life & Times blog (September 14, 2005), http://tomwatson.typepad.com/tom_watson/2005/09/just_one_photog.html.

Mark Glaser, "NOLA.com Blogs and Forums Help Save Lives after Katrina,"
    Online Journalism Review (September 13, 2005),
        www.ojr.org/ojr/stories/050913glaser/.

"Donors Give Online at Record Levels for Hurricane Katrina Relief
    Efforts," Convio.com press release (September 1, 2005),
        www.convio.com/convio/news/releases/hurricane-katrina-
        relief-efforts.html.

Hurricane Katrina Archive, Nola.com,
        www.nola.com/katrina/archive/.

"New Orleans Is a Ghost Town," People Get Ready blog (September 26,
    2005),
        http://peoplegetready.blogspot.com/2005/09/new-orleans-is-
        ghost-town.html.

Tom Watson, "Hilton Symposium Celebrates Success, and Highlights
    Development Challenges," onPhilanthropy.com (September 13,
    2007),
        www.onphilanthropy.com/site/News2?page=NewsArticle&id=7229.

Don Tapscott and Anthony Williams, *Wikinomics: How Mass Collaboration
    Changes Everything* (Portfolio Hardcover, December 28, 2006),
    pp. 11, 15.

Tom Watson, "Facebook Generation: Will Social Networks Change the
    Nature of Philanthropy?" onPhilanthropy.com (June 13, 2007),
        www.onphilanthropy.com/site/News2?page=NewsArticle&id=7133.

"Americans Scrutinize Business Practices in Deciding What to Buy," Cone
    Communications press release (July 9, 2007),
        www.coneinc.com/content76.html.

Jill Eisnaugle, "Time of Greatest Need," Hellicane blog (September 1, 2005),
        http://hellicane.blogspot.com/2005_09_01_archive.html.

Chapter 2

Rebecca McNamara, "MED Student Awarded Soros Fellowship," *BU
    Today* (March 31, 2008),

www.bu.edu/today/2008/03/28/med-student-awarded-soros-fellowship,

Brian Braiker, "Facebook-ing Philanthropy," *Newsweek* (October 26, 2007), www.newsweek.com/id/62168.

Om Malik, "Sean 'Wild Boy' Parker Returns," GigaOm (March 19, 2007),

http://gigaom.com/2007/03/19/sean-parker-new-startup/.

Michael Arrington, "Project Agape: Sean Parker to Apply Virality to Altruism," TechCrunch (March 29, 2007),

www.techcrunch.com/2007/03/29/project-agape-sean-parker-to-apply-virality-to-altruism/.

Nancy Scola, "Interview: Joe Green of Project Agape and Facebook's Causes App," MyDD.com blog (June 3, 2007),

www.mydd.com/story/2007/6/3/225443/4586.

Charles Leadbeater, *We-Think: The Power of Mass Creativity* (Profile Books Ltd., February 2008), p. 211.

Stowe Boyd, "Tim Berners-Lee on Social Graph: Okay, I Give," /Message blog (November 23, 2007),

www.stoweboyd.com/message/2007/11/tim-berners-lee.html.

Allison Fine, *Momentum: Igniting Social Change in the Connected Age* (Jossey-Bass, September 29, 2006), p. 12.

Clay Shirky, *Here Comes Everybody: The Power of Organizing Without Organizations* (Penguin Press, 2008), p. 31.

Mark Hefflinger, "Project Agape Gets $5 Million for Online Political/Social Activism," *DMW Daily* (March 31, 2008),

www.dmwmedia.com/news/2008/03/31/project-agape-gets-$5-million-online-political/social-activism.

J.D. Lasica, *Darknet: Hollywood's War Against the Digital Generation* (John Wiley & Sons, 2005), p. 260.

Michael Arrington, "Causes Reports on Its First Year—$2.5 Million for 20,000 Charities and Nonprofits," TechCrunch (May 28, 2008),

www.techcrunch.com/2008/05/28/causes-reports-on-its-first-year/.

Chapter 3

"An Open Letter to His Excellency Hu Jintao," Save Darfur Coalition (February 12, 2008),

www.savedarfur.org/page/content/china_open_letter/.

Leslie R. Crutchfield and Heather McLeod Grant, *Forces for Good* (Jossey-Bass, October 19, 2007), p. 126.

Beth Kanter, "Jonathon Colman to Beth Kanter," Beth's Blog (February 24, 2008),

http://beth.typepad.com/beths_blog/2008/02/interview-with.html.

Catherine Holahan, "Click Here to Save Darfur," *BusinessWeek* (February 14, 2008),

www.businessweek.com/technology/content/feb2008/tc20080213_617723.htm.

Lova Rakotomalala, "Rising Voices, Digital Media and Foko," Foko blog (December 29, 2007),

www.foko-madagascar.org/?p=175.

Beth Kanter, "Why You Didn't Hear About Cyclone Ivan's Destruction in Madagascar and How to Help Support Relief Efforts," Beth's Blog (February 24, 2008),

http://beth.typepad.com/beths_blog/2008/02/devastating-des.html.

Beth Kanter, "Foko Madagascar: It Takes a Village to Raise an Idea," BlogHer.com (February 3, 2008),

www.blogher.com/foko-madagascar-it-takes-village-raise-idea.

Chris Mooney, "The Intersection" (April 4, 2007),

http://scienceblogs.com/intersection/2007/04/media_ignoring_madagascan_cycl.php.

Robert S. Boynton, "How to Make a Guerrilla Documentary," *New York Times Magazine* (July 11, 2004).

Allison Fine, *Momentum: Igniting Social Change in the Connected Age* (Jossey-Bass, September 29, 2006), p. 41.

Ned Sherman, "The DMW Interview with Filmmaker Robert Greenwald," DigitalMediaWire (June 19, 2007),

> www.dmwmedia.com/news/2007/06/19/the-dmw-interview-with-filmmaker-robert-greenwald.

Joel Barkin, "Interview with Robert Greenwald," Progressive States Network (2006),

> www.progressivestates.org/people/346/filmmaker-robert-greenwald.

Chapter 4

Lynette Holloway, "A Small Bronx School That Succeeds Where Its Predecessor Failed Is Offered More Freedom," *New York Times* (February 10, 1999),

> http://query.nytimes.com/gst/fullpage.html?res=9E05EFDA103BF933A25751C0A96F958260.

Tim Ferriss, "How to Dine with Queen Noor, Chill with Oprah, and Change the World," *Huffington Post* (July 19, 2007),

> www.huffingtonpost.com/tim-ferriss/how-to-dine-with-queen-no_b_56926.html?view=print.

Stephanie Strom, "Matching Givers with Those in Need: Some See a Web-Based Charity as the Future of Philanthropy," *New York Times* (July 2, 2002).

Matt Flannery, "Kiva and the Birth of Person-to-Person Microfinance Innovations," *MIT Press Journals* (Winter/Spring 2007, Vol. 2, No. 1-2), pp. 31–56,

> www.mitpressjournals.org/doi/abs/10.1162/itgg.2007.2.1-2.31.

Jeffrey O'Brien, "The Only Nonprofit That Matters," *Fortune* (February 26, 2008),

> http://money.cnn.com/magazines/fortune/fortune_archive/2008/03/03/103796533/index.htm.

Sean Stannard-Stockton, "Kiva.org and the Social Capital Markets," Tactical
    Philanthropy blog (January 30, 2008),
        http://tacticalphilanthropy.com/2008/01/kivaorg-and-the-social-
            capital-markets.
Nicholas Kristof, "You, Too, Can Be a Banker to the Poor," *New York Times*
    (March 27, 2007).

Chapter 5

Aparna Kumar, "He Said, She Said, Web Dread," *Wired* (February 23,
    2001),
        www.wired.com/techbiz/media/news/2001/02/41997.
"A Portrait of 'Generation Next': How Young People View Their Lives,
    Futures and Politics," Pew Research Center for the People and the
    Press (January 2007).
Clive Thompson, "The Age of Microcelebrity: Why Everyone's a Little
    Brad Pitt," *Wired* (November 27, 2007),
        www.wired.com/techbiz/people/magazine/15-12/st_thompson.
Morley Winograd and Michael Hais, *Millennial Makeover: MySpace, YouTube
    and the Future of American Politics* (Rutgers University Press, 2008).
Amanda Lenhart, Mary Madden, Alexandra Rankin Macgill, and Aaron
    Smith, "Teens and Social Media," Pew Internet and American Life
    Project (December 19, 2007),
        www.pewinternet.org/pdfs/PIP_Teens_Social_Media_Final.pdf.
Allison Fine, "Social CitizensBETA—Civic Participation in a Digital Age,"
    Case Foundation (April 28, 2008),
        http://blog.socialcitizens.org/file_download/1/Social-Citizens-
            Discussion-Paper.pdf.
Nancy Scola, "Interview: Joe Green of Project Agape and Facebook's
    Causes App," MyDD.com blog (June 3, 2007),
        www.mydd.com/story/2007/6/3/225443/4586.

Mark Hugo Lopez and Karlo Barrios Marcelo, "Youth Demographics," Center for Information and Research on Civic Learning and Engagement (November 2006),

> www.civicyouth.org/PopUps/youthdemo_2006.pdf.

"free rice," lazylaces blog (Wednesday, October 17, 2007),

> www.lazylaces.com/article.asp?p=2972.

Kristen Nicole, "Razoo is a Community for Causes," Mashable.com (August 31, 2007),

> http://mashable.com/2007/08/31/razoo/.

Tom Watson, "A Deeper Commitment: At Gathering of Philanthropists, Personal Involvement Is the Message," onPhilanthropy.com (July 12, 2007),

> www.onphilanthropy.com/site/News2?page=NewsArticle&
> id=7155.

Chapter 6

Britt Bravo, "Interview with Eric Mattson," NetSquared.org (January 17, 2008),

> www.netsquared.org/blog/britt-bravo/nonprofits-outpacing-
> business-use-social-media-interview-eric-mattson.

Eric Mattson and Nora Barnes, Ph.D., "Blogging for the Hearts of Donors: Largest U.S. Charities Use Social Media," University of Massachusetts Dartmouth Center for Marketing Research,

> www.umassd.edu/cmr/studies/blogstudy4.cfm.

Joan D. Mandle, How Political Is the Personal?: "Identity Politics, Feminism and Social Change," Colgate University

> http://userpages.umbc.edu/~korenman/wmst/identity_pol.html.

Michael D. Shea and Tim Craig, "Allen on Damage Control After Remarks to Webb Aide," *Washington Post* (August 16, 2006),

> www.washingtonpost.com/wp-dyn/content/article/2006/08/15/
> AR2006081501210.html.

Michael Scherer, "Salon Person of the Year: S.R. Sidarth," Salon.com (December 16, 2006),

www.salon.com/opinion/feature/2006/12/16/sidarth/index.html.

Andrew Sullivan, "Video Power: The Potent New Political Force," *Sunday Times* (February 4, 2007),

www.timesonline.co.uk/tol/comment/columnists/andrew_sullivan/ article1321781.ece.

Jay Rosen, "From Off The Bus to Meet the Press," PressThink blog (April 15, 2008),

http://journalism.nyu.edu/pubzone/weblogs/pressthink/ 2008/04/15/mayhill_fowler.html.

Mayhill Fowler, "Obama: No Surprise That Hard-Pressed Pennsylvanians Turn Bitter," *Huffington Post* (April 11, 2008),

www.huffingtonpost.com/mayhill-fowler/obama-no-surprise- that-ha_b_96188.html.

James Rainey, "Barack Obama Can Thank 'Citizen Journalist' for 'Bitter' Tempest," *Los Angeles Times* (April 15, 2008),

www.latimes.com/news/politics/la-na-bitterweb15apr15,0,3231174, full.story.

Matthew Mosk, "Obama Rewriting Rules for Raising Campaign Money Online," *Washington Post* (March 28, 2008),

www.washingtonpost.com/wp-dyn/content/article/2008/03/27/ AR2008032702968.html?wpisrc=newsletter.

Joshua Green, "The Amazing Money Machine," *Atlantic Monthly* (June 2008), www.theatlantic.com/doc/200806/obama-finance.

Kenneth P. Vogel, "Ron Paul Becomes $6 Million Man," Politico.com (December 16, 2007),

www.politico.com/news/stories/1207/7421.html.

Micah Sifry, "Getting the Download from Joe Trippi," techPresident blog (March 30, 2008),

www.techpresident.com/blog/entry/23374/getting_the_download_ from_joe_trippi.

Alexander Brunk, "The Challenge for the Rightosphere," TheNextRight blog (June 4, 2008),

    www.thenextright.com/node?page=1.

Tristan Louis, "Demographic Shift," TNL.net blog (May 19, 2008),

    www.tnl.net/blog/2008/05/19/demographic-shift/.

Micah Sifry, "The Deaning of America," *The Nation* (April 12, 2004),

    www.thenation.com/doc/20040412/sifry.

Ronald Brownstein, "The First 21st-Century Campaign," *National Journal* (April 19, 2008),

    www.nationaljournal.com/njmagazine/cs_20080416_3324.php.

Marc Ambinder, "HisSpace: How Would Obama's Success in Online Campaigning Translate into Governing?" *Atlantic Monthly* (June 2008),

    www.theatlantic.com/doc/200806/ambinder-obama.

Mark Glaser, "How Our Next President Should Use Participatory Media," PBS MediaShift (February 18, 2008),

    www.pbs.org/mediashift/2008/02/open_source_ideashow_our_new_p.html.

Steve Gilliard, "What Are People Afraid Of?" The News Blog (January 17, 2007),

    http://stevegilliard.blogspot.com/2007/01/what-are-people-afraid-of.html.

Tom Watson, "Power of Information: New Taskforce and Speech," tom-watson.co.uk blog (March 31, 2008),

    www.tom-watson.co.uk/?p=1945.

Chapter 7

Kevin Poulson, "Firsthand Reports from California Wildfires Pour through Twitter," *Wired* (October 23, 2007),

    http://blog.wired.com/27bstroke6/2007/10/firsthand-repor.html.

Britt Bravo, "Interview with Nate Ritter," NetSquared.org (January 18, 2008),

    www.netsquared.org/blog/britt-bravo/twitter-and-san-diego-fires-interview-nate-ritter.

Don Tapscott and Anthony Williams, *Wikinomics: How Mass Collaboration Changes Everything* (Portfolio Hardcover, December 28, 2006), p. 15.

Molly Hennessy-Fiske, "Tough Calls in Transplant Case: A Northridge Teen Dies Shortly after Her Insurer Reverses Its Refusal to Pay for a Treatment It Called Experimental," *Los Angeles Times* (December 22, 2007),

    www.latimes.com/business/la-fi-transplant22dec22,1,3777077.story?track=crosspromo&coll=la-headlines-business&ctrack=1&cset=true.

Eve Gittelson ("nyceve"), "Though We Mourn, People-Power Triumphed: You Made the Ground Tremble," DailyKos.com blog (December 21, 2007),

    www.dailykos.com/storyonly/2007/12/21/92628/467.

Tom Watson, multiple posts 2004–5, My Dirty Life & Times blog,

    http://tomwatson.typepad.com.

Nicholas Kristof, "Banding Together for Mukhtaran Bibi," *New York Times* (September 29, 2004),

    www.nytimes.com/2004/09/29/opinion/29kris.html.

Samantha Henig, "Banding Together for Mukhtaran Bibi," Columbia Journalism Review (June 16, 2005),

    www.cjr.org/blog_report/banding_together_for_mukhtaran.php?page=all.

Jeremy McDermott, "Colombia's Rebels: A Fading Force?" BBC News (February 1, 2008),

    http://news.bbc.co.uk/2/hi/americas/7217817.stm.

Jenny Carolina Gonzalez and Simon Romero, "Marches Show Disgust with a Colombian Rebel Group," *New York Times* (February 4, 2008),

    www.nytimes.com/2008/02/04/world/americas/05colombiaweb.html.

Jennifer Woodard Maderazo, "Facebook Becomes Catalyst for Causes, Colombian FARC Protest," PBS MediaShift (February 22, 2008), www.pbs.org/mediashift/2008/02/socialgood_networkingface-book.html.

Chapter 8

Tom Watson, "Skoll at Oxford: A Changing Time for Philanthropy," onPhilanthropy.com (April 2, 2007),
  www.onphilanthropy.com/site/News2?page=NewsArticle&id=7010.
Dr. Susan Raymond, "Google's Philanthropy," onPhilanthropy.com (September 20, 2006),
  www.onphilanthropy.com/site/News2?page=NewsArticle&id=6731.
Matthew Miller and Tatiana Serafin, "The 400 Richest Americans," *Forbes* (September 21, 2006),
  www.forbes.com/lists/2006/54/biz_06rich400_The-400-Richest-Americans_land.html/.
"U.S. Charitable Giving Reaches $295.02 Billion in 2006," GivingUSA Foundation (June 25, 2007),
  www.aafrc.org/press_releases/gusa/20070625.pdf.
"Family Foundations Expected to Top 33,000 in 2005," *Philanthropy News Digest* (November 30, 2005),
  http://foundationcenter.org/pnd/news/story.jhtml?id=124000010.
"America's Millionaires Are on a Roll," Spectrem Group (April 19, 2006),
  www.spectrem.com/custom.aspx?id=30.
Sonny Cloward, "Will Change.org Change ... Well, Anything?" Nonprofit Technology Network (March 3, 2007),
  www.nten.org/blog/2007/03/20/will-change-org-change-well-anything.
Ben Rattray, "Conference Season," Change.org blog (March 31, 2008),
  www.blogforchange.org/?p=13.

Vinay Bhagat, "The Real Impact of the Internet," onPhilanthropy.com
(February 24, 2004),
www.onphilanthropy.com/site/News2?page=NewsArticle&id=5197.

Susan Carey Dempsey, "The Guys and the Globe," onPhilanthropy.com
(September 21, 2006),
http://flip.onphilanthropy.com/news_onphilanthropy/2006/09/
the_guys_and_th.html.

Roxanne Clark, "Oxfam Targets Major Donors Online," philanthropy | UK
(September 2007),
www.philanthropyuk.org/Newsletter/Sep2007Issue30/Oxfamtarg
etsmajordonorsonline.

Daniel A. Rabuzzi, "Looking for Likely Allies: New Capital for the Social
Sector," onPhilanthropy.com (August 20, 2004),
www.onphilanthropy.com/site/News2?page=NewsArticle&id=5343.

"Rising Star: GlobalGiving," FastCompany.com (December 2007),
www.fastcompany.com/social/2008/profiles/globalgiving.html.

"Give Like an Entrepreneur," Forbes.com (December 14, 2007),
www.forbes.com/entrepreneurs/2007/12/14/philanthropy-giving-
donations-ent_mf_1214charity.html.

Lindsey McCormack, "Global Warming: Forget Fruitcakes, Earmuffs, and
Amazon Gift Cards—Sometimes the Best Gifts Are the Ones That
Give Back," 02138.com (Winter 2007),
www.02138mag.com/magazine/article/1090.html.

Carla E. Dearing, "Schwabification of Philanthropy," *Worth* (February 1,
2007),
www.worth.com/Editorial/Money-Meaning/Philanthropy/
Thought-Leaders-Philanthropy-Schwabification-of-
Philanthropy.asp.

Alan Benamer, "Economy 2.0 and Consumer Philanthropy = My Startup,"
Non-Profit Tech Blog: Confession of a Nonprofit IT Director
(December 6, 2006),

www.nonprofittechblog.org/economy-20-and-consumer-philan-
thropy-my-startup.

Mario Morino and Bill Shore, "High-Engagement Philanthropy: A Bridge
to a More Effective Social Sector," Venture Philanthropy Partners and
Community Wealth Ventures (June 2004),
    www.vppartners.org/learning/reports/report2004/report2004_
    essay.pdf.

Lucy Bernholz, "Is Philanthropy Going Open Source?" *Stanford Social
Innovation Review* (March 31, 2008),
    www.ssireview.org/opinion/entry/is_philanthropy_going_open_
    source/.

Susan Davis, *Hilton Foundation Humanitarian Symposium Proceedings*
(September 12, 2007),
    www.hiltonfoundation.org/conferences/16-PDF3.pdf.

Kristi Heim, "A Web of Giving," *Seattle Times* (December 18, 2006),
    http://community.seattletimes.nwsource.com/
    archive/?date=20061218&slug=techphil18.

Chapter 9

Chris Anderson, "Definitions: The Final Round!" The Long Tail blog
(January 09, 2005),
    http://longtail.typepad.com/the_long_tail/2005/01/definitions_
    fin.html,

Chris Anderson, "The Long Tail," *Wired* (October 2004),
    www.wired.com/wired/archive/12.10/tail.html.

"Giving Challenges Inspire 80,000 People to Give," Case Foundation
(February 21, 2008),
    http://giving.casefoundation.org/givingchallenge/press.

Beth Kanter, "The Kids in Cambodia Say Thank You via Video Clip!"
Beth's Blog (March 13, 2008),
    http://beth.typepad.com/beths_blog/cambodia/index.html.

Charles Leadbeater, *We-think: The Power of Mass Creativity* (Profile Books, February 2008), p. 83.

Marnie Webb, "Four Lessons Learned: Social Media and Nonprofit Meme," ext 337 blog (January 14, 2008),
http://ext337.org/article/four-lessons-learned-social-media-and-nonprofit-meme.

Geoff Livingston, Now Is Gone: A Primer on *New Media for Executives and Entrepreneurs* (Bartleby Press, November 12, 2007), p. 147.

Susan Herr, "Live from Sundance: Are Your Donors Going Hollywood on You?" onPhilanthropy.com (January 24, 2007),
www.onphilanthropy.com/site/News2?id=6891&page=NewsArticle.

Chapter 10

Peter Deitz, "Root Causes vs. Facebook Causes," *Stanford Social Innovation Review* (April 30, 2008),
www.ssireview.org/opinion/entry/root_causes_vs_facebook_causes/.

David Kirkpatrick, "Technology and the Developing World," *Fortune* (December 22, 2006),
http://money.cnn.com/2006/12/20/magazines/fortune/kirkpatrick_UN_speech.fortune/index.htm.

Amra Tareen, "The allvoices Team," allvoices.com (December 2007),
www.allvoices.com/team.

Ray Richmond, "Bottom Line: These Aren't Real Empathetic Souls. They Just Play Them on TV. Be Very Afraid," *Hollywood Reporter* (February 28, 2008),
www.hollywoodreporter.com/hr/television/reviews/article_display.jsp?&rid=10733&imw=Y.

Phil Cubeta, "Oprah's Big Give," Gift Hub blog (March 1, 2008),
www.gifthub.org/2008/03/oprahs-big-give.html.

Jaron Lanier, "Digital Maoism: The Hazards of the New Online Collectivism," Edge.org (May 30, 2006),

www.edge.org/3rd_culture/lanier06/lanier06_index.html.

Charles Leadbeater, *We-think: The Power of Mass Creativity* (Profile Books Ltd., February 2008), p. 40.

Index

AVC, 71
Acumen Fund, 139
Admic Nacional, 75
Al-Abdullah, Rania, 138
Alinsky, Saul, 112
AllAfrica.com, 50
Allen, George, 97–101
Allvoices.com, 186, 187, 199
Alva, Tony, 6, 158, 168
Amazon.com, 72, 160
Ambinder, Marc, 111
America Online, 18, 20, 163, 175
American Humane Association, 11
American Red Cross, 3, 7, 11, 12, 76
American Society for the
    Prevention of Cruelty to
    Animals, 11
America's Giving Challenge,
    163, 164
Amnesty International, 132
Amoss, Jim, 8
Anderson, Chris, 160, 161
Anderson, Elizabeth, 88
Anderson, Scott Edward, 78
Application programming interface
    (API), 172, 180
Armstrong, Lance, 174

Arnold, Matthew, 137
Arrington, Michael, 29
Ashoka, 138, 203
Asian-American Network Against
    Abuse of Human Rights, 129
AsianAve.com, 105
AskTheCandidates.org, 48

Baby Boomers, 19, 85, 91, 105
Bacon, Kevin, 175
Badges, 44, 46, 48, 122, 175
Banks, Tyra, 175
Barnes, Nora, 156
Beijing Olympics, 44–46
Benamer, Allan, 152, 153
Bernholz, Lucy, 153, 154
Best, Charles, 60–64, 72–74, 78
BetterPlace.org, 199
Beyerstein, Lindsay, 131
Bhagat, Vinay, 148
Bibi, Mukhtaran, 127–133, 185
BlackPlanet, 105
BloggersBlog, 3
BlogPulse, 3
Blue Girl, 168
Bono, 174, 176
Bowbrick, Steve, 131

Boyd, Stowe, 35
BRAC-USA, 155
Branson, Richard, 174
Brave New Films, 53–55
Bright Hope International, 55–57,
    84, 175
Brilliant, Larry, 138
BringLight, 181, 199, 201
Brown, Gordon, 115
Brownstein, Ron, 109
Brunk, Alexander, 108
Buffett, Warren, 65, 140–141, 163,
    174, 188
Burnham, Brad, 74
Bush, George W., 2, 3, 55, 99, 103,
    112, 128
BuzzFeed, 202

Calacanis, Jason, 125, 126
California wildfires, 119–121
Callejon, Donna, 155
Cambodia, 165, 166
Cambodia4kids, 166
Campaign for Cancer Research,
    25, 26
Cancer research fundraising, 23–28
Care2, 181, 199
Carnegie, Andrew, 141
Case, Jean, 18, 163, 164
Case, Steve, 18, 163
Case Foundation, 18, 83,
    163–166, 203
Cause marketing, 18, 153, 188
Causes Giving Challenge, 163, 164
Causes on Facebook, 16, 24–39, 89,
    144, 163, 164, 182, 183, 199
CauseWired
    meaning of, 12–14
    web site, 202

Celebrities, involvement of, 42, 102,
    173, 175, 176
Cell phones, 82, 83, 93, 94, 106,
    185, 187, 194
Chambers, Ray, 74
Change.org, 14, 17, 19, 48, 144–146,
    179, 181, 182, 192, 199
Changing Our World, Inc., 93, 116,
    164, 203
ChangingthePresent, 19, 144, 181,
    182, 190, 199
Charity Navigator, 57
Chavez, Cesar, 31, 32
Chavez, Hugo, 134
Chen, Steve, 99
Chervokas, Jason, 20, 33, 111,
    131, 169
Cheyer, Adam, 144
China
    and allvoices.com, 187
    Beijing Olympics, 44–46
    and Darfur, 43–46
    earthquake (May 2008), 154
ChipIn, 200
Christianity.com, 92
Clinton, Bill, 42, 75, 102, 104, 142
Clinton, Hillary, 71, 101–103,
    106–110, 126
Clinton Global Initiative, 140, 142,
    143, 188, 203
Cloward, Sonny, 146
Coalition for the Homeless, 152
Colbert, Stephen, 71
Colman, Jonathon, 49
Colombia, 134, 135
ColombiaSoyYo, 135
Community Wealth Ventures, 152
CompuMentor, 171
Cone Communications, 18, 85, 86

Confessions of a Nonprofit IT Director, 152, 202
Consumer philanthropy, 152–154
Convio, 11, 148, 200
Craigslist, 11, 74, 116, 183, 204
Creative control, 171
Crutchfield, Leslie, 49, 176
Cubeta, Phil, 189
Cunningham, Bill, 175
Cyclone Ivan, 50, 52

DailyKos, 2, 68, 99, 101, 125, 131
Dar, Ami, 74
Darfur, 17, 26, 28, 41–49, 56, 141, 146
Darfur Peace and Accountability Act, 43
Dash, Anil, 74
Davis, Susan, 14, 155
Dean, Howard, 107, 108, 162, 163
Dearing, Carla, 151, 156
Deitz, Peter, 179–183
Del.icio.us, 33, 130, 204
DellHell, 136
DeMarco, Ralph, 131
DemocracyinAction, 181, 200
Demographics
    Baby Boomers, 91, 105
    and donor patterns, 73
    millennials, 84–86, 88–92, 94, 106
    and social networks, 105
Dempsey, Susan Carey, 88, 153
Dickinson, Tim, 162
Digby's Hullabaloo, 112
Digg.com, 33, 48, 105, 123, 204
Digital democracy, 138, 189, 190, 192, 193

Dimas, Mark, 144
Ding, Eric, 23–28, 36, 39
Direct mail, 36, 72, 76, 145, 148
DMI. *See* Drum Major Institute for Public Policy (DMI)
Dodd, Chris, 54
Donors. *See also* Philanthropy in the U.S.
    and impact of gift, 155
    online, 147, 148, 153, 184
    statistics on wealth and giving, 142, 143
DonorsChoose.org
    administrative fee, 70
    and allvoices.com, 187
    creation of, 60–63
    donations, 72, 73
    donors, 71–73
    future of, 73
    media attention, 71
    as model for online philanthropy, 14, 149
    national expansion, 70
    and nature of philanthropy, 19
    project example, 69, 70, 72
    and Social Actions, 179, 182
    and social entrepreneurship, 17, 144
    and Web 2.0, 63, 64
    web site, 200
DoSomething, 19
Douglas, Kirk, 174
Drayton, Bill, 138
Drum Major Institute for Public Policy (DMI), 114, 115, 189, 203
Duvall, Robert, 175
Dyer, Craig, 55–57, 84, 175, 176
Dyer, Kevin, 56

Earthquake relief
  China, 154
  Pakistan, 186
eBay, 68, 74, 137, 138, 140, 157
Echeverri, Felipe, 134
Edwards, John, 31, 126, 127
80/20 rule, 161
Eisnaugle, Jill, 22
Email, 13, 26, 27, 93, 115, 116, 122,
  130–133, 185, 193
Eons, 105, 204
Essembly.com, 31
ext337 blog, 171, 202
Extreme Makeover: Home Edition,
  188, 189

Facebook
  and Bright Hope International,
    55–57, 175
  Causes on Facebook, 16, 24–39,
    44, 45, 48, 89, 122–126, 163,
    164, 182, 183, 199
  and Change.org, 145
  creation of, 24, 25, 30
  and flash causes, 134–136
  and FLiP, 88, 89
  "friend" terminology, 37, 161
  and Genocide Intervention
    Network (GI-NET), 43
  and Hurricane Katrina, 21
  Kiva group, 76–78
  and Millennium Village, 94
  mini-feed, 36, 37, 80
  mini-feeds, 80, 81
  and peer pressure, 36, 141
  and philanthropy, 19, 156
  and political campaigns, 105,
    106, 115

  Save Darfur Causes, 43–49
  and social entrepreneurship, 17
  use of, 14, 172, 193
  user profile, 36, 48, 80, 87, 89,
    115, 123, 135, 164. *See also*
    User profiles
  web site, 204
Faithbase, 105
Family foundations, 142
Fanning, Shawn, 29
Feed the Children, 11
Fighting Dems network, 99
Figueroa, Temo, 162
Fine, Allison, 35, 53, 83, 84, 201
FireDogLake, 101, 113
Firefox, 48
FirstGiving, 19, 181, 182, 200
Flannery, Jessica, 64–68
Flannery, Matt, 64–69, 74, 75,
  77, 78
Flash causes online, 121–124
  characteristics of, 136
  examples, 124–135
Flickr.com, 3, 11, 12, 14, 33, 47,
  105, 172, 183, 204
FLip (Future Leaders in
  Philanthropy), 17, 88, 202
Flowers, Lennon, 94
Foko Madagascar, 50–52, 185
Founders Fund, 16, 30
Fowler, Mayhill, 102–104
Fox, Michael J., 173
Freecycle, 200
Freerice.com, 86, 87
FriendFeed, 33, 204
Friending, 37, 161
Friends of New Orleans, 21
Friendster, 19, 30, 43, 204

Fuerzas Armadas Revolucionarias de Colombia (FARC) — Ejército del Pueblo, 134, 135
Fundable, 181, 182, 200
Future Leaders in Philanthropy (FLiP), 17, 88, 202

Gabriel, Peter, 138
Gadbois, Karen, 21
Gandelman, Joe, 131
Ganz, Marshall, 31
Gates, Bill, 140–141, 163, 174, 188
Gates, Melinda, 188
Gates Foundation, 141, 188
Gen Next, 81–85
Gen X, 85, 91
Genocide in Darfur. *See* Darfur
Genocide Intervention Fund, 42
Genocide Intervention Network (GI-NET), 43, 44, 47
Geragos, Mark, 125
Gibson, William, 197
Gift Hub, The, 189, 202
Gilliard, Steve, 113, 114, 117, 131
Gittelson, Eve, 125
GiveForward, 200
GiveMeaning, 181, 200
Giving USA, 142
GivingNet, 151
Glaser, Mark, 7, 111, 134
Global Voices Online, 51, 166
GlobalGiving, 154, 155, 157, 164, 165, 179, 181, 200
Gold, Matt, 131
Google, 20, 21, 99, 111, 122, 138, 140, 146, 155, 160, 171, 183
Google Blog Search, 171
Google.org, 140

Gotham Gal, 169
Government, 115, 116
Grameen Bank, 64, 65, 138
Grameen Foundation, 155
Green, Joe, 16, 24, 28, 30–32, 35–39, 85
Green Skeptic, The, 202
Greenstein, Howard, 63, 202
Greenwald, Glenn, 113
Greenwald, Robert, 53–55
Gulf Coast Housing Recovery Act, 54
Gupta, Rajiv, 144

Hais, Michael, 90, 91
Half the Sky Foundation, Children's Earthquake Relief Fund, 154, 155
Hamsher, Jane, 112
Hanis, Mark, 42, 43, 46, 47, 57
Harris, Josh, 79, 80
Heifer Foundation, 150
Heifer International, 150
Heiferman, Scott, 77, 108, 195
Hellicane, 22
Helpalot, 181, 182, 200
Hendrie, Nancy, 166
Henig, Samantha, 132
Hildebrand, Steve, 163
Hill, Declan, 129
Hope Equity, 150, 151
Huffington, Arianna, 103
Huffington Post, 131
Huijnk, Julius, 182
Hurley, Chad, 99
Hurricane Katrina
    destruction caused by, 1, 2
    online donations, 7, 12, 13, 20, 148

Hurricane Katrina (*Continued*)
  online reaction to, 2–11
  online video, impact of, 54, 55
  social networks, impact of, 11,
    12, 20–22

IceRocket.com, 3, 171
Idealist.org, 74, 204
Idol Gives Back, 188
International trends, 185
Intersection, The, 52
iTunes, 72, 160, 190

Jarvis, Jeff, 131, 136
Jintao, Hu, 45
Jolie, Angelina, 176
JustGiving, 200
Justmeans, 200

Kanter, Beth, 50, 52, 165–167, 172,
    201
Karmadu, 19, 200
Kerry, John, 10, 28, 30, 31, 128
Kidman, Nicole, 175
King, Martin Luther, Jr., 97, 114,
    195
Kirkpatrick, David, 185
Kiva
  and allvoices.com, 187
  appeal of, 77, 78
  creation of, 67, 68
  impact of, 19
  loan examples, 75–77
  as model for online
    philanthropy, 14, 149–151
  and Social Actions, 179, 181, 182
  and social entrepreneurship,
    17, 144

  success of, 74
  website, 200
Kivafriends.com, 78
Klein, Ezra, 131
Knowmore.org, 200
Kraban Support Foundation, 76
Kristof, Nicholas, 42, 43, 76,
    127–129, 131, 133

Lanier, Jaron, 192
Lasica, J. D., 38
LastFM, 33, 190, 204
Lazylaces, 87
Leadbeater, Charles, 161, 170, 193
Leadership, 159–177
Lincoln, Abraham, 141
LinkedIn, 17, 19, 33, 105, 204
LiveJournal, 47
Livingston, Geoff, 172
Long-tail pattern, 71, 72, 160, 161
Louis, Tristan, 109

M.A. Peel, 168
"Macaca moment," 98–101
Madagascar, 50–52
Maderazo, Jennifer Woodard,
    134, 135
Mahalo, 126, 204
Mainoo, Abena, 42
Make The Difference Network
    (MTDN), 201
Malik, Om, 29
Mannion, Lance, 131, 168
Mash-ups, 17, 34, 102, 179
Mashable.com, 92
Masonis, Todd, 29
Mattson, Eric, 156
Mayor.tv, 115

McCain, John, 102, 107, 109, 112
McLeod, Heather, 49, 176
Media Grok, 111
MediaShift, 111, 134
Meetup.com, 77
Mercy Corps, 129
Message boards, 157
Michael J. Fox Foundation, 173
Micro-credit programs, 186
Micro-endowments, 150
Micro-philanthropists, 184
Microcelebrity, 81
MicroGiving, 181, 182, 201
Microsoft Live, 171
MiGente.com, 105
Milken, Michael, 173
Milken Global Forum, 143,
    173, 174
Milken Institute, 203
Millennials, 84–86, 88–92, 94, 106
Millennium Village, 94
Mini-feeds, 36, 37, 80
Moderate Voice, The, 113
Montes, Óscar, 135
Mooney, Chris, 52
Moore, Garth, 93
Morales, Oscar, 134
Morino, Mario, 152
Moulitsas, Markos, 2, 131
MoveOn.org, 53, 55
Musharraf, Pervez, 129, 131, 132
My.BarackObama.com (MyBo),
    105, 106, 112, 162, 163
MyDD, 31, 101, 113
MySpace
    Causes on MySpace, 39
    and flash causes, 122, 136
    and friend terminology, 37, 161

and Genocide Intervention
    Network (GI–NET), 43, 46, 47
and philanthropy, 19
and political campaigns, 90, 105,
    106, 108
and social entrepreneurship, 17
user profile, 33, 87. *See also* User
    profiles
website, 204

Napster, 16, 29
Nature Conservancy, The, 48, 49
Navy–Marine Corps Relief
    Society, 11
Neddie Jingo, 169
Net–native generation, 18, 19, 184
Netroots, 112–115
NetSquared, 120, 156, 171, 203
Network for Good, 21, 146, 164,
    175, 201
Newcritics.com, 167–170, 202
Newmark, Craig, 74
NextGen, 88, 92. *See also*
    Millennials
Nguyen, Minh, 29
Nicole, Kristen, 92
Nola.com, 8, 9
Novogratz, Jacqueline, 139
NPowerNY, 146
NTEN (Nonprofit Technology
    Network), 146, 203
Nurses' Health Study, 24
@NY, 20
Nyceve, 125

Obama, Barack, 38, 71, 90,
    101–112, 116, 126, 143, 144,
    162, 163, 190, 192

O'Brien, Jeffrey, 72
O'Donnell, Rosie, 175
OffTheBus, 103
Omidyar, Pierre, 138
O'Neill, Ellen, 168
Online social activism, 14, 15, 35, 43, 60, 84, 87–90, 92, 160, 161, 165, 172, 180, 184, 188–196
OnPhilanthropy.com, 17, 88, 140, 152, 153, 202
OpenLeft, 113
Oprah's Big Give, 189. *See also* Winfrey, Oprah
Overdyke, Scott, 92
Oxfam, 149
OxfamAmerica, 21

Paez, Jason, 84
Pakistan, 127, 129–133, 185–187
Paley Center for Media, 168
Pandora, 33, 205
Parade.com, 165
Parker, Pamela, 131
Parker, Sean, 16, 24, 28–30, 32, 35, 37
Party4APurpose.com, 84
Paul, Ron, 107–109
PayPal, 68, 74, 99, 146
Peer-to-peer philanthropy, 59–78. *See also* DonorsChoose.org; Kiva
People Get Ready blog, 9
Perlmutter, David, 113
Personal Democracy Forum, 106, 203
Pew Internet & American Life Project, 83, 87, 88, 203

Pew Research Center for the People and the Press, 81, 82
PhilanthroMedia, 202
Philanthropreneurs, 138
Philanthropy in the U.S., 139–143, 148, 152, 155, 156
Phoenix of New Orleans, 21
PincGiving, 181, 182, 201
Pitt, Brad, 174
Planet Green, 49
Plaxo, 16, 29, 32, 33
PledgeBank, 181, 182, 201
Podcasts, 90, 157, 188, 194
Political campaigns
    bloggers, impact of, 112–114
    Clinton campaign, 101–103, 106–110. *See also* Clinton, Hillary
    network, impact of, 101
    new ways of political organizing, 96, 97
    Obama campaign, 101–112, 116, 162, 163. *See also* Obama, Barack
    party politics and old system of political access, 95, 96
    Paul, Ron, 107–109
    and policy setting, 110–117
    YouTube, impact of, 97–101
Politico.com, 108
PressThink, 103
Project Agape, 16, 28, 163
Projects Direct, 149, 150
Pseudo, 79
Public online identities, 80

Rabuzzi, Daniel, 151
Rakotomalala, Lova, 51

Rasiej, Andrew, 74
Rattray, Ben, 14, 15, 144, 145, 147,
    192, 194
Raymond, Susan, 140, 141
Razafimharo, Joan, 50, 52
Razoo, 19, 92, 93, 122, 144, 181,
    182, 201
Relief International, 186
Reville, Lyndsey, 88
Rice, Condoleeza, 131
Ring, Cameron, 30
Rising Voices, 51
Ritter, Josh, 121
Ritter, Nate, 120, 202
Rosen, Jay, 103
Rospars, Joe, 106
Route Out of Poverty for
    Cambodian Children, 165
Ruffini, Patrick, 109

Salon.com, 100, 113
Sarkisyan, Nataline, 124–127
Saunders, Vicky, 181
Save Darfur, 26, 44, 45
Scherer, Michael, 100
Schlesinger, Andrea Batista, 114,
    115, 189, 191
Schneider, Will, 88
"Schwabification" of philanthropy,
    151, 156
Scoble, Robert, 131
Sedgwick, Kyra, 175
Self-Styled Siren, 169
September 11, 2001 terrorist
    attacks, 4, 9, 61, 82, 128, 148
Shah, Premal, 68, 73, 74
Shakepeare's Sister, 131
Shamus, The, 169

Sharing Foundation, 165, 166
Shirky, Clay, 37, 161, 202
Shore, Bill, 152
Sidarth, Shekar Ramanuja,
    97–101
Sifry, Micah, 74, 91, 107
Simpson, Jessica, 175
SixDegrees.org, 175, 181, 201
Skoll, Jeffrey, 137–139
Skoll Centre, 138
Skoll Foundation, 138, 203
Skoll World Forum, 137–139, 143
Smith, Christy Hardin, 113
Social Actions, 19, 179–183, 201
Social enterprise, 14, 62, 64, 65,
    139, 190
Social entrepreneurship, 13, 14, 17,
    51, 65, 73, 74, 137–140, 143,
    144, 195, 196
Social graph, 35
Social networks, generally
    online, 4, 11, 12, 16, 18, 19
    public nature of, 80–82
    and social causes, 28–32, 43, 92,
    93, 190
SocialEdge, 202
SocialVibe, 201
Soros, Jonathan, 74
Spradlin, Greg, 150, 151
Squandered Heritage, 21
STAND, 43
Stannard-Stockton, Sean, 74
Structure and hierarchy in online
    organizing, 170–172
Sudan. *See* Darfur
Sullivan, Andrew, 101
Supercommunicators, 83
Sustainablog, 202

Tabios, Divine, 88
Tactical Philanthropy, 203
TakingItGlobal, 201
Talking Points Memo, 101, 113
TalkLeft, 113
Tapscott, Don, 14, 15, 122
Tareen, Amra, 186, 187
Tattered Coat blog, 6
Technorati.com, 3, 12, 107, 122,
    130, 171, 205
TechPresident.com, 106, 107, 203
TechSoup, 171, 204
Telephone canvassing, 47
Texas SPCA, 11
Text messaging, 46, 82, 83, 93, 122,
    148, 194
TheMiddleClass.org, 115
ThePoint, 181, 182, 201
Thomas, Sarah, 150
Thompson, Clive, 81
Toffler, Alvin, 15, 49
Tolmach, Robert, 190, 191
Traeger, Sebastian, 92
Transparency, 124, 151, 196
Trickster, 169
Trippi, Joe, 108
Twitter, 14, 48, 52, 78, 81, 120, 122,
    125, 205
Typepad.com, 205

UJA Federation, 11
United Nations
    Millennium Development
        Goals, 94
    World Food Programme, 52,
        86, 87
Upscale philanthropy, 174, 175

Urban Institute, 21
Usenet, 33
User profiles, 16, 25, 26, 29, 30, 33,
    34, 36, 48, 80, 81, 87, 89, 115,
    122, 123, 135, 164, 172, 175

Venture philanthropy, 14
Venture Philanthropy Partners, 204
Video blogs, 157
Viscount LaCarte, 169
Vitter, David, 55

Watson, Tom, 115, 116, 132,
    133, 203
Watson, Veronica, 75, 76, 191, 197
We Live in Public, 80
Web 2.0, 4, 47, 63, 73, 147,
    156, 161
Webb, James, 98–101
Webb, Marnie, 171
Whittle, Dennis, 157
Widgets, 49, 106, 148, 155, 164–166,
    172, 188, 193
Wikimedia Foundation, Inc., 15
Wikipedia, 4, 15, 170, 171, 192, 205
Wikis, 4, 93, 111, 157
Williams, Anthony, 14, 15, 122
Wilson, Fred, 71
Winfrey, Oprah, 62, 75, 174,
    176, 189
Wings Academy, 59, 60
Winograd, Morley, 90, 91
Wolcott, James, 131
Woods, Tiger, 174
Wordpress, 167–168, 205
World Economic Forum, 140
WorldChanging.com, 19

Yahoo!, 11, 171, 180
YouTube, 205
  and Darfur, 47
  and Hurricane Katrina, 3, 12,
    21, 54
  and Kiva, 78
  and Madagascar cyclone, 52
  and political campaigns, 90, 98,
    99, 102, 105, 107, 125, 126

  and Robert Greenwald,
    53, 54
  use of, 14, 33, 123, 125, 172
Yunus, Muhammad, 64, 65, 138

Zapata, Salvador, 135
Zazengo, 181, 201
Zuckerberg, Mark, 25, 30,
  32, 35

DATE DUE	RETURNED